AF378164

HOW TO DRAW
Sci-Fi Fantasy Mecha

SPACESHIPS, AIRPLANES, CARS, SUBMARINES AND MORE!

KENICHI SOMEMORI

SHIN YOSHIMURA

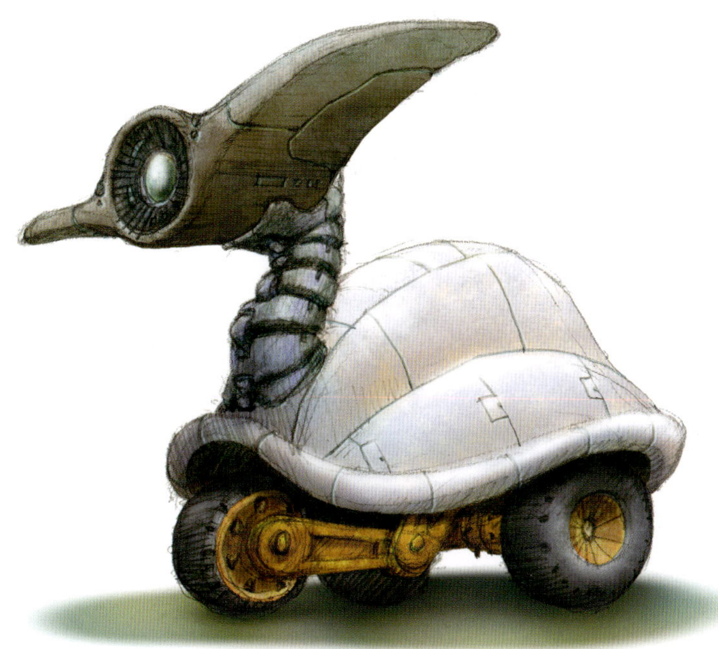

TUTTLE Publishing

Tokyo | Rutland, Vermont | Singapore

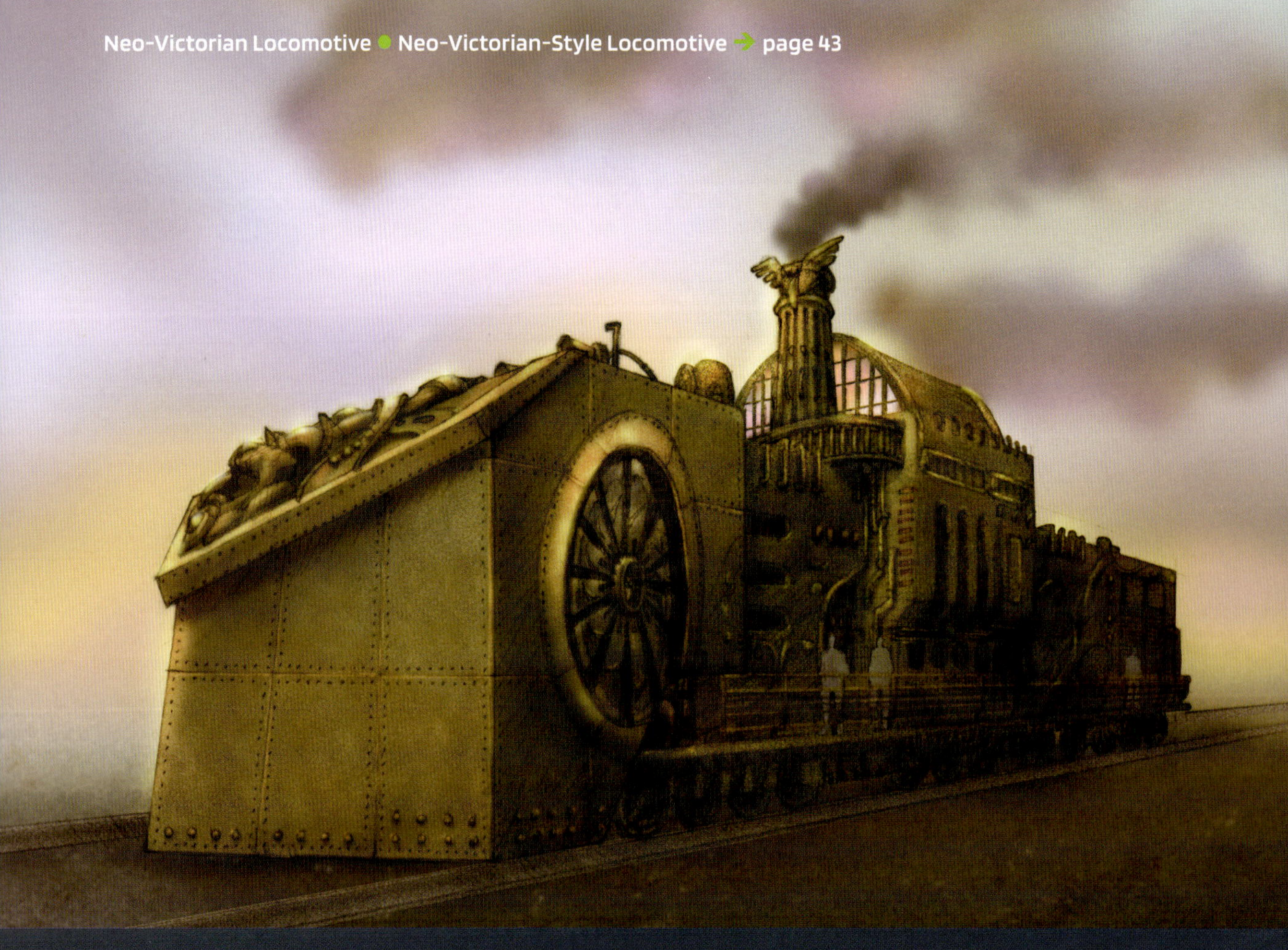

Neo-Victorian Locomotive ● Neo-Victorian-Style Locomotive → page 43

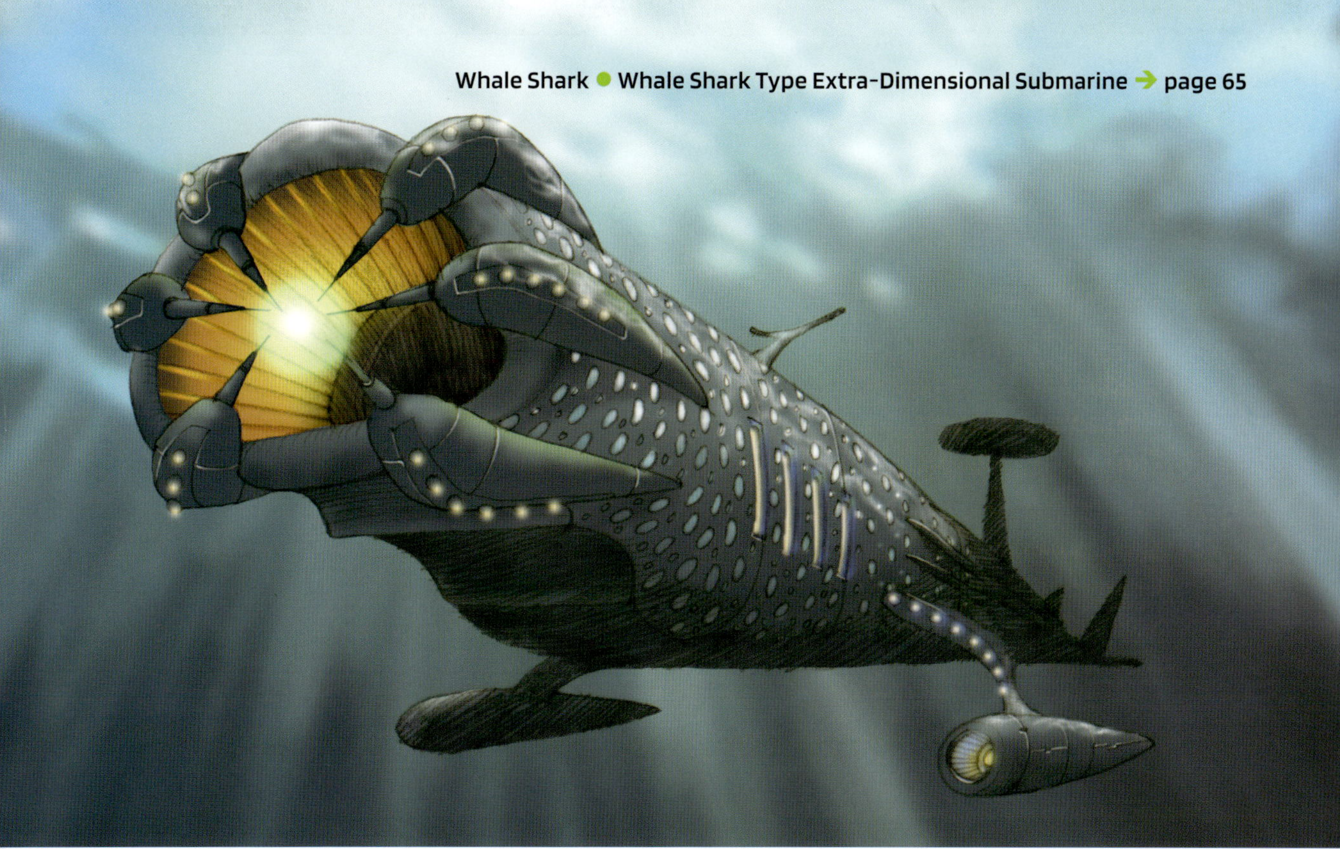

PART 2   # FORM, FUNCTION AND DESIGN: SOME HINTS

PART 3   ILLUSTRATION TECHNIQUES

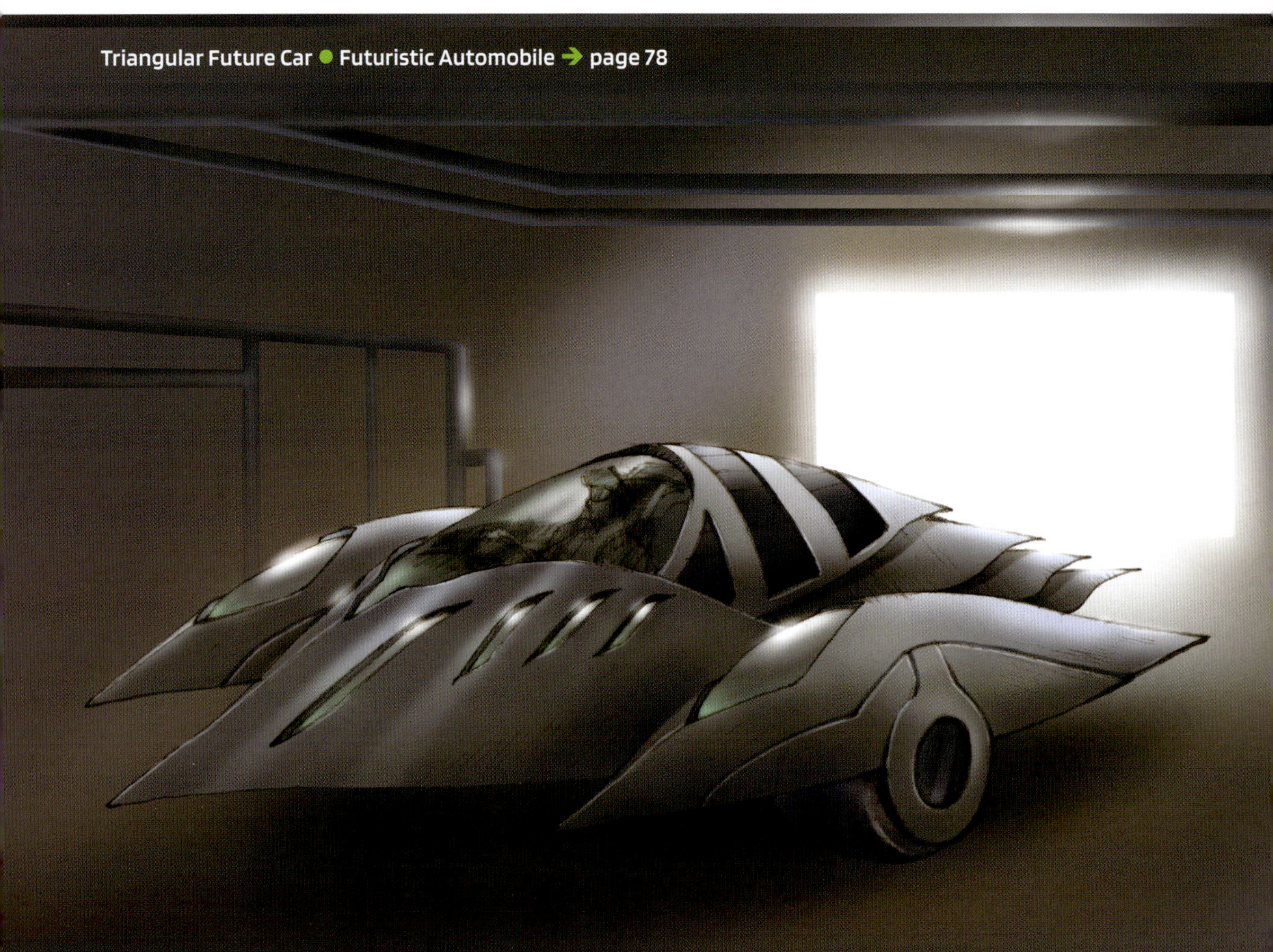

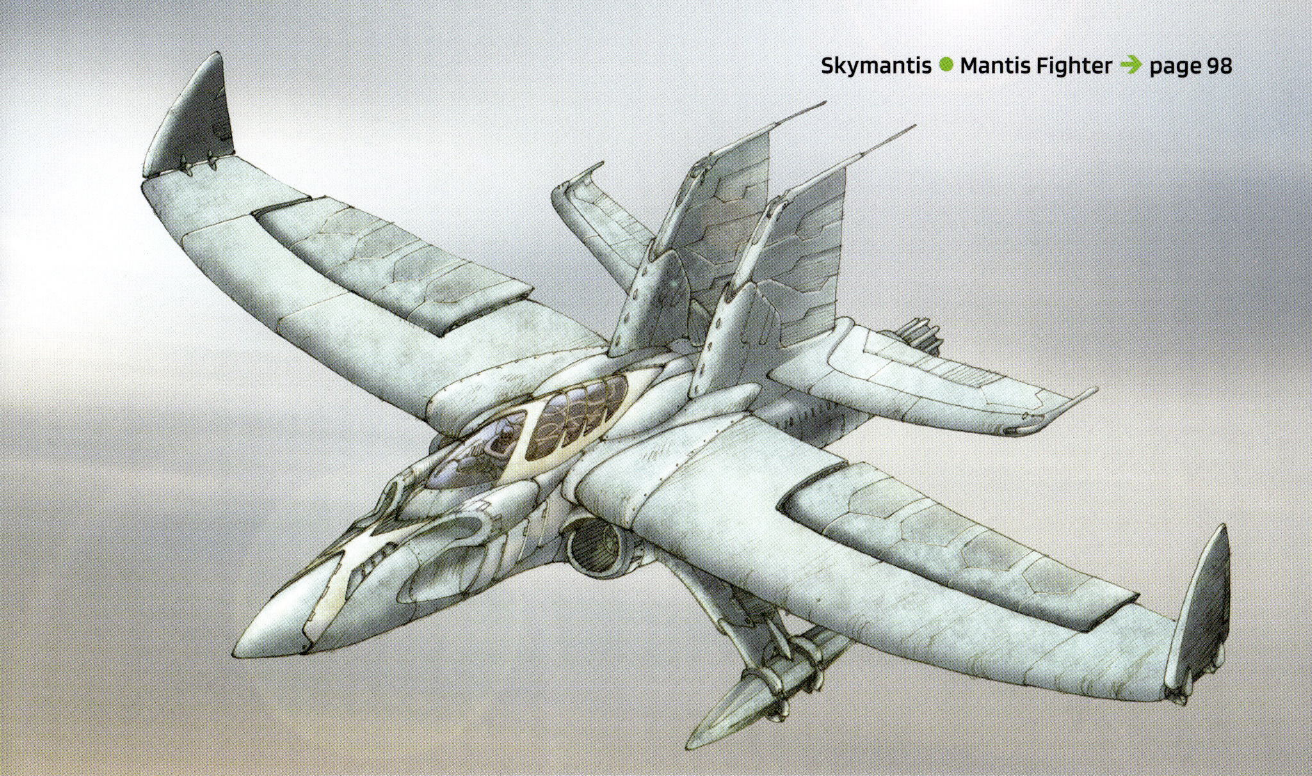

PART 4 PRACTICAL ASSESSMENTS

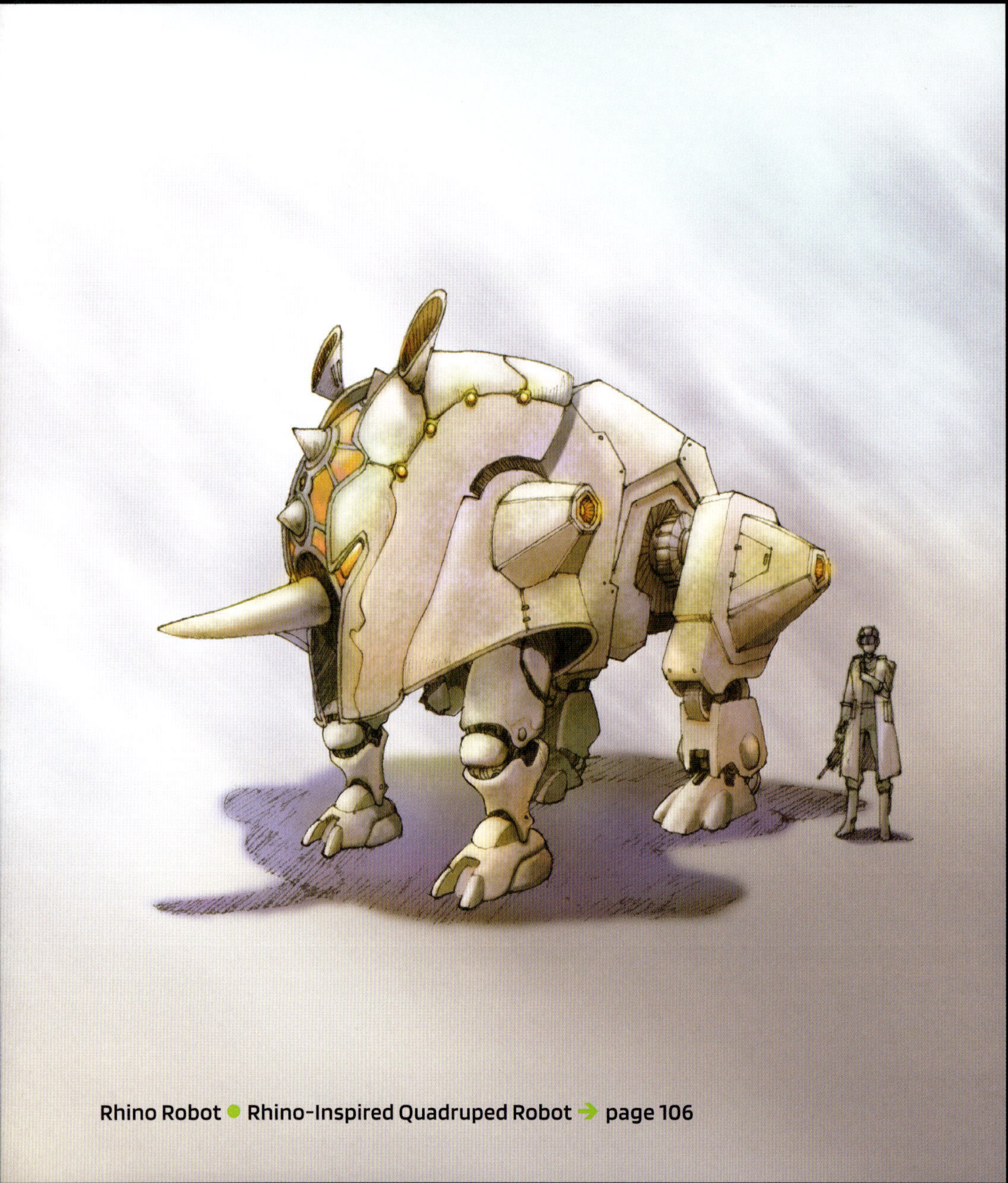

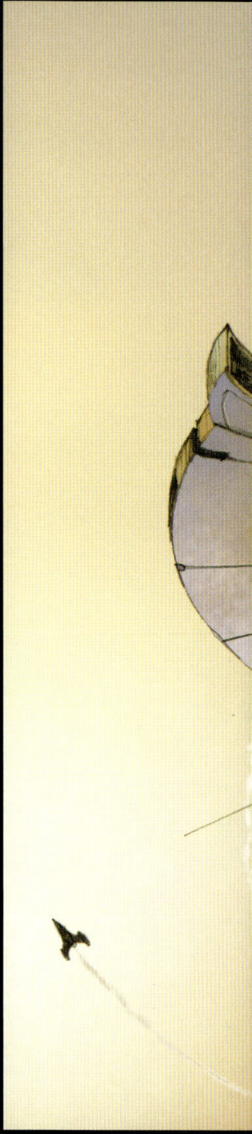

Rhino Robot ● **Rhino-Inspired Quadruped Robot** → page 106

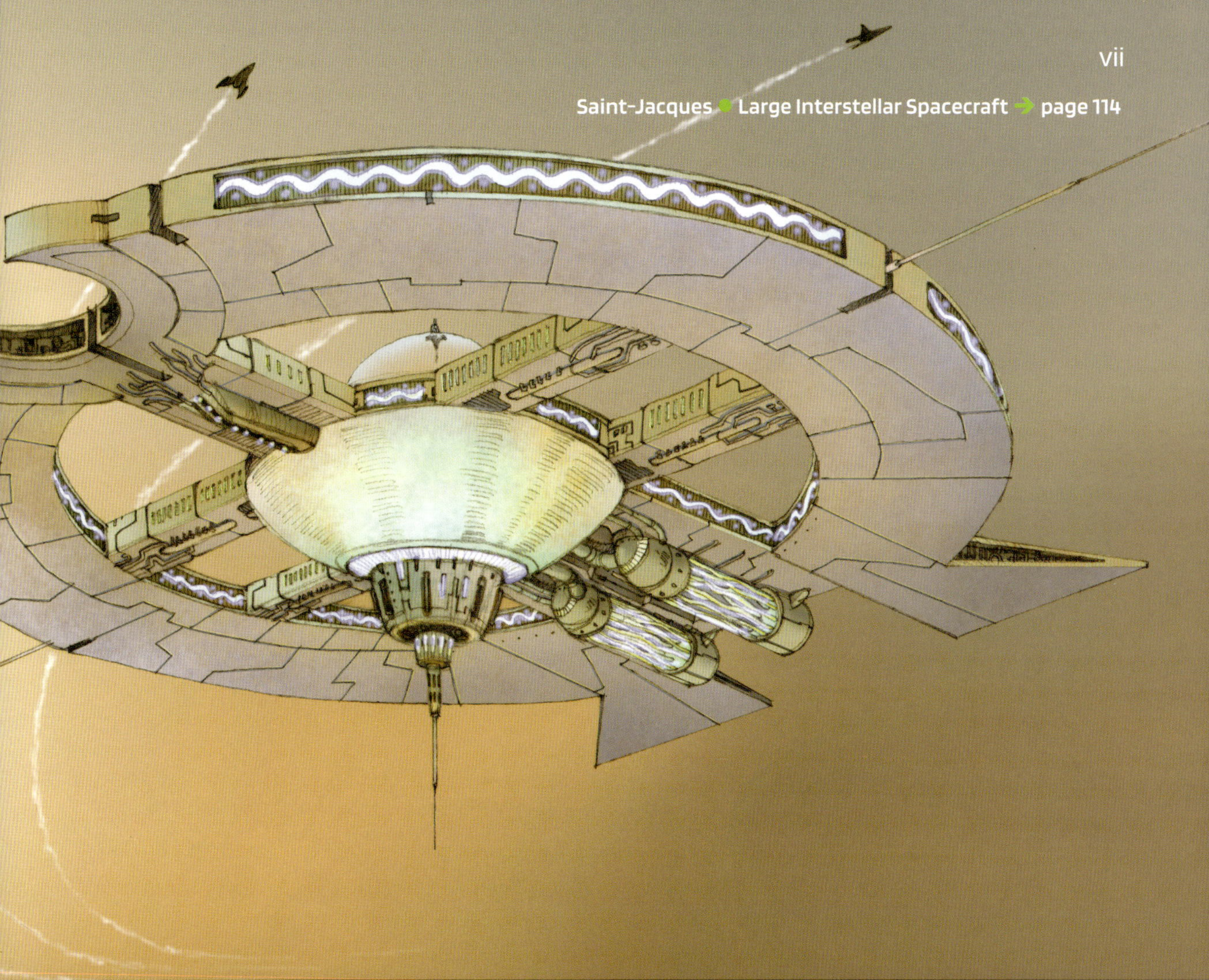

LARGE INTERSTELLAR SPACECRAFT

Anyone can learn to draw, if you learn the right way. We all know the formula: learn the techniques, practice them, then keep on practicing them. Over and over again. Here, various methods of representing three-dimensional objects on paper or onscreen are explained using concrete examples and procedures. The basics of drawing are the same for all the mecha mash-ups presented here, so once you master them, you'll be able to apply them to any original design.

The mecha and vehicles that appear in science fiction and fantasy, the subject of this book, have been brought to life by various creators in the world of novels, movies and animation. Examining many of these works, I realize over and over how deeply influenced they are by the history of art and design. Then, of course, there's the ultimate inspiration: the forms found in nature. Whether in form or color, from the microscopic to the macroscopic, everything that nature creates is a never-ending source of imagistic inspiration. The fantasy vehicles and mashup machines here are hybrid creations, fusing the organic and the manufactured, the earthbound and the aerial, the animate and the not so animate. Fantasy fusions for flights of fancy. Where will your imagination soar to next?

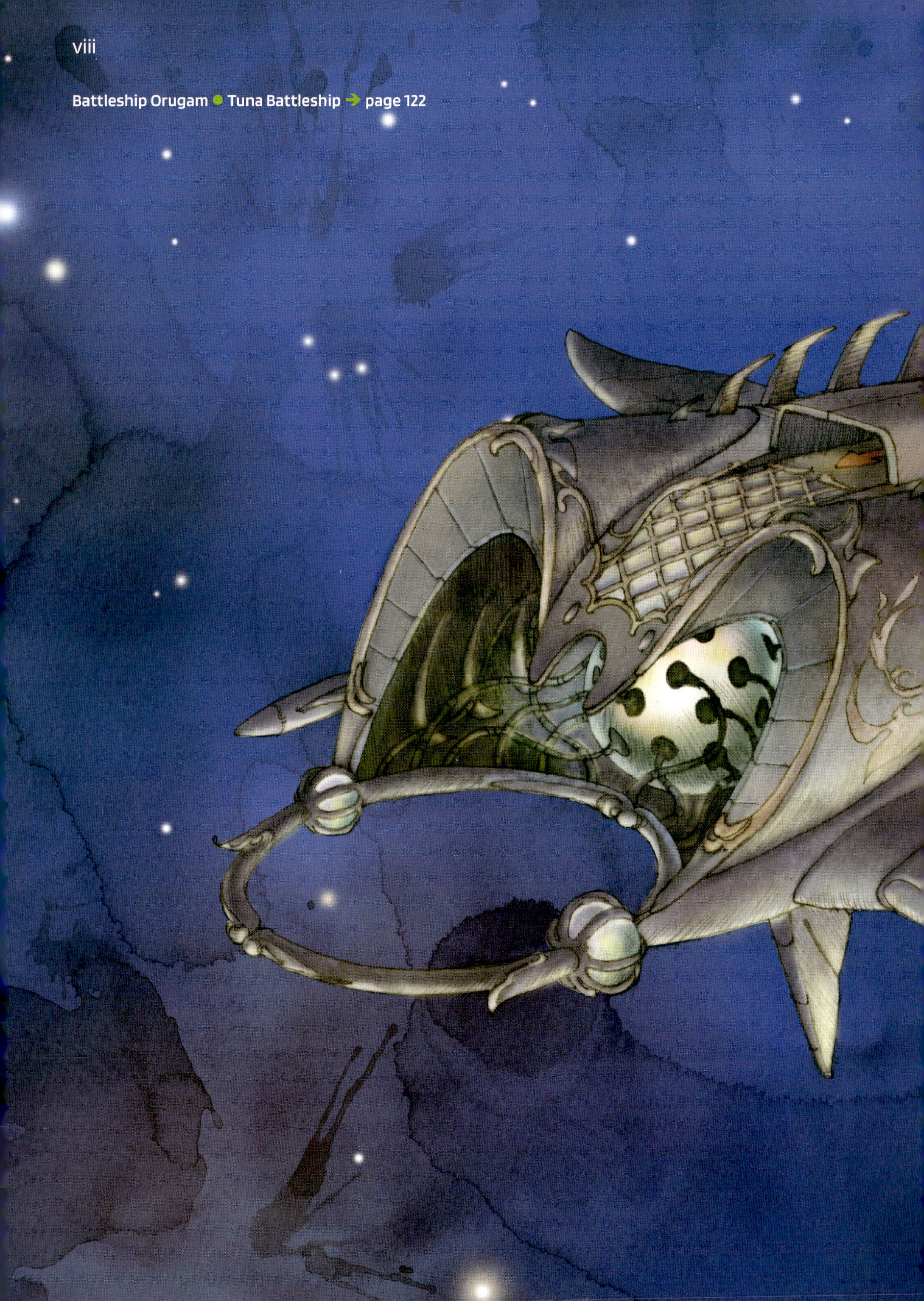

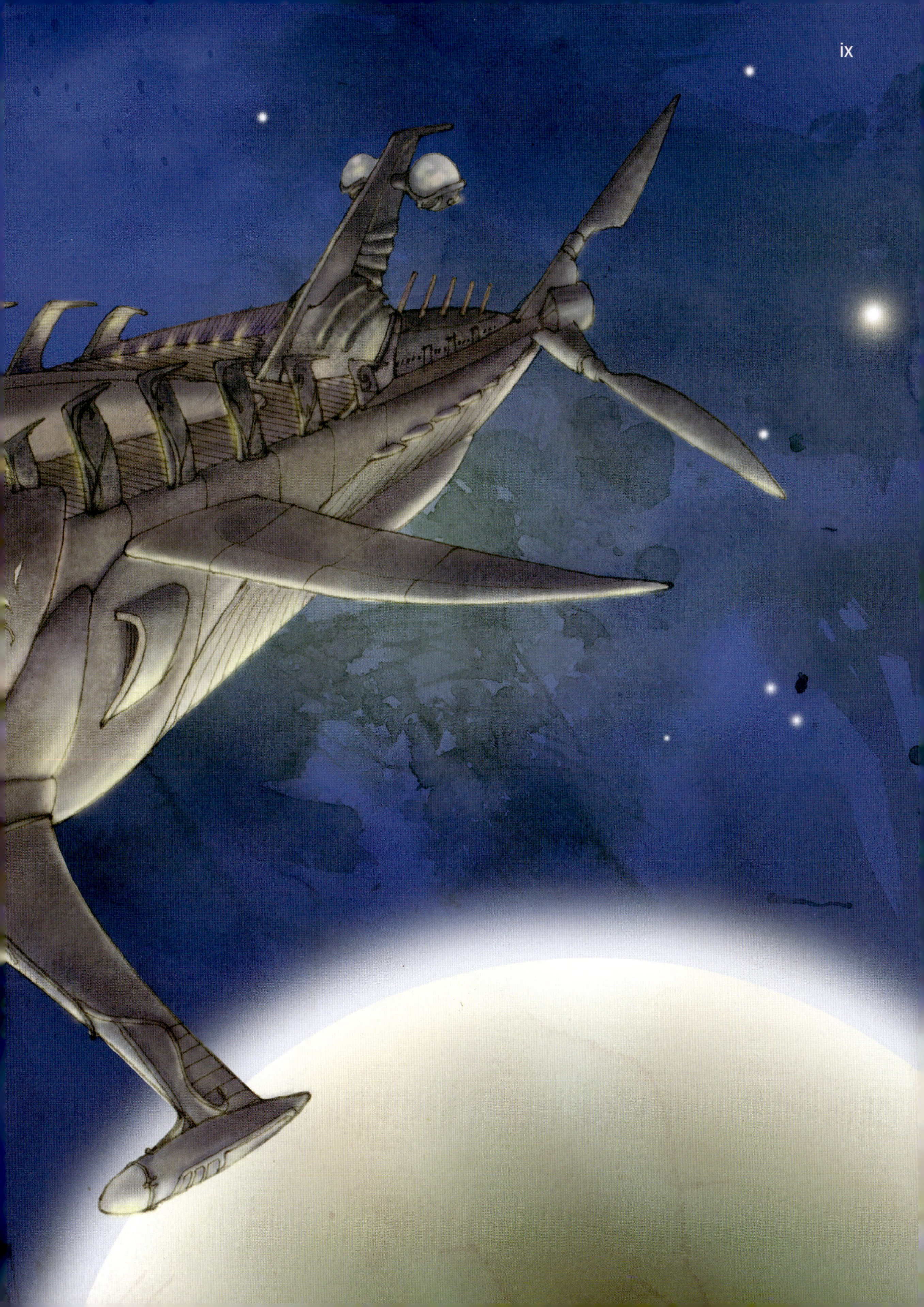

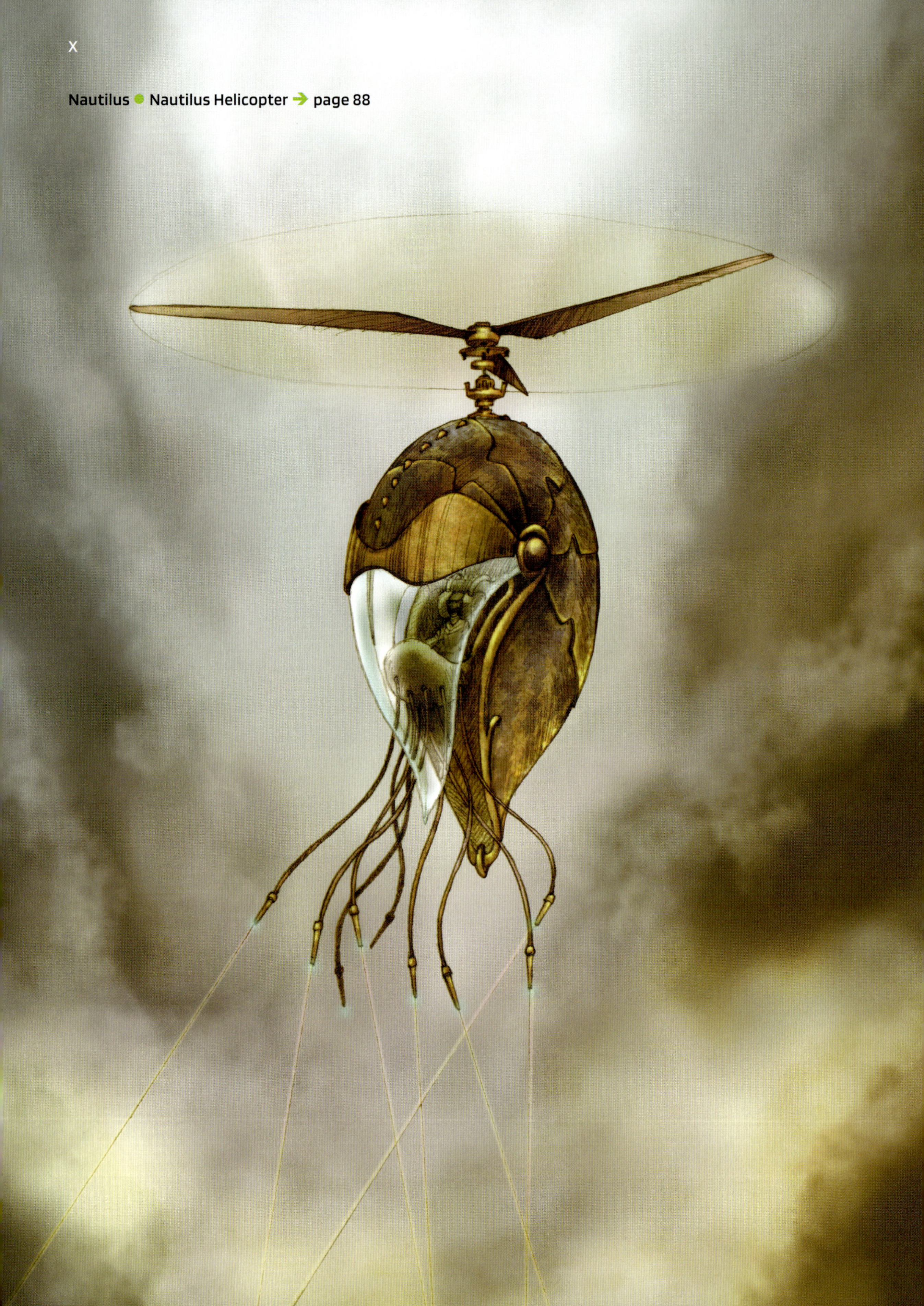

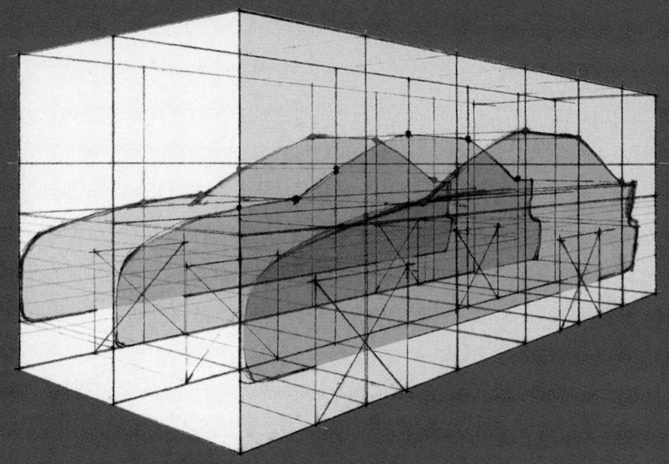

Part 1

BASIC FORMS AND TECHNIQUES

All three-dimensional objects are made up of a
collection of basic shapes. Here, we'll look at how to
approach the design of three-dimensional objects
and how to draw them based on the concept of
diagrammatic representation.

1-1   DRAWING 3D OBJECTS

It's often easiest to approach three-dimensional objects in terms of form.
So let's first consider the relationship between three-dimensional space
and form.

Drawing a Three-Dimensional Object

Everything around us is three-dimensional. If we express it in dimensions, it's length by width by
height. Designs on clothing, patterns on furniture and walls, figures drawn on paper, anything
represented on a flat surface is a two-dimensional rendering of a three-dimensional space.
One-dimensional renderings are limited to the straight and curved lines that collectively create
patterns, shapes and images.

■ **1D, 2D, 3D**

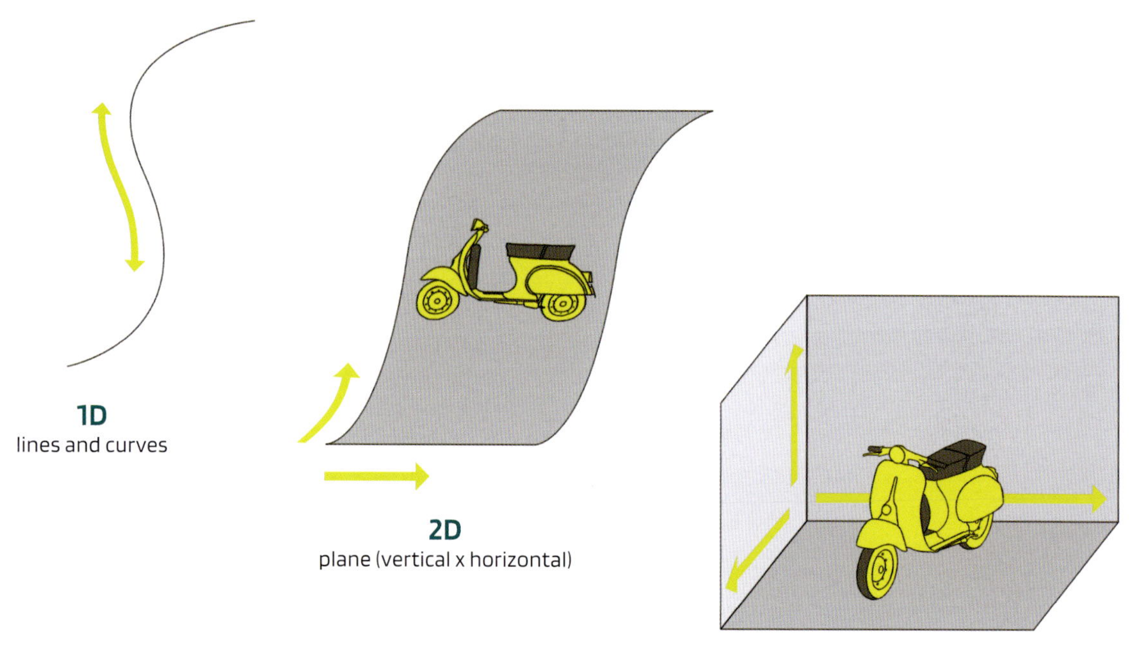

Representing a three-dimensional object on a
two-dimensional plane is analogous to taking
a photograph or drawing a picture.

Types of 3D Expression

When illuminated, a three-dimensional object casts a shadow. This method is called projection or shadow projection and is known as a drawing that represents a three-dimensional object in three planes (a blueprint-style overview, front view and side view). Drawings and maps can show a three-dimensional object more accurately in detail. There are many types of projections other than drawings. The Kantian drawing method (including perspective drawing), which we'll look at a little bit later, is one of the methods of turning drawings and designs into three-dimensional objects.

Figure 1-1: 3D Objects and Their Blueprint, Side, and Front Views

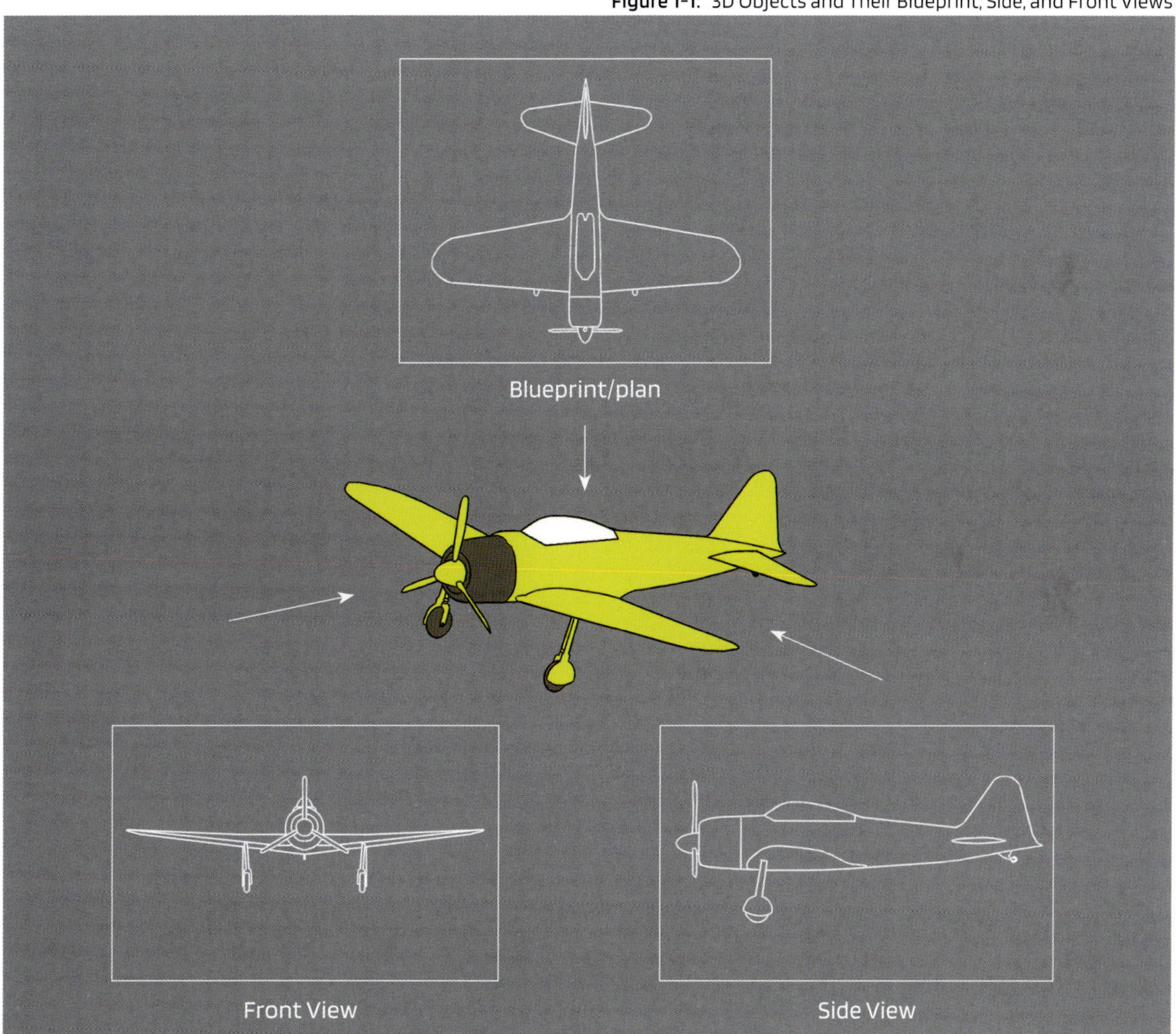

A view of a three-dimensional object from directly above is often called a plan or blueprint view, while the side view and the front view are sometimes referred to as the elevation views.

Basic Forms

When attempting to draw three-dimensional objects such as machines or vehicles, it's important to understand that there are various fundamental shapes contained within them.

Basic shapes include circles, triangles and rectangles, while basic solids include spheres, cylinders, cones, regular tetrahedrons, triangular pyramids, cubes (regular hexahedrons), and rectangular prisms. Additionally, there are applied solids created based on these basic forms.

● Basic Shapes and Basic Solids

Circles, equilateral triangles and squares are the fundamental flat shapes. Variants of these include ellipses, scalene triangles, rhombuses, parallelograms and trapezoids. By adding thickness or rotating these basic shapes, they become basic solids.

Basic solids also include regular polyhedrons. Examples are the tetrahedron, octahedron and icosahedron made up of equilateral triangles; the hexahedron (cube) made of squares; and the dodecahedron made of pentagons.

Figure 1-2: From Basic Shapes to Basic Solids

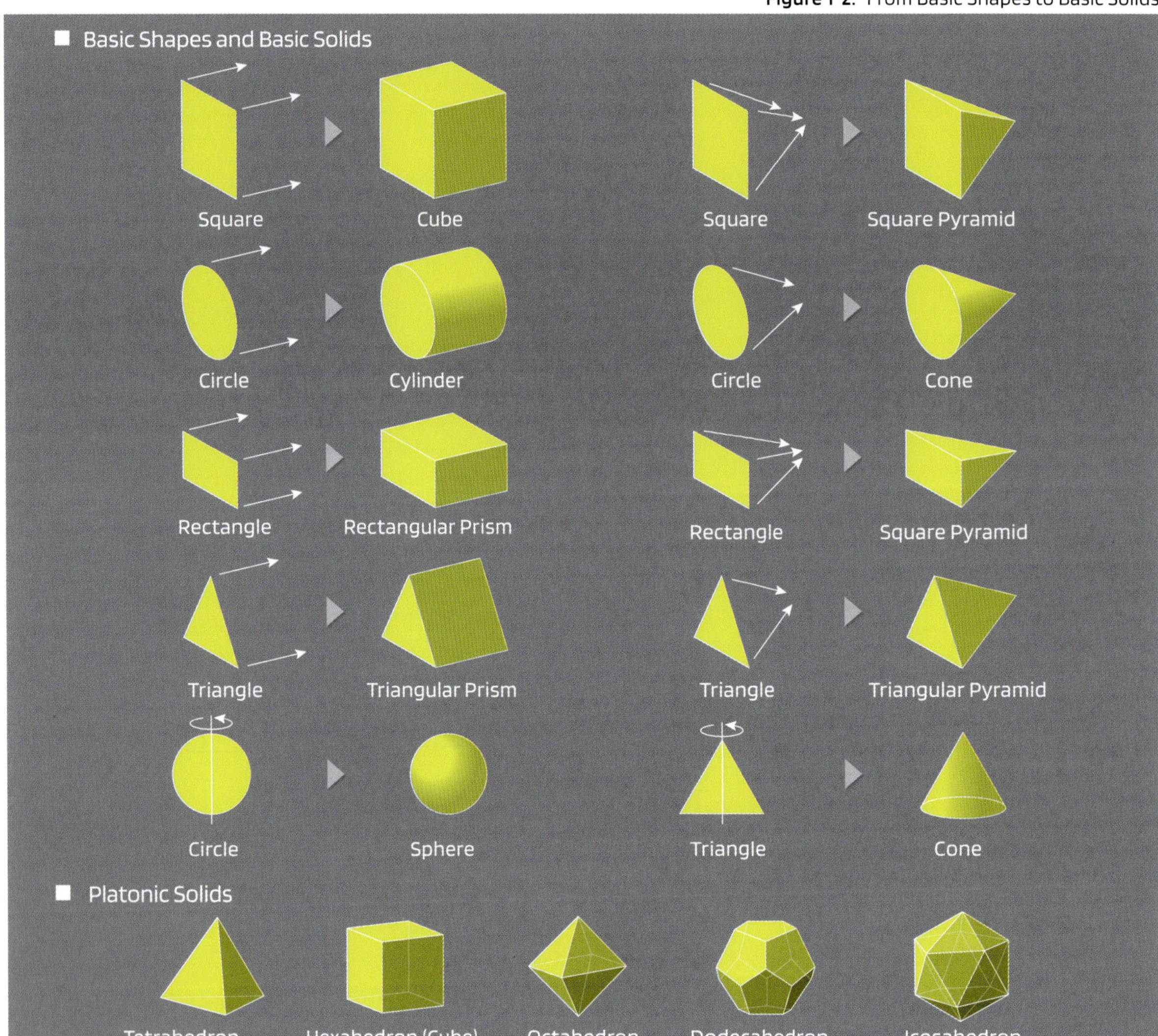

● Applied Solids

Basic shapes and basic solids can be represented by basic mathematical formulas, while forms found in living organisms, human-made forms and those found in inorganic substances are called realistic forms. Human-made forms are based on pure geometric and natural forms.

    These are referred to as applied solids. When it comes to vehicles where air and water resistance is a factor, the designs assume streamlined forms like raindrop or spindle shapes or designs that are low at the front or pointed, such as a dustpan or a wedge. Many other applied solids, like donut, barrel, bell and spring shapes, are commonly used in industrial products.

■ Examples of Applied Solids

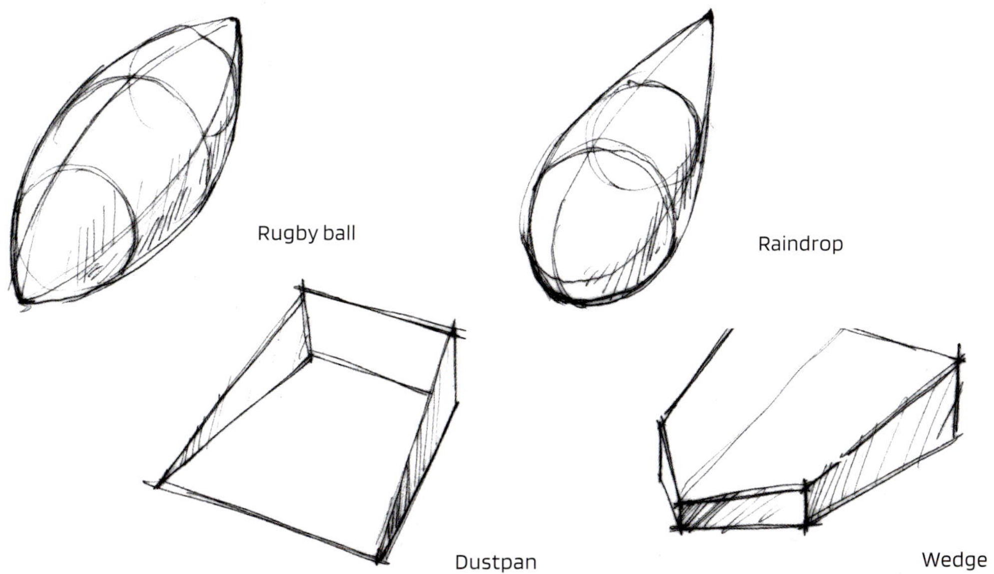

Figure 1-3: Forms Derived from Basic Shapes

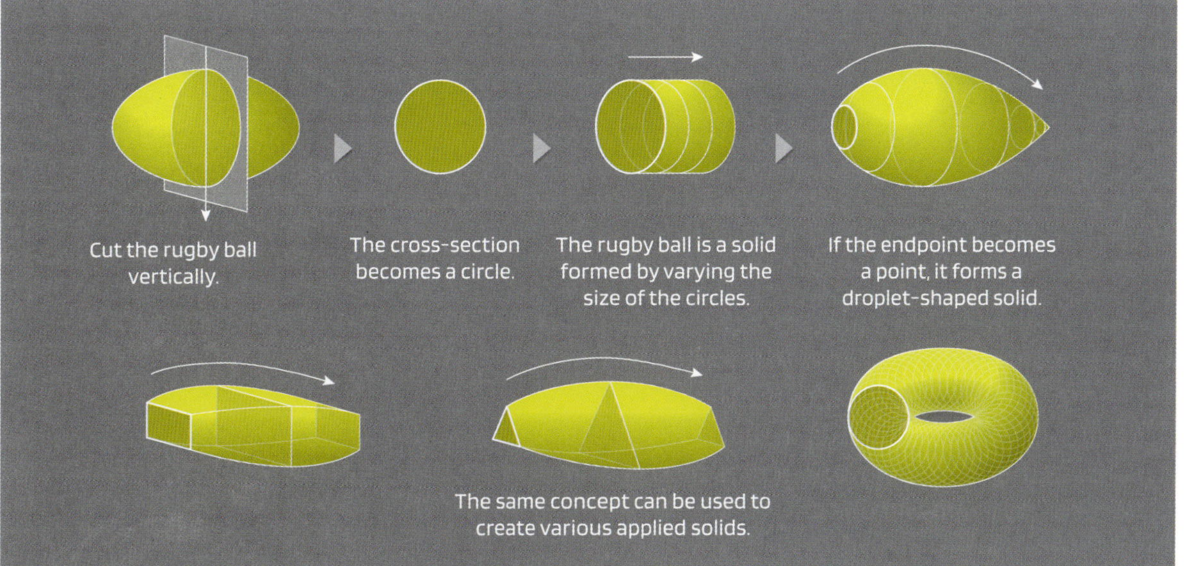

 | # Finding Basic Forms in 3D Objects

Here we've isolated the basic solid shapes that make up the medieval cannon in the photo. Analyzing and breaking down the forms integrated within a three-dimensional object like this will be extremely useful in the following chapters.

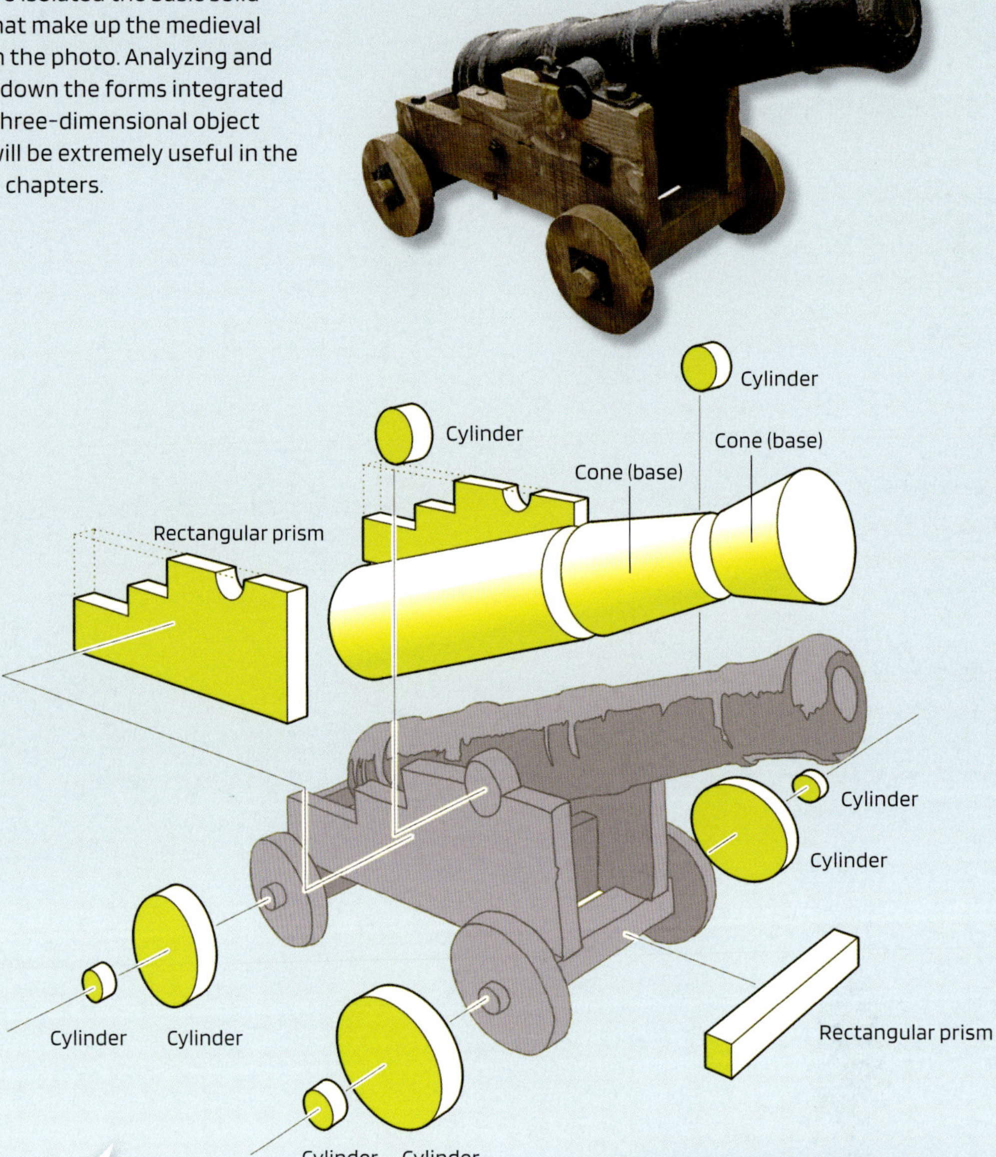

Even parts that appear to have complex shapes can be broken down into basic solid shapes.

DID YOU KNOW?

When identifying the shapes that make up a three-dimensional object, start with the basic shapes → basic solids → applied solids, in that order for each part. In other words, move your perspective from larger parts to smaller ones.

1-2   THREE EASY-TO-USE DIAGRAMS

For certain three-dimensional shapes, simply shifting the shape vertically or horizontally transforms the vehicle. Let's add to our understanding of 3D design by looking at the parallel shifting of vertical and horizontal shapes. Then we'll move on to perspective projection (or perspective view), which represents the form as seen by the human eye.

Military Diagrams

Oblique projection refers to methods that depict a three-dimensional shape by shifting side or plane views in parallel or vertically, without altering their original shapes. There are two types of oblique projection: the cavalier projection, which shifts the front or side view, and military projection, which shifts the plan view.

Cavalier projection shifts the front view diagonally in the depth direction. Military projection first tilts the plan of top view and then shifts its height. With cavalier projection, the angle and dimensions of the front view remain unchanged, while with military projection, the angle and dimensions of the plan/top view remain unchanged. Which method to use depends on whether you want to show the front or the bird's-eye view of the object.

Figure 1-4: Cavalier and Military Projections

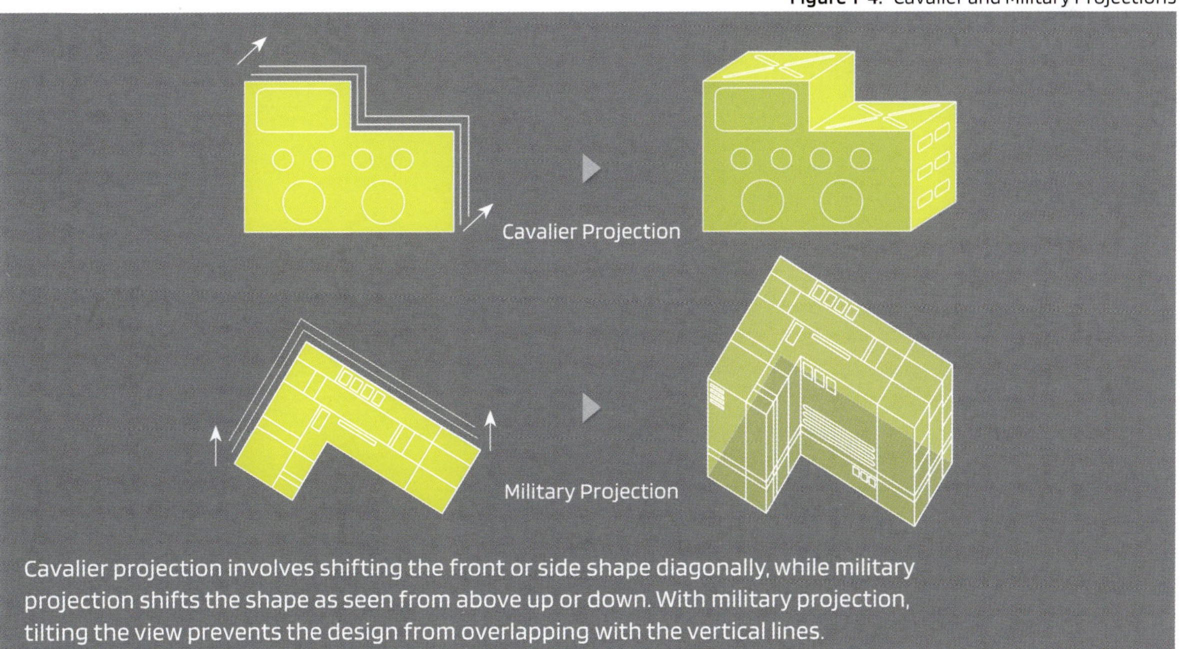

Cavalier projection involves shifting the front or side shape diagonally, while military projection shifts the shape as seen from above up or down. With military projection, tilting the view prevents the design from overlapping with the vertical lines.

■ Drawing a Handgun Using Cavalier Projection

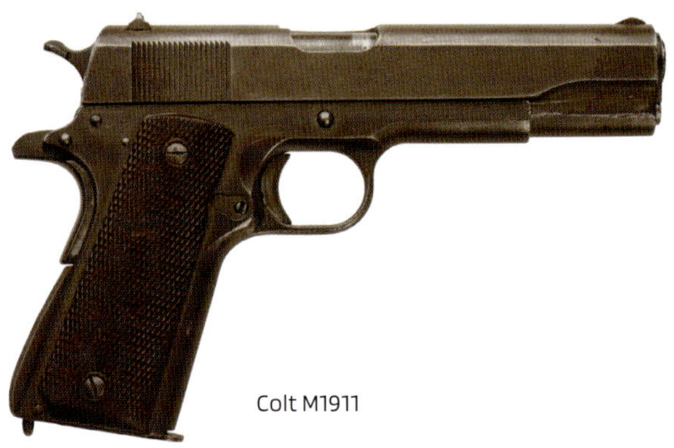

Colt M1911

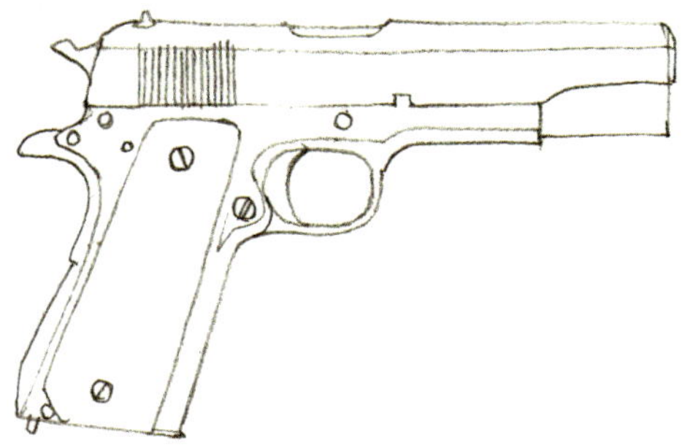

1 Draw the side view of the pistol using photos or diagrams as reference. Set the angle and length offset at 45° and half the actual size, respectively, as the default.

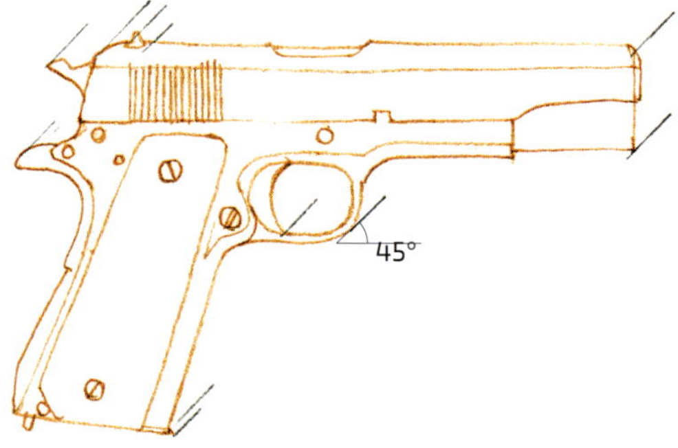

2 Draw a 45° guide line to the upper right.

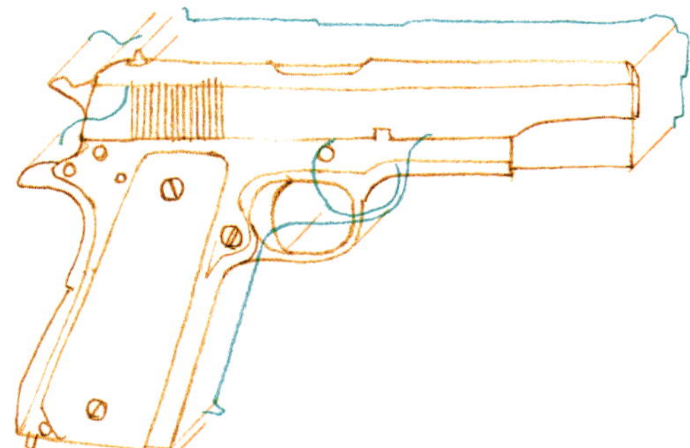

3 Move the top and right contour lines along the guide line.

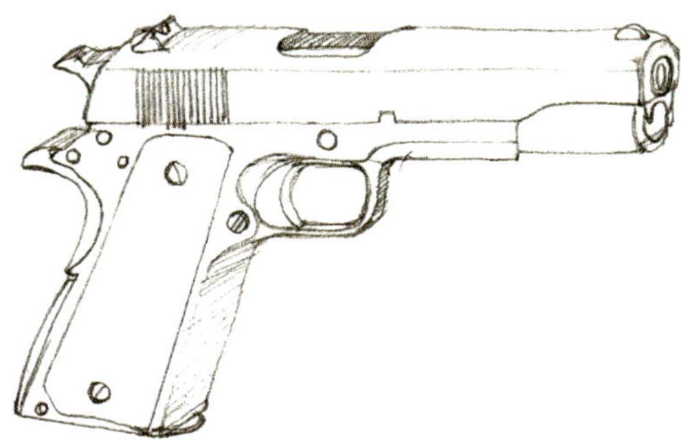

4 Adjust and refine specific areas, such as the trigger, to make them thinner.

■ Drawing a Tank Using Military Projection

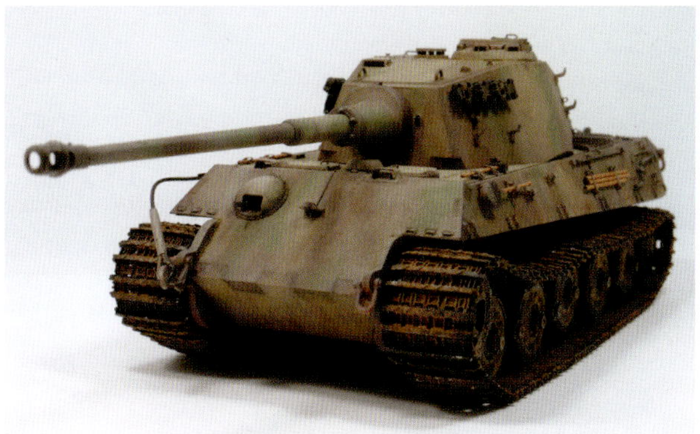

Tiger II

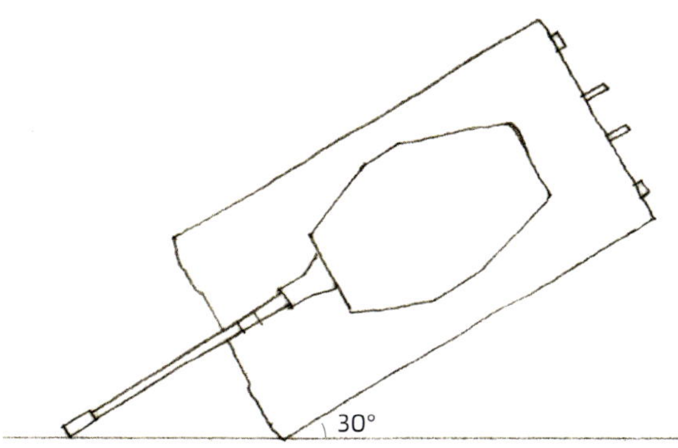

1 Tilt the plan view (the tank as seen from directly above) by 30°.

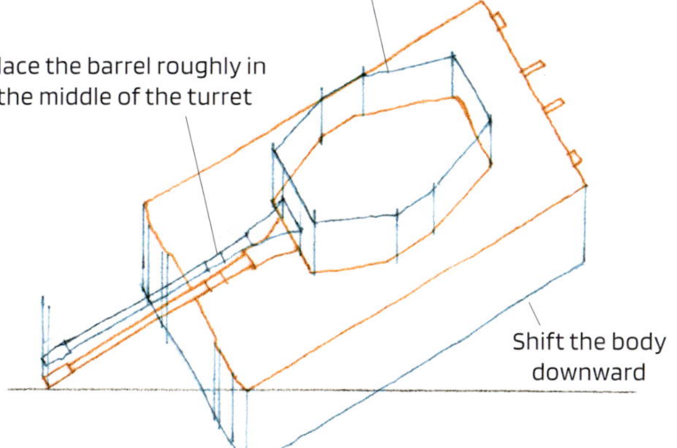

2 Draw the body shifted downward and the turret shifted upward. Adjust the shift so that the barrel aligns roughly in the center of the turret.

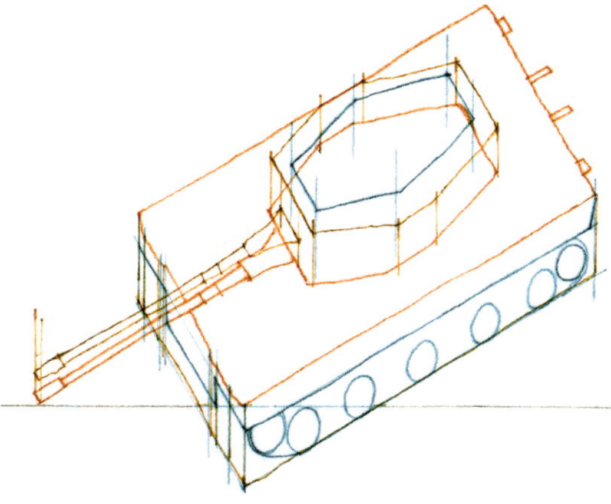

3 Draw the top of the smaller turret. Add caterpillar tracks on the sides.

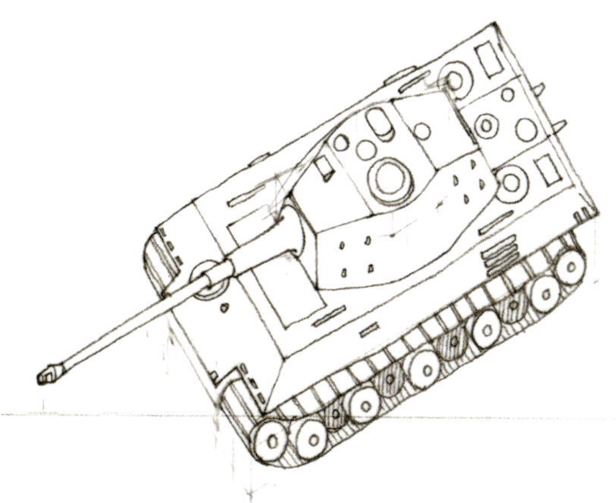

4 Round out the caterpillar track area and add details to the whole image.

Axial and Linear Measurement

As with military projection, where the shape/plane is shifted vertically, axonometric projection involves tilting the shape of a three-dimensional object along the horizontal line and compressing it vertically to create distortion (see below). In the case of a cube, the square shape becomes a parallelogram. Axonometric projection is a method that represents three-dimensional objects by widening the angles at the corners of the planes and elevations.

When drawing axonometric projections, there is no fixed rule for tilting the image, setting the angles or determining the dimension ratios.* This is similar to cavalier projection, where the key is to choose a combination that makes the object or desired view feel the most natural. Additionally, understanding how to draw axonometric projections and tilt shapes/planes provides a foundation for learning perspective drawing.

* With axonometric projection, the tilting of the shape is generally optional, but when set to angles of 30°, 120° and 30°, it's called an isometric projection (also known as isometric drawing or iso view). Isometric projections offer the advantage of using actual dimensions for the lengths and heights.

Figure 1-5: Axonometric Projection

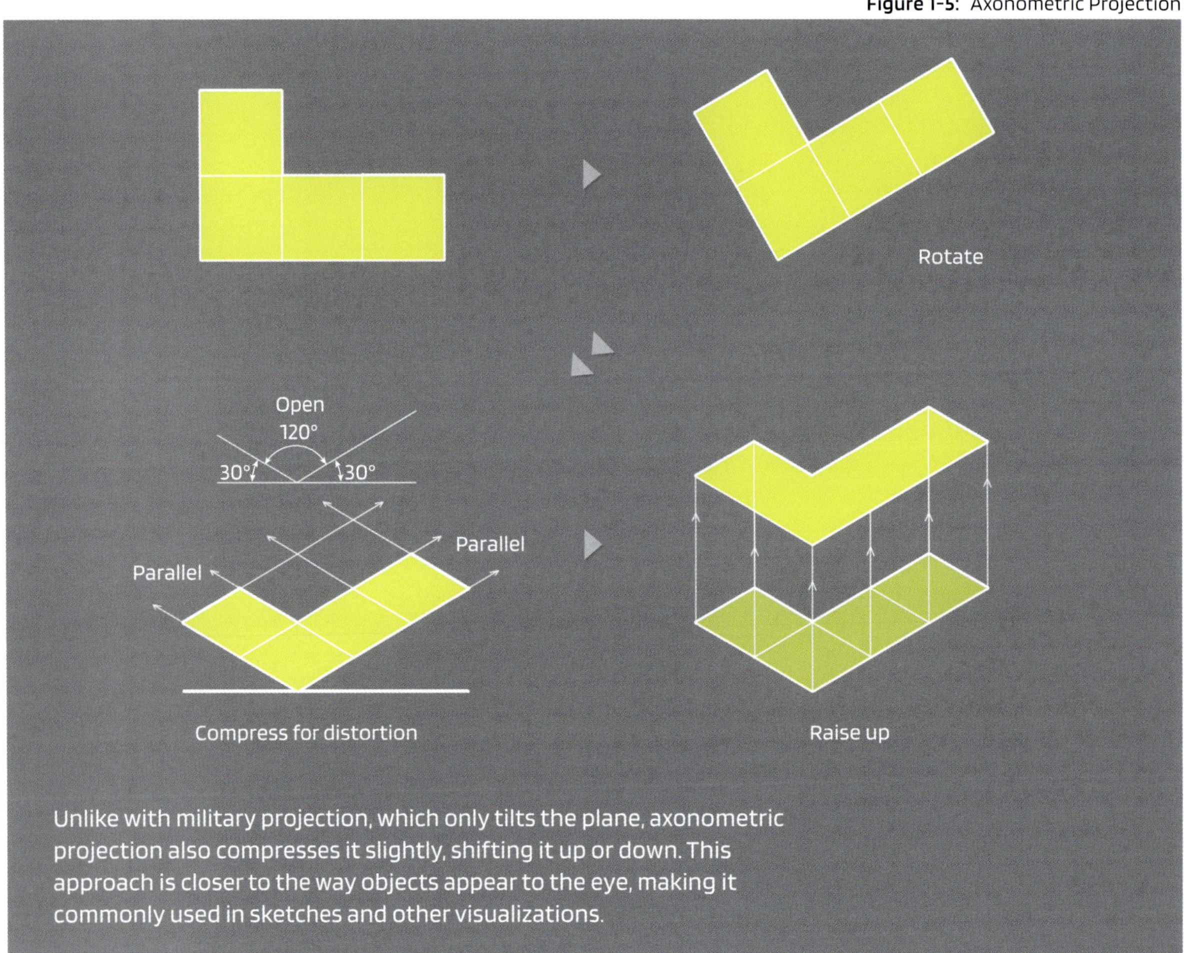

Unlike with military projection, which only tilts the plane, axonometric projection also compresses it slightly, shifting it up or down. This approach is closer to the way objects appear to the eye, making it commonly used in sketches and other visualizations.

■ Drawing an Airplane Using Axonometric Projection

Prepare a plan view and draw a grid. The grid size is arbitrary. Aligning the center and both ends of the shape to the grid will simplify the subsequent steps.

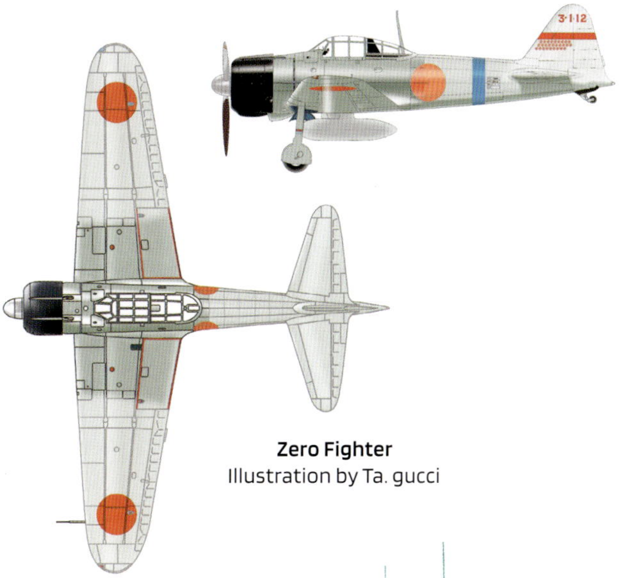

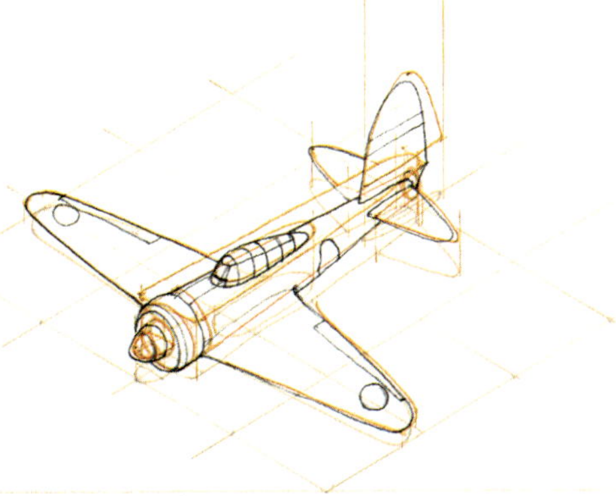

Zero Fighter
Illustration by Ta. gucci

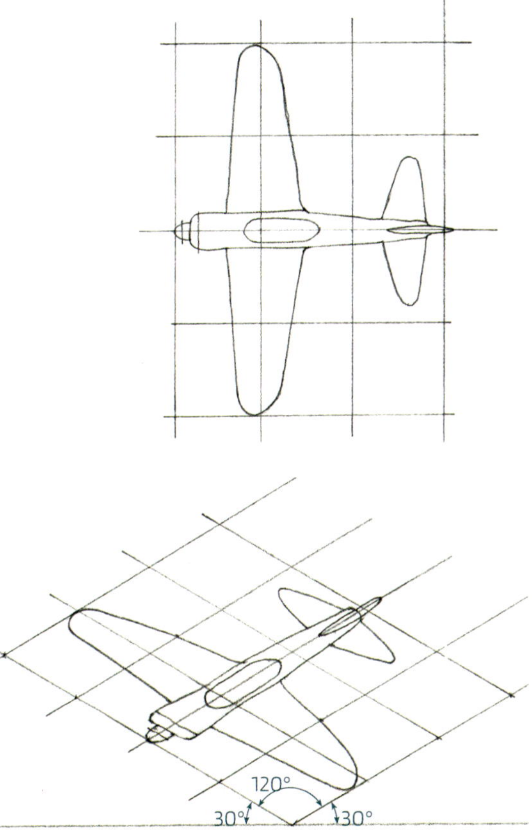

1 Compress the grid to angles of 30°, 120° and 30°. Place in plan view, using the grid for alignment.

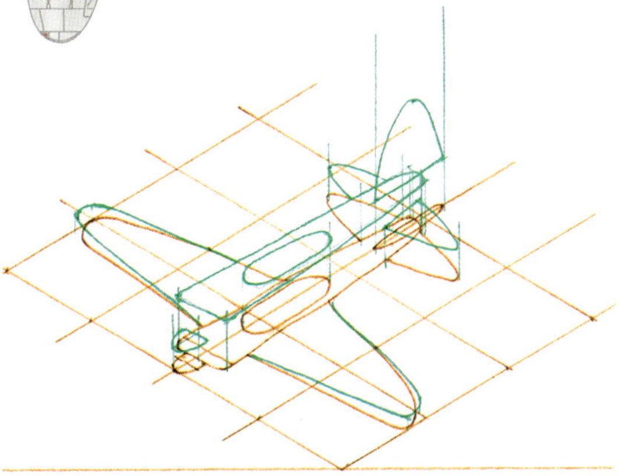

2 Raise each part. Shift the fuselage up by the width of the front section. Lift the wing tips slightly, connecting them to the base.

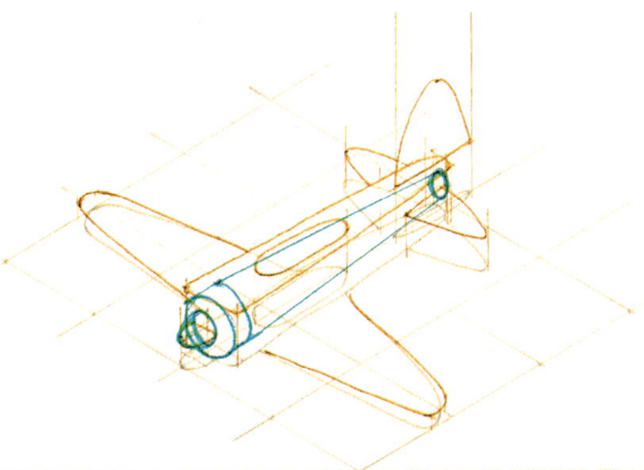

3 Round out the fuselage, which is a rectangular prism. Since the fuselage narrows toward the rear, draw the back circle smaller and connect it with a line to the front.

4 Expand the cockpit. Lower the vertical stabilizer slightly to match the drop in the rear fuselage.

Perspective Grid Method

With cavalier, military and axonometric projections, the lines representing the depth of a cube remain parallel. However, to our eyes, lines that aren't parallel to our viewpoint seem to converge as they recede into the background. When extended, these lines meet at a single point, called the vanishing point. A drawing with lines converging toward the vanishing point is called a perspective drawing.

■ Difference Between Cavalier, Military, Axonometric and Perspective Drawings

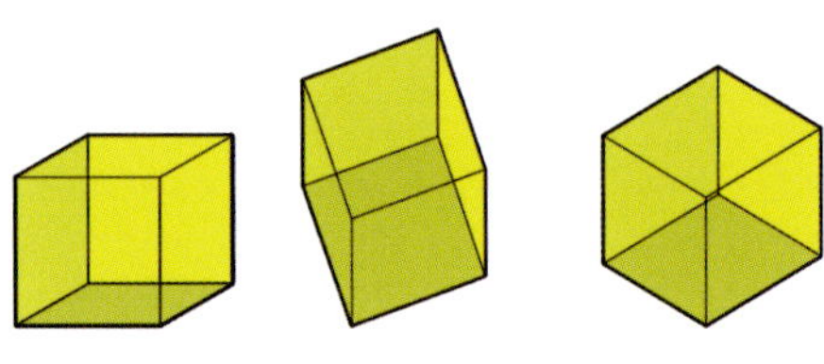

Cavalier, Military, and Axonometric Projections

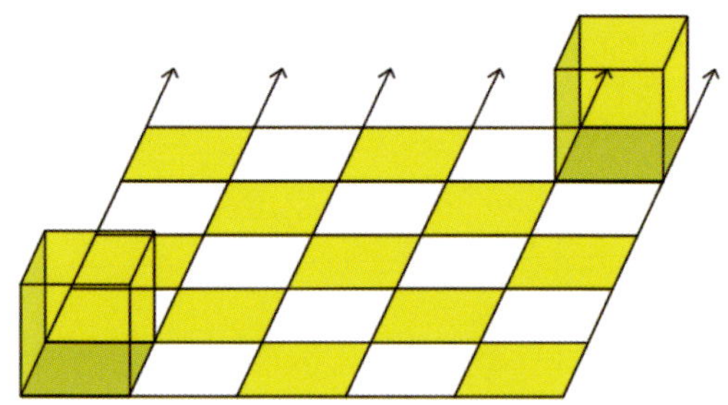

Depth lines are parallel indefinitely, and the cube's size remains the same.

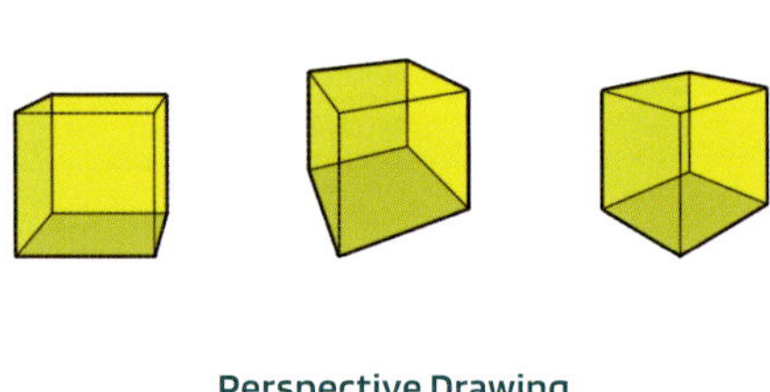

Perspective Drawing

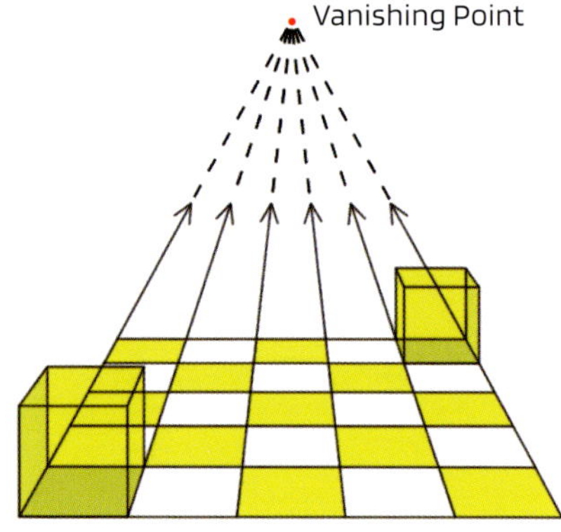

Depth lines converge at the vanishing point, and the cube gets smaller.

Thinking of a checkered pattern helps in understanding perspective drawings. Representing this checkered pattern as straight lines creates a grid. Using this grid to draw three-dimensional objects is called the perspective grid method. With this approach, it becomes relatively easy to draw perspective views of ellipses or complex curves.

● How to Create a Perspective Grid

The number of grid lines can be adjusted according to the object you're drawing. Here, the base line is divided into four sections, connecting them to the vanishing point to create a 4-by-4 grid. Draw guidelines to create a large square that appears natural and then add parallel lines at the intersections of the diagonals and vanishing lines to form the perspective grid.

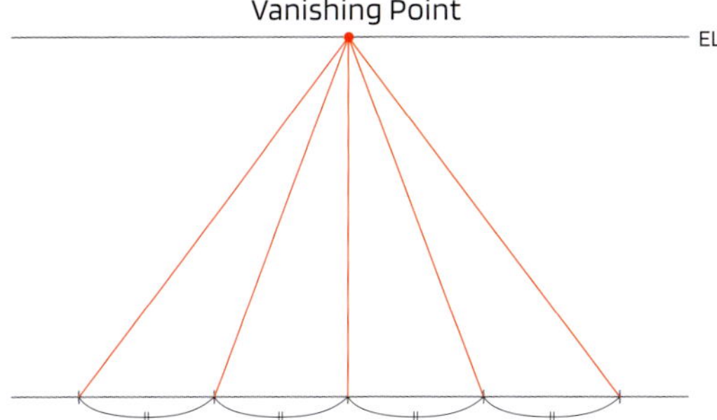

1 Draw the eye level (EL) line at any height you choose, and connect points on the divided base line to the vanishing point.

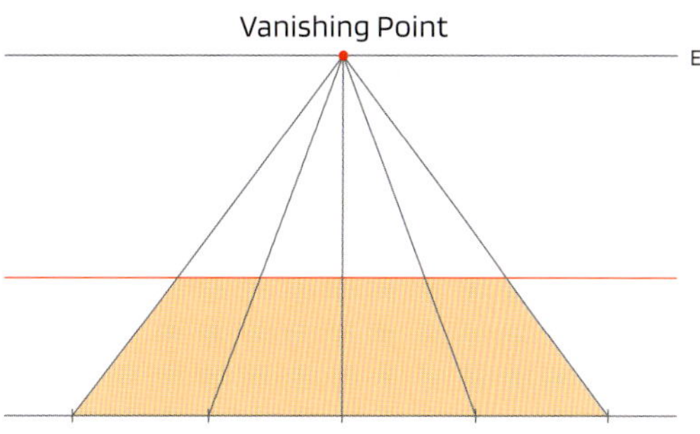

2 Draw a base line (red line) on one side to appear as a rectangle (orange section).

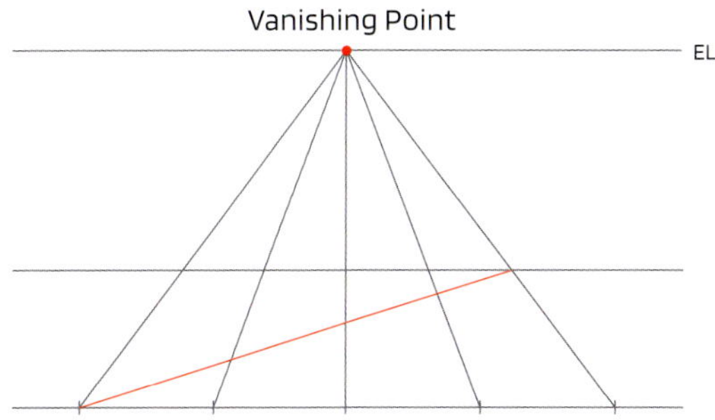

3 Add a diagonal line (red line) within the square.

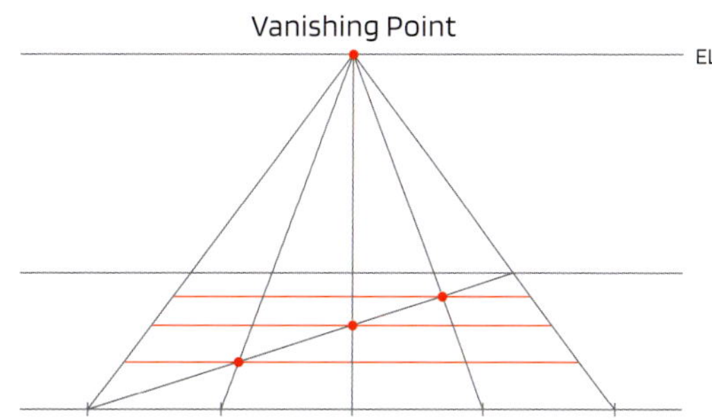

4 Place parallel lines at points where the vanishing and diagonal lines intersect.

■ Expanding the Perspective Grid

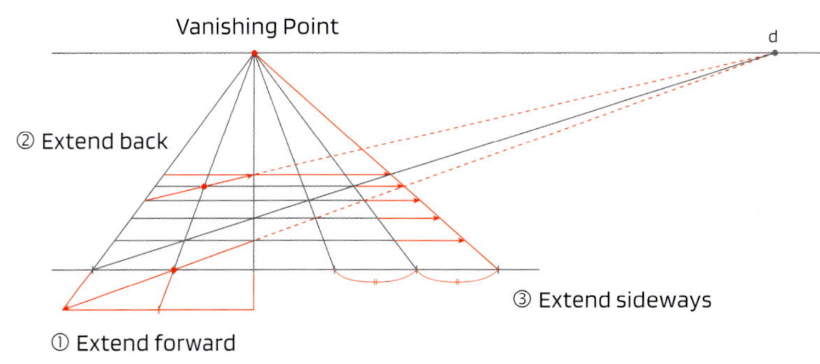

The perspective grid can be freely expanded even after it's complete. To extend it forward or backward, connect the intersection points on the grid to point d on the EL line. To expand it horizontally, keep adding equal-length divisions to the base line in the front.

● Converting to a Perspective Grid

Now let's consider how to convert a top-view plan into a perspective grid by placing points onto the grid. First, draw grid lines onto the shape you want to create.

Then, transform these grid lines into a perspective grid and replace the curves along the way. To do this, make the grid finer in some areas and find the intersection points between the grid lines and the curves. Divide the grid into quarters as a unit for more detail.

■ Drawing Curves by Connecting Points

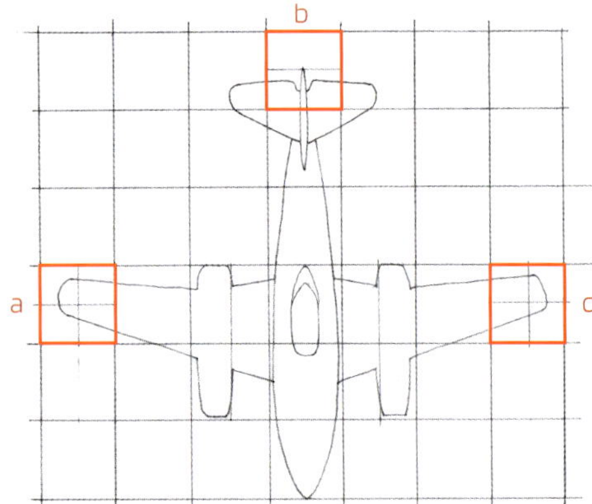

1 Draw a grid using the top-view plan. Place the grid wherever it's easy to draw, not necessarily centered. Here, two lines are set on either side, with points distributed from the front.

For areas like the wingtip and tailfin where the shape doesn't align with the grid, subdivide the grid in these sections (points a, b and c).

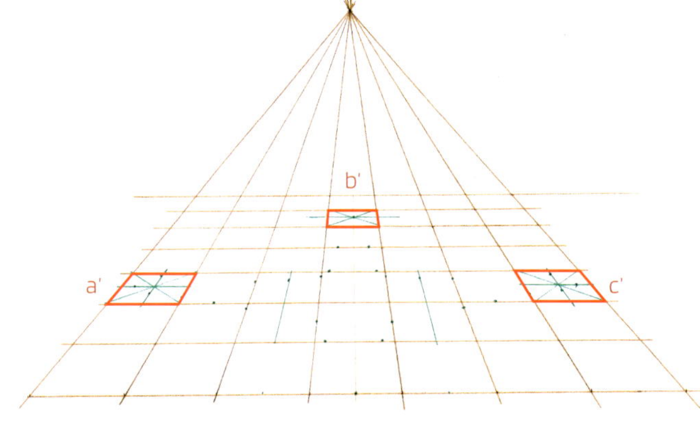

2 Using the grid in Step 1 as a reference, mark the points where the one-point perspective grid intersects the object's contour (a', b' and c' correspond to a, b and c in one-point perspective).

3 Connect each point naturally to form a smooth curve for the rounded areas.

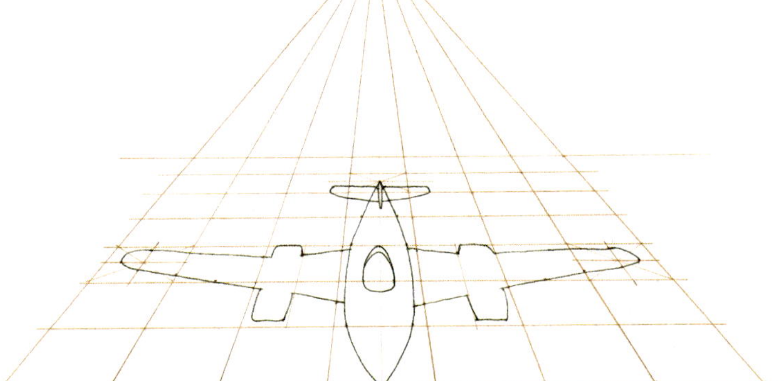

● Three-Dimensional Objects on a Perspective Grid

So far, we've used a one-point perspective grid, but remember that one-point and two-point perspective grids (those with two vanishing points) both exist on the same plane. The illustration below shows a cube placed on both one-point and two-point perspective grids.

A one-point perspective grid is useful when drawing interiors or cityscapes from the front but is less suitable for objects drawn from the side. Since this book focuses on motifs that show depth from a side view, we use a two-point perspective grid.

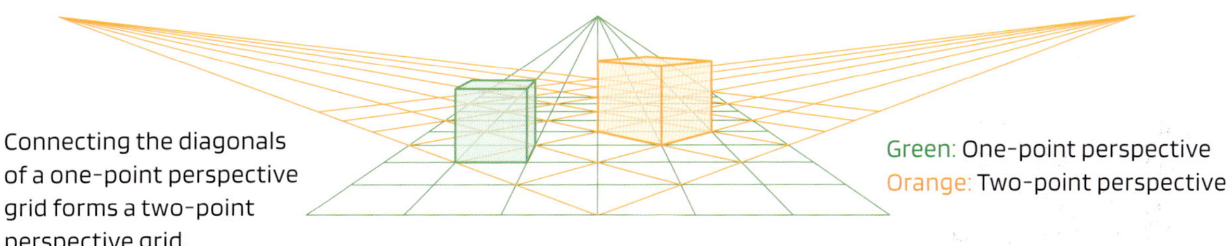

Connecting the diagonals of a one-point perspective grid forms a two-point perspective grid.

Green: One-point perspective
Orange: Two-point perspective

Circles in a Perspective Grid

When drawing circles in perspective, start with a four-part perspective grid. In perspective, circles always appear as true ellipses, not distorted ones. As shown in Figure 1-6, draw grid lines that intersect with the circle and create a four-part grid as the base. Once the grid is replaced with perspective, draw an ellipse that touches the perspective grid. Note that the ellipse's actual center (●) and the center of the ellipse within the perspective grid (diagonal intersection, ✖) do not align.

Figure 1-6: Circles on a Perspective Grid

Circles in a Two-Point Perspective Grid

In a tilted perspective grid, such as two-point perspective, be aware of the circle's central axis direction and draw an ellipse that's perpendicular to it. Here, too, the intersection of the grid's diagonal lines doesn't align with the ellipse's center.

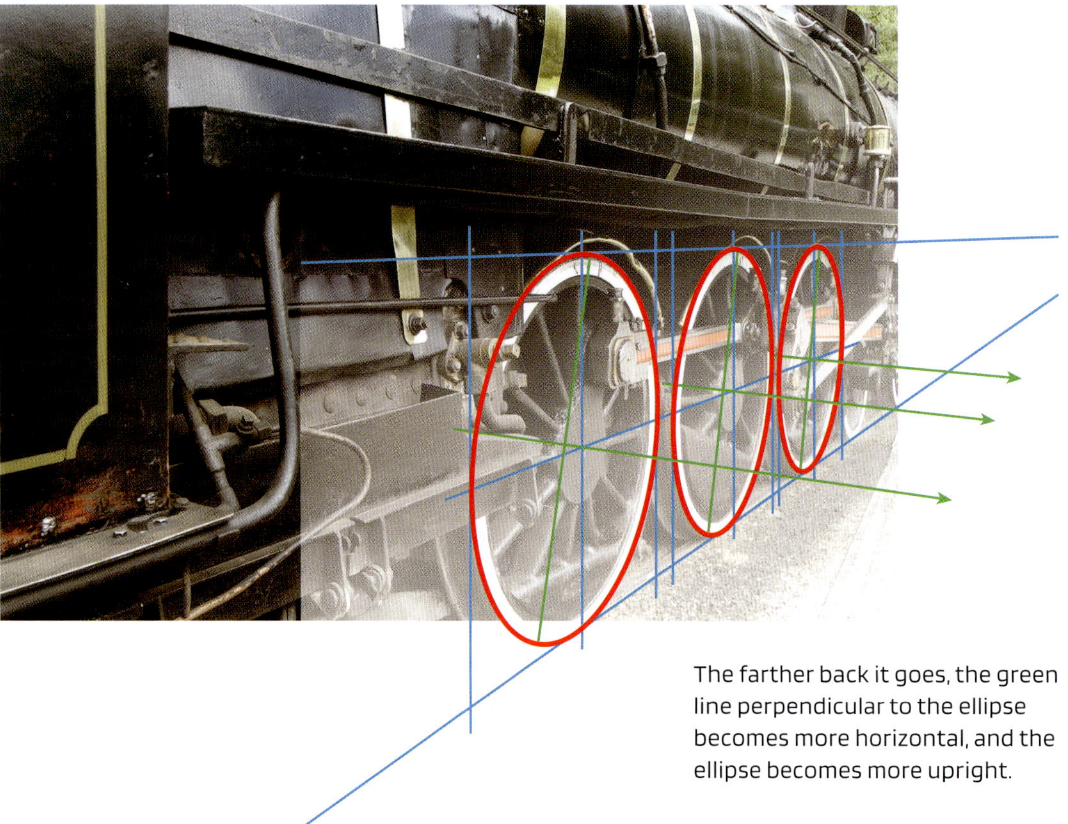

The farther back it goes, the green line perpendicular to the ellipse becomes more horizontal, and the ellipse becomes more upright.

PRO TIP Ellipses within a Square Grid

An ellipse drawn in perspective remains consistent in shape, irrespective of the angle, in both one-point or two-point perspective planes. The line from the center point of the ellipse to the vanishing point is always perpendicular and symmetrical. This emphasizes the importance of initially enclosing an ellipse within a square grid when drawing it.

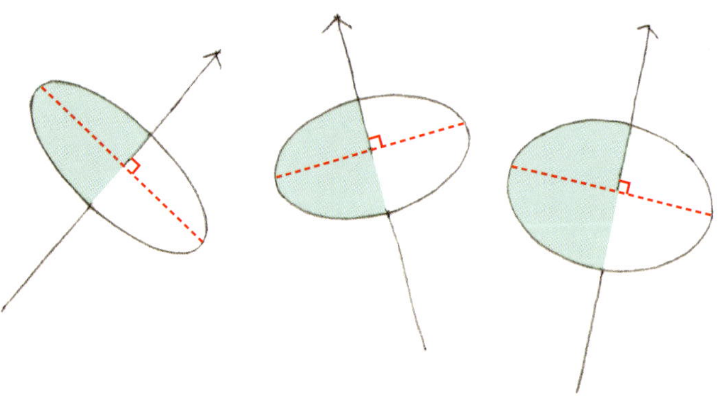

An ellipse is always symmetrical around its perpendicular guide line.

1-3 DRAWING WITH A THREE-DIMENSIONAL PERSPECTIVE GRID

Let's consider a scenario where a perspective grid for a cube has lines for height, width and depth as well as two vanishing points.

The 3D Grid and the Motif

The vehicle is represented as a rectangular prism drawn using two-point perspective. Imagine applying the front, side and top views to each face of this prism.

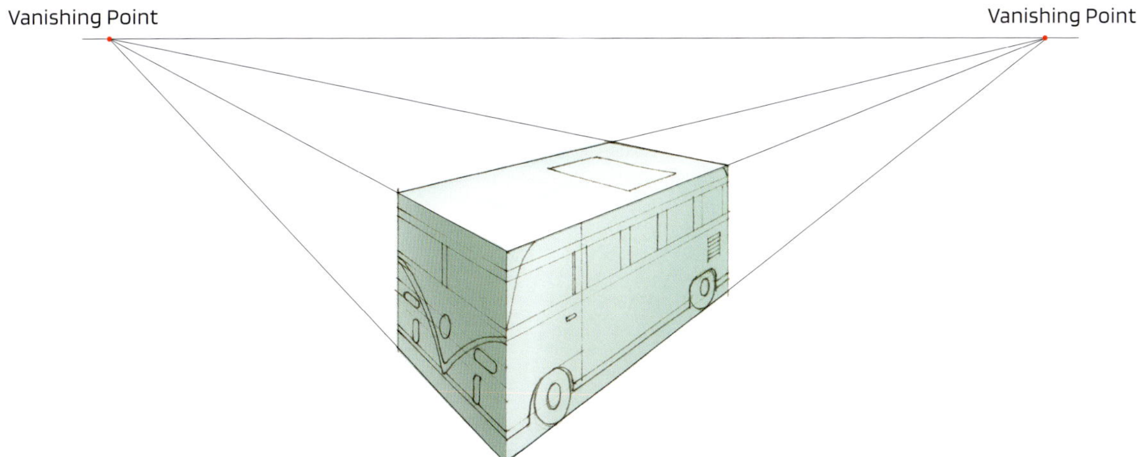

This setup introduces an issue. Currently, the depth appears distorted, making the vehicle look unnatural. The primary reason for this distortion is the incorrect distance to the vanishing points and between the vanishing points on the grid. The observer's viewpoint and the range (the distance between the two vanishing points) are not naturally aligned for a realistic view (see Figure 1-7).

Figure 1-7: Appearance and Distortion Based on Viewpoint and Range

Figure 1-8 shows how a cube appears based on the relationship between the viewpoint (SP) and the vanishing points (VP). When the two vanishing points are close together, the visible range is narrow, causing distortion at the edges of the cube. Conversely, when the vanishing points are farther apart, there's less distortion, but the shape may appear small and flat.

● Viewpoint and Vanishing Points

Figure 1-8: The Relationship Between the Viewpoint and Vanishing Points

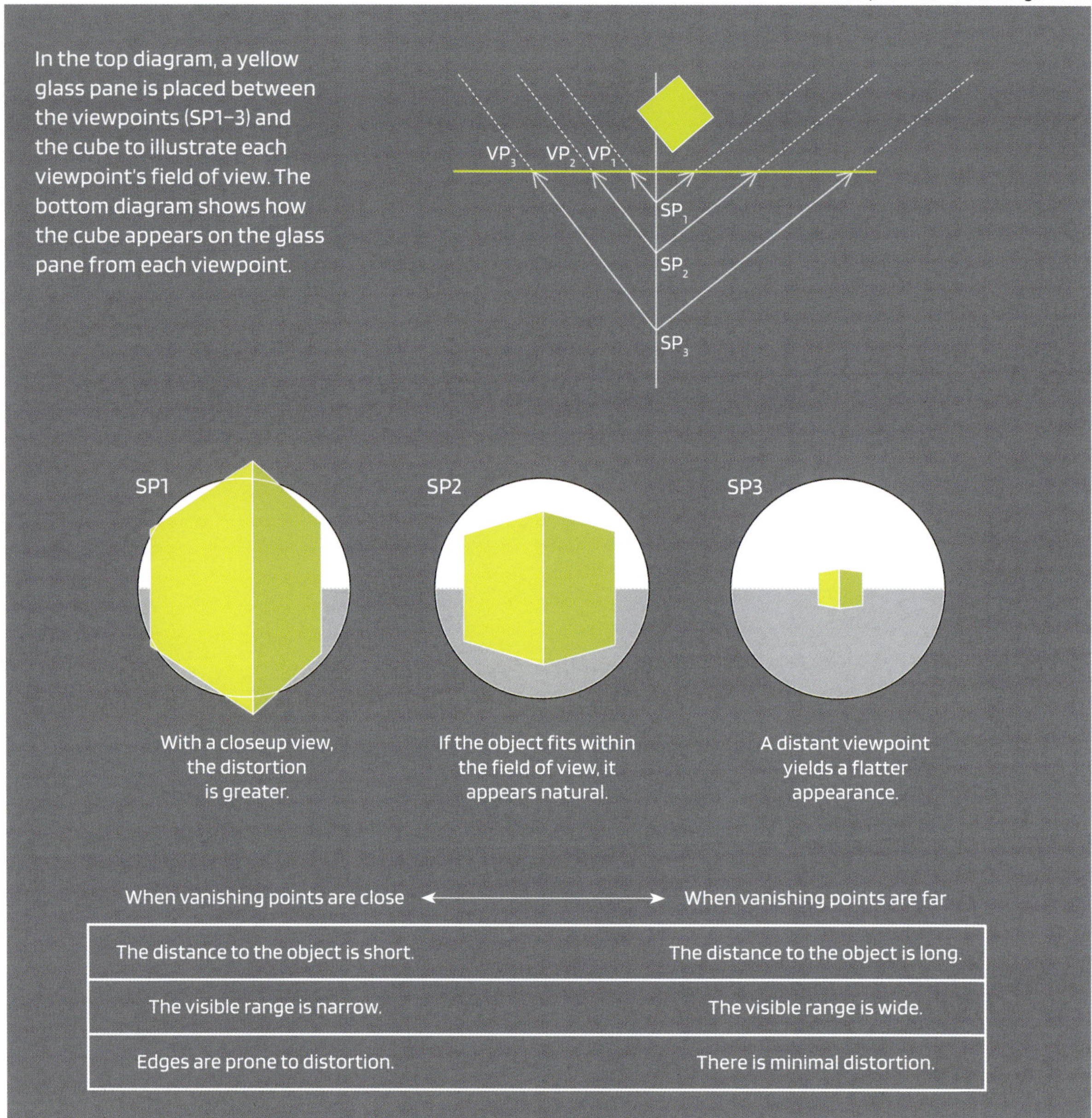

When vanishing points are close	When vanishing points are far
The distance to the object is short.	The distance to the object is long.
The visible range is narrow.	The visible range is wide.
Edges are prone to distortion.	There is minimal distortion.

The lessons and tutorials presented here aim for drawings with no distortion, where the entire form appears natural and impactful. Therefore, the ideal approach is to set a moderate distance between the two vanishing points, filling the field of view with the subject and placing it within the perspective grid of the cube.

Creating the Basic 3D Perspective Grid

The diagram below shows a basic two-point perspective grid, frequently used as a base in the final section: Practical Assessments. The field of view and distance between the vanishing points are set to make the designs appear more natural. The grid consists of six squares toward the right and left vanishing points and three upward squares, forming a three-dimensional structure with internal grids in vertical, horizontal and depth directions. Each face of this 3D grid includes top, front and side views, which help place the subject within it. Dimensions are noted to be used as a draft in actual drawings.

■ Basic 3D Perspective Grid Used in This Book (Dimensional Diagram)

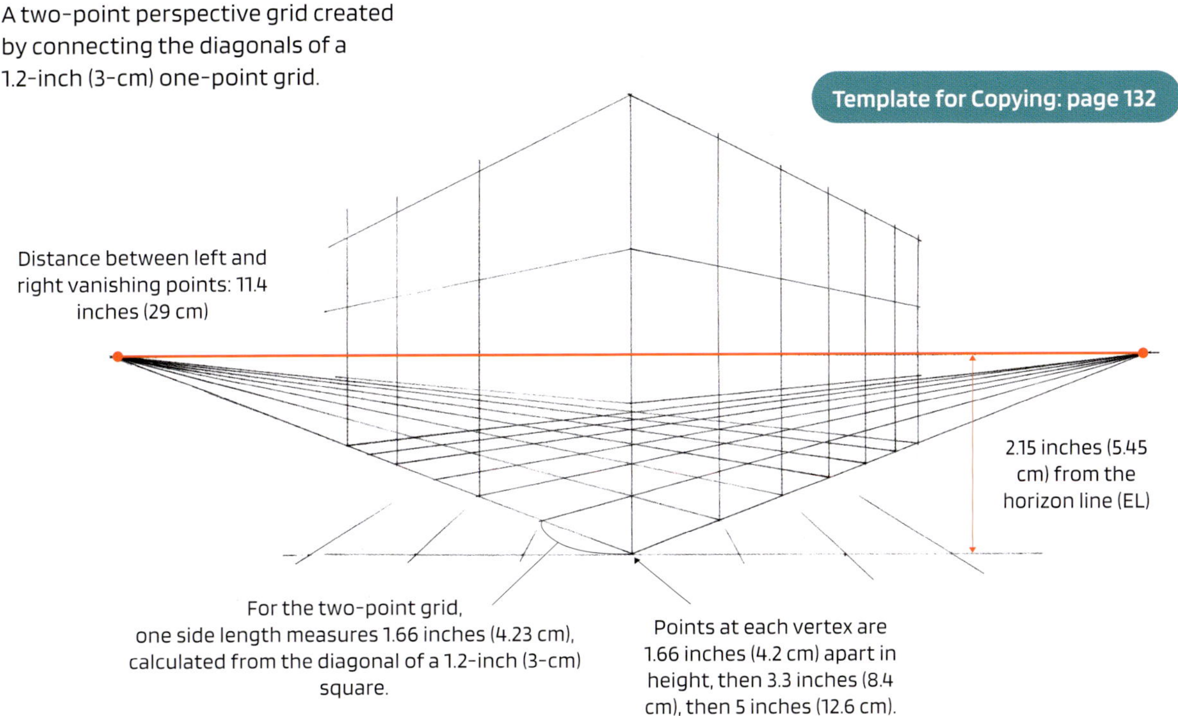

* Note: A copy-ready 3D perspective grid is provided on page 132 at 120% enlargement for actual-size use.

Depth in 3D space includes three directions: left-right in the horizontal direction and one vertical direction. This results in a three-point perspective with vanishing points in three directions for the most accurate perspective. However, drawing in three-point perspective introduces many grid lines leading to vanishing points, making it an often complex process. Here, we've used a simpler two-point perspective grid, focusing on the central area in order to reduce distortion.

Painting Procedures: The 3D Perspective Grid Method

This section provides a step-by-step explanation of how to use a 3D perspective grid based on the front, side and top views. Catalogs for cars displayed at dealerships often feature three-view diagrams like the one shown below, which can also be used for practice.

■ Front, Side and Top Views of the Car

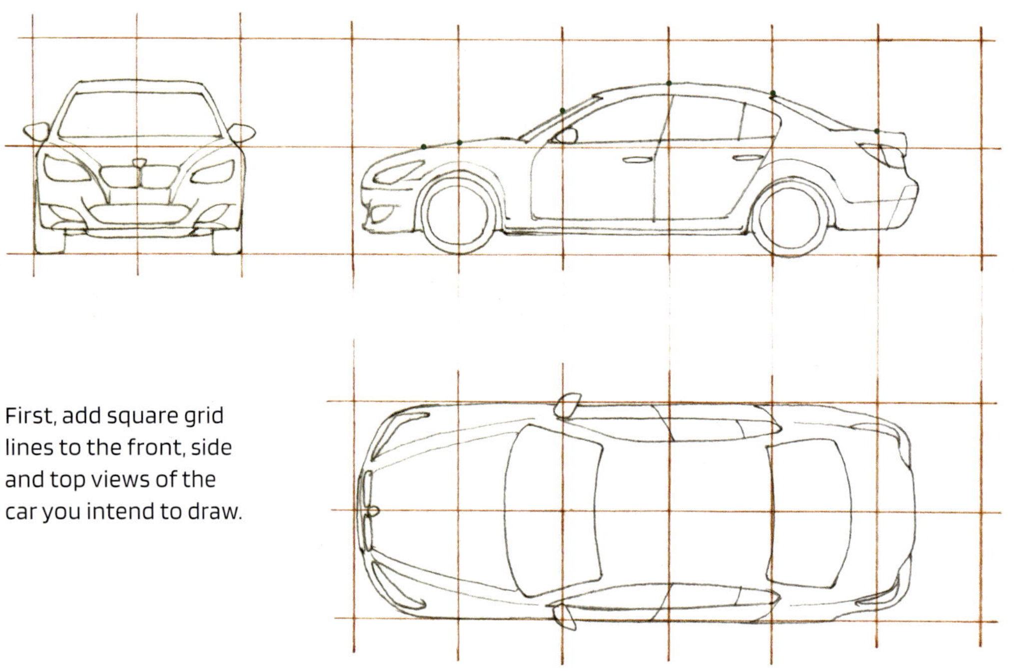

First, add square grid lines to the front, side and top views of the car you intend to draw.

■ Drawing Steps

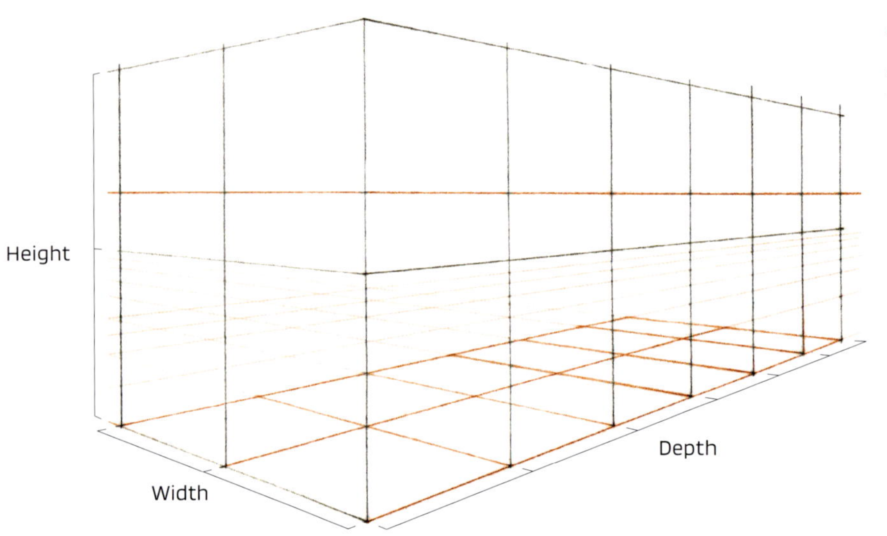

1 Draw a 3D perspective grid with dimensions of width 2 × depth 6 × height 2.

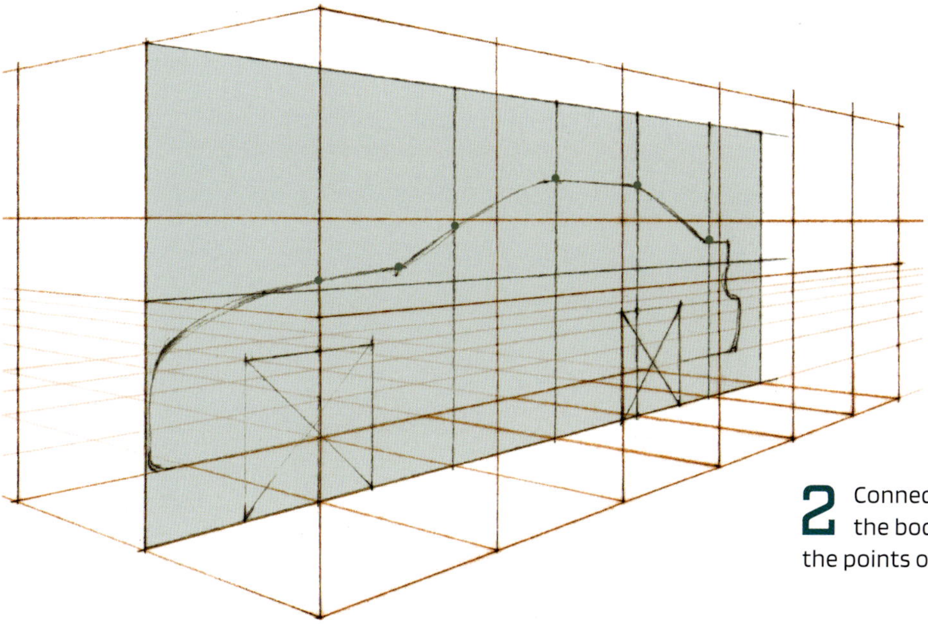

2 Connect the curves of the body by referring to the points on the side view.

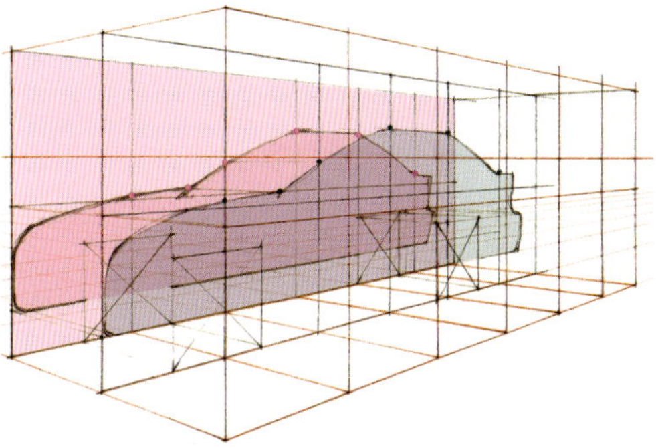

3 Transfer the side view to the back face. Focus on the intersections with the grid. Draw a line extending from the green point in the direction of the vanishing point and connect it to the intersection with the back grid (the pink).

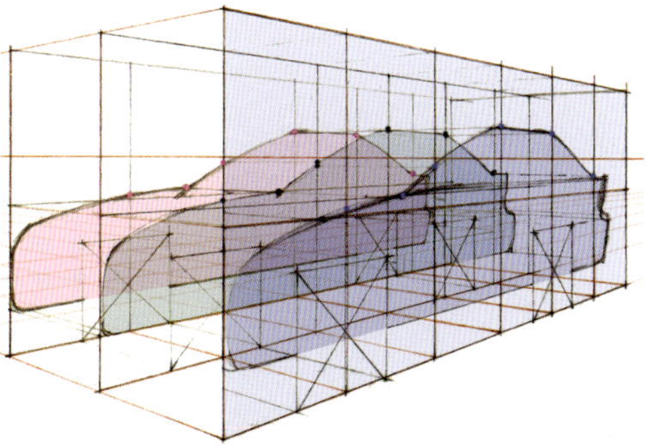

4 Transfer the side view to the front face. Draw a line extending from the green point in the direction of the vanishing point toward the front and connect it to the intersection with the front grid (the blue).

5 Transfer the front view. This is done to show the front and to adjust the width of the roof section for the seating area.

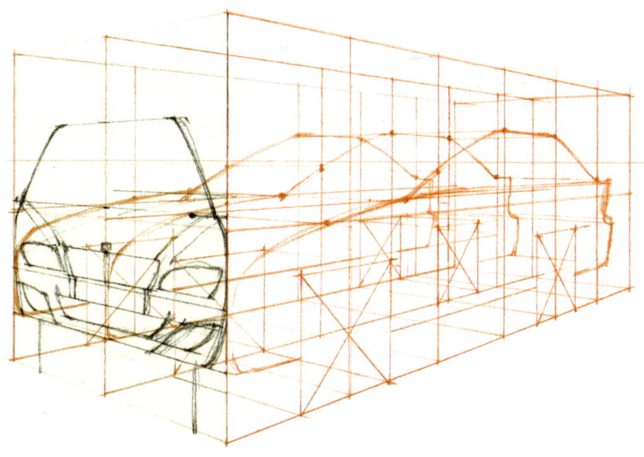

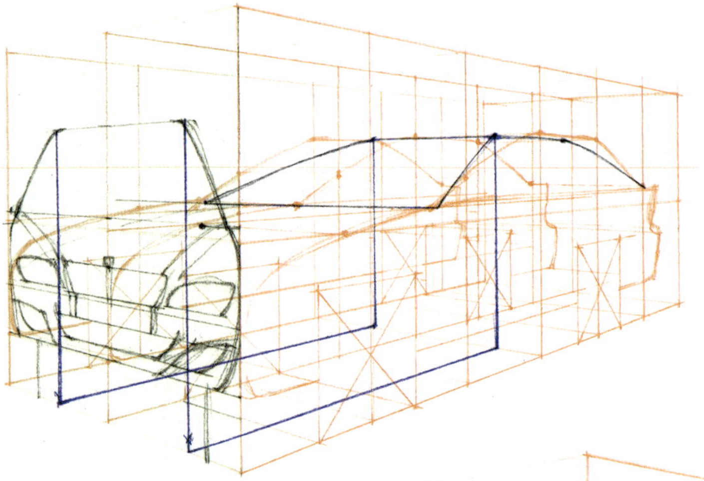

6 Transfer the width of the roof. Ideally, you would extend this width in the direction of the vanishing point and take the intersection point for the roof's width. However, since the roof appears flattened in this drawing, this method would be inaccurate. Instead, lower the point temporarily, move in the direction of the vanishing point, and then rise up from directly underneath the roof to determine the roof's width.

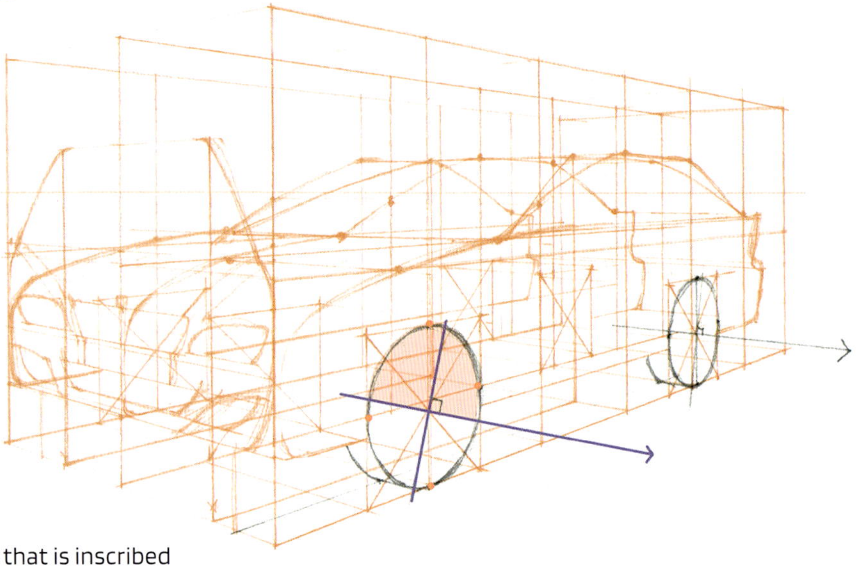

7 For the tires, draw a circle that is inscribed within a square. This circle will pass through the four points at the top, bottom, left and right of the square. Additionally, it will become an ellipse divided in half by the vanishing line that runs toward the axle. Unfortunately, the rear tire will not be visible from this angle.

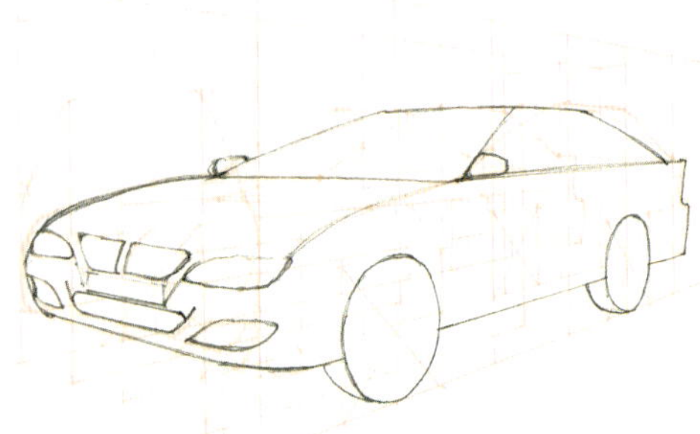

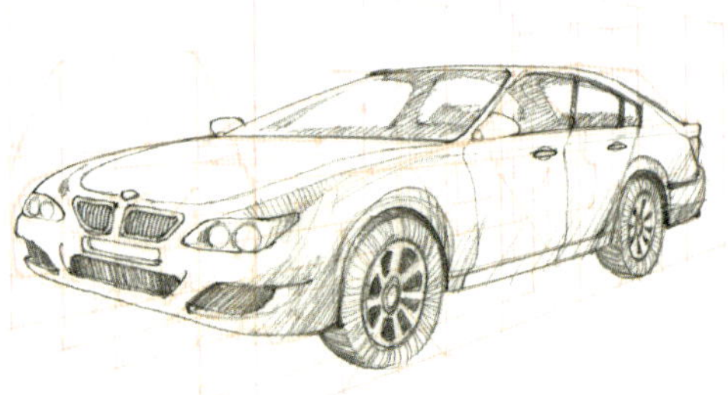

8 Transfer the width of the tires from the front view and organize the lines temporarily.

9 Pay attention to the direction of the vanishing point as you add details and nuances.

● Adjusting the 3D Perspective Grid to Accommodate Various Motifs

Depending on the size and shape of the vehicle or mecha mashup you're drawing, you may find that you need more depth in the grid or want to reduce its height. Understanding how to increase or decrease the grid as shown below will help you adapt your design.

■ Increasing and Decreasing the 3D Perspective Grid

● Increasing the 3D Perspective Grid

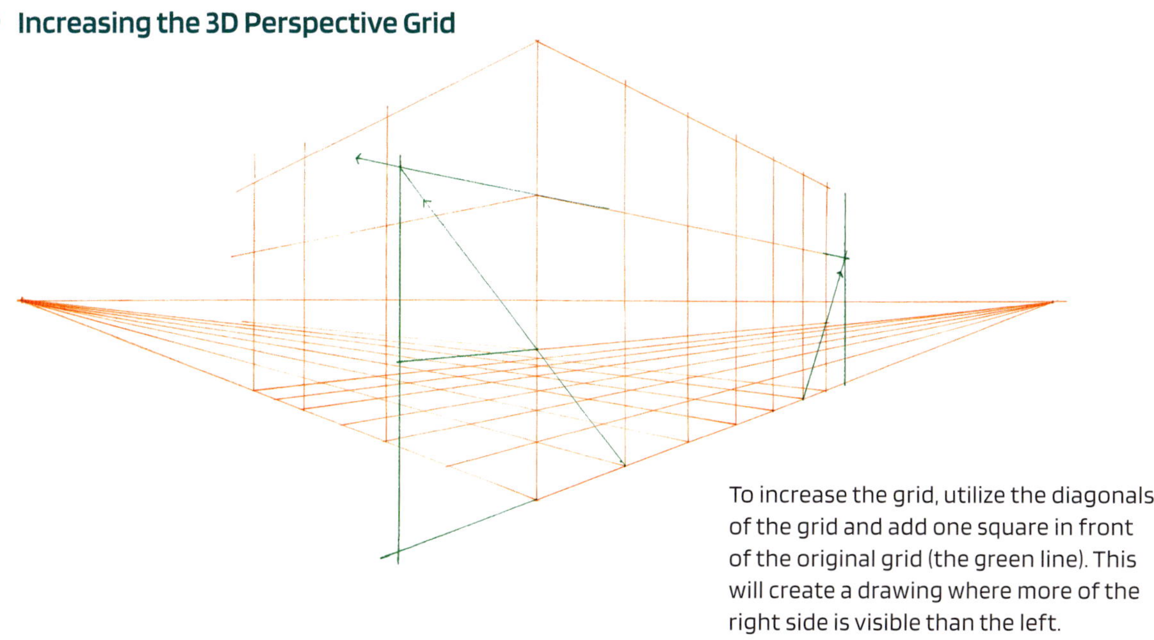

To increase the grid, utilize the diagonals of the grid and add one square in front of the original grid (the green line). This will create a drawing where more of the right side is visible than the left.

● Decreasing the 3D Perspective Grid

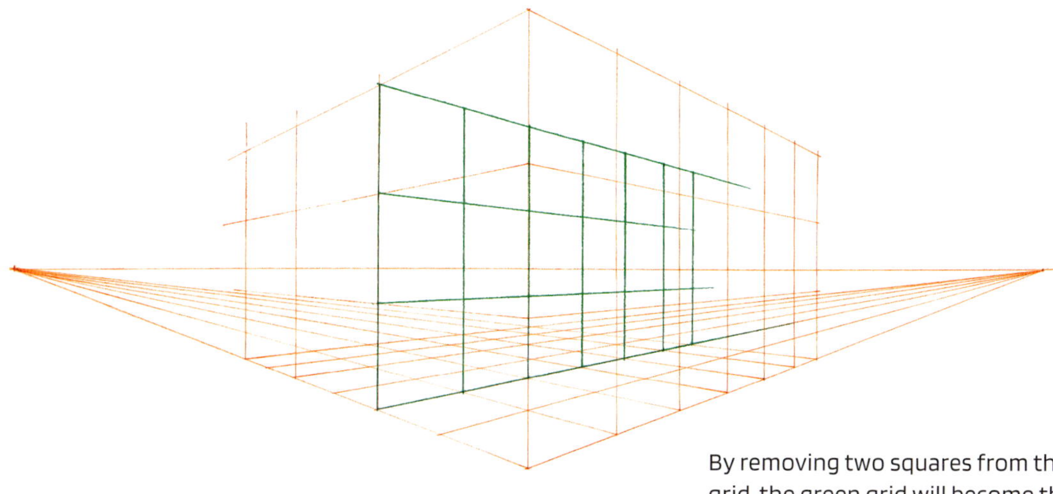

By removing two squares from the front grid, the green grid will become the side grid. Compared to the original grid, this allows you to create a drawing that appears to be viewed more from the side.

TAKE A CLOSER LOOK | Perspective in Japanese Painting and Illustration

Perspective drawing was invented during the Renaissance in 15th-century Italy. Although we tend to think that renderings using perspective are characteristic of Western painting, the history of painting using perspective is only about 600 years old. There were no paintings using perspective in ancient civilizations, nor in the Greek and Roman periods. The Age of Exploration, which coincided with the Renaissance, brought perspective paintings to the East. It wasn't a technique or a method of drawing that was introduced, but a finished painting. Traditionally, Chinese painting emphasized spirituality rather than realistic expression, and spatial representation of buildings was done in a manner similar to oblique projection. Landscape paintings may appear realistic at first glance, but when you actually stand in the place where they were created, you'll see that the scenery from various viewpoints has been combined and edited into a single composite image.

These qualities are also evident in traditional Japanese painting and ukiyoe. In Japan during the Edo period (1603–1868), Western books and paintings were brought to Japan via China. These were called ukiuki-e or kokumi-e in Japan at the time and were sometimes used as models by Japanese painters and ukiyoe artists. Famous examples include works by Katsushika Hokusai and Maruyama Okyo. Later, painters emerged who studied and implemented perspective. By the end of the Edo period, painters began to create more accurate pictures in perspective, and Western-style spatial expression took root.

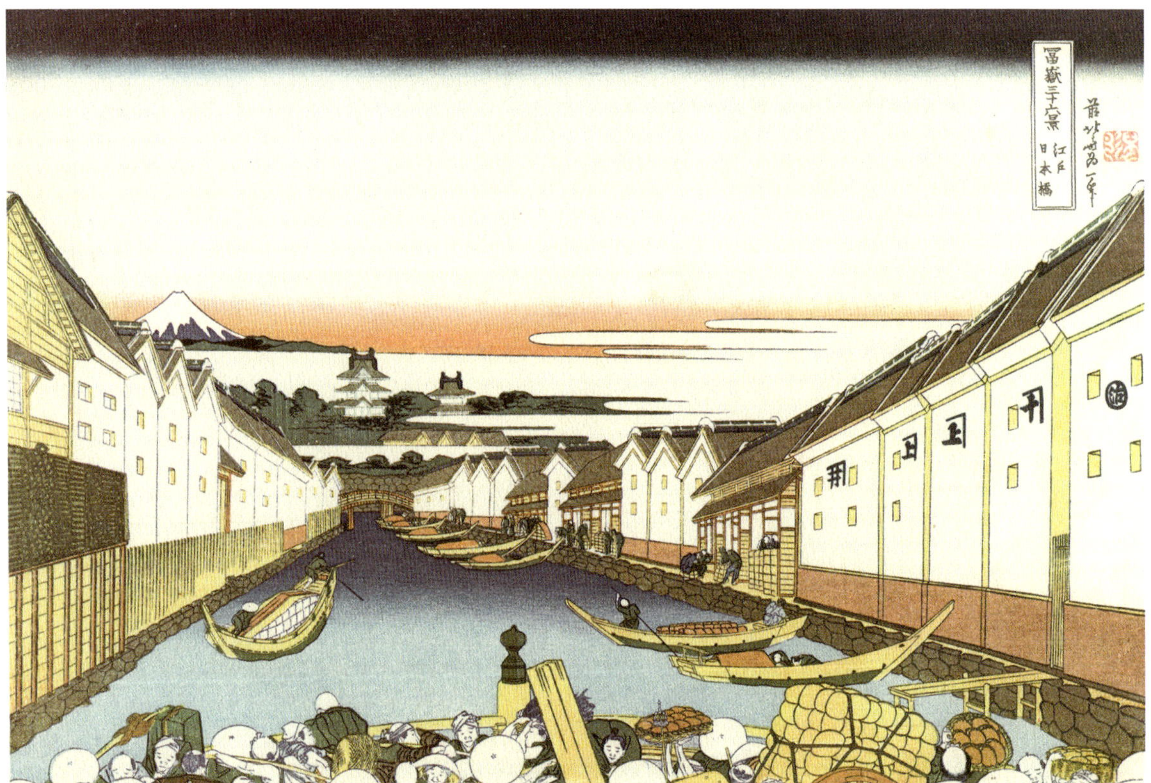

Katsushika Hokusai, *Fugaku Sanjurokkei (Thirty-six Views of Mt. Fuji), Edo Nihonbashi*

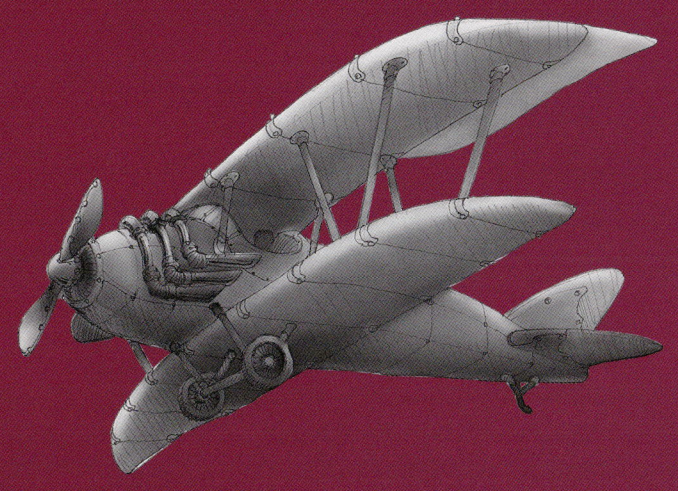

Part 2

FORM, FUNCTION AND DESIGN: SOME HINTS

One way to get started on your original mecha creation or sci-fi fantasy vehicle is to think of a theme, motif or subject matter. Then develop your design according to that concept. Here, we'll share some useful hints and give you some examples of fusing function, fantasy and form.

2-1 LEARNING FROM STANDARDS

So how do I get started? There's no one answer, but perhaps the best way is to look to the world around you, the masterpieces and classics, the pop culture products and aesthetic traditions—known as standards. Observe, study and absorb their characteristics and strengths as references for your own designs. Collect materials and resources, such as photographs and drawings, regularly of anything that inspires you or fuels your imagination.

Formal Trends

Forms are influenced by functionality but also by the passage of time. Mechanical designs and vehicles have evolved not only due to advancements in function and materials but also through changes in consumer preference. Understanding the trends that have influenced various forms and then integrating these visual traditions into your own designs is one key source of inspiration. At the same time, remember that forms and designs from earlier times can appear innovative in a different or modern context or among those who prize simplicity in design.

● Evolution of the Tōkaidō and Sanyō Shinkansen Vehicles

To understand how forms change over time, let's look at the various trains that have crisscrossed Japan since the late twentieth century. The vehicles of the Tōkaidō and Sanyō Shinkansen, now a vital artery of the nation's archipelago, initially appeared with rounded forms and evolved to become more aerodynamically efficient over time. While the pursuit of cutting-edge technology certainly alters their shapes, it's also very interesting to consider the influence of aesthetics and marketing in their evolution.

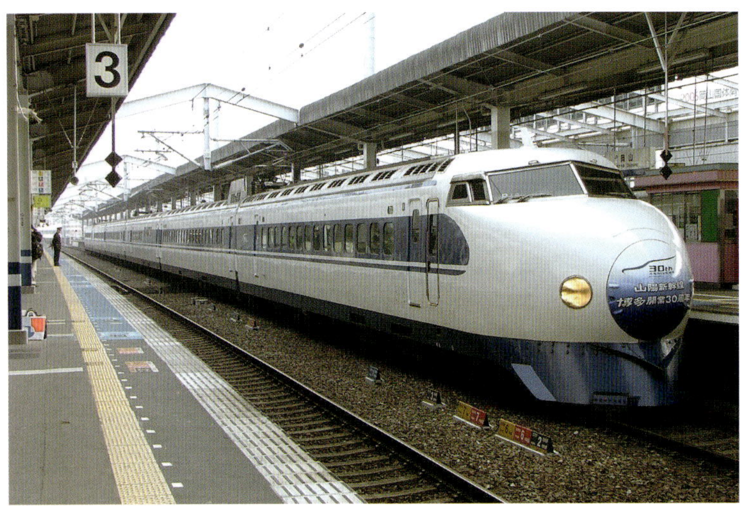

0 Series Hikari
The first-generation Shinkansen Hikari. Viewed from the front, the driver's cab windows give a gentle rounded face. On the other hand, the blue-painted skirt adds solidity and weight. At the time, it was an extremely futuristic design that was completely different from previous trains, but from our present perspective, it now looks somewhat retro and nostalgic.
(Commercial operation began in 1964.)

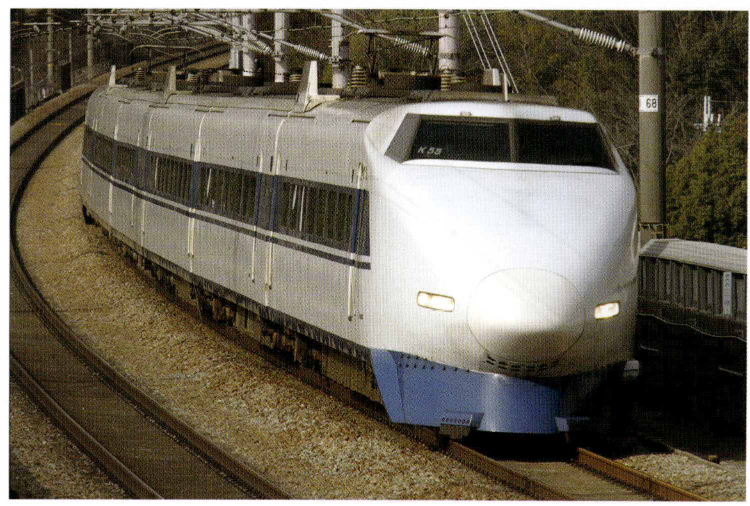

100 Series Kodama

The bullet-shaped nose helped define this model. The painting generally follows the design of the 0 series, but the pointed tip and elongated lights convey a sense of speed, marking a new era of Shinkansen.
(Commercial operation began in 1985.)

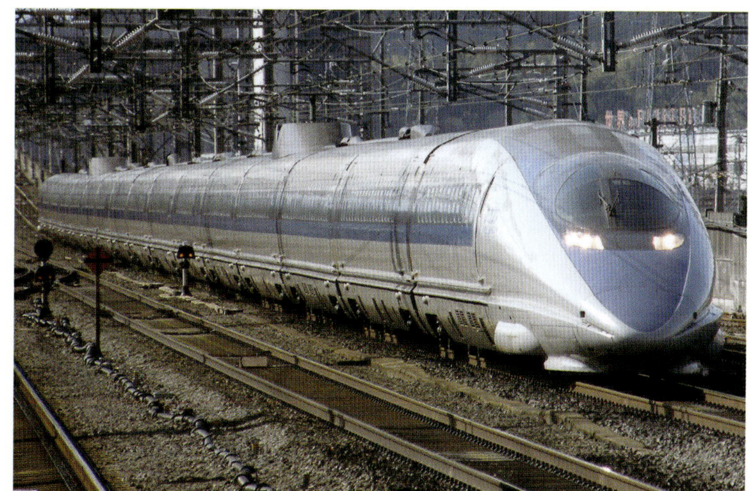

500 Series Nozomi

This design suggests a rounded, metallic capsule. The form features a sharp taper from the middle of the body to the tip, resembling a fighter jet.
(Commercial operation began in 1997.)

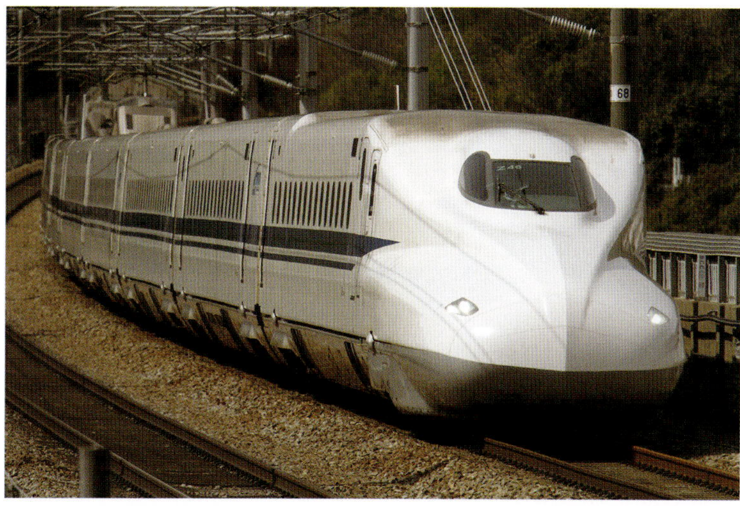

N700 Series Nozomi

The front shape, based on fluid dynamics, suggests a platypus. This design is the evolution of a form that has been meticulously refined based on complex calculations to achieve both high-speed operation and noise reduction.
(Commercial operation began in 2007.)

Standard Appreciation and Observation

There are many excellent features in the forms and designs of past classics and masterpieces of the form. When creating mechanical designs and vehicles, referencing and reinventing the best designs and outstanding standards is one way of advancing your vision and setting your designs apart.

● Two-Wheeled Vehicle (Honda Dream CB750 FOUR)

A masterpiece of a motorcycle with a 750cc engine, it was first produced by Honda Motor Co. in 1969. Until then, large motorcycles had been the domain of Western companies, but this marked the beginning of larger Japanese models. The design highlights the size and high-performance, instantly recognizable by its four-cylinder engine with four exhaust pipes (two on each side).

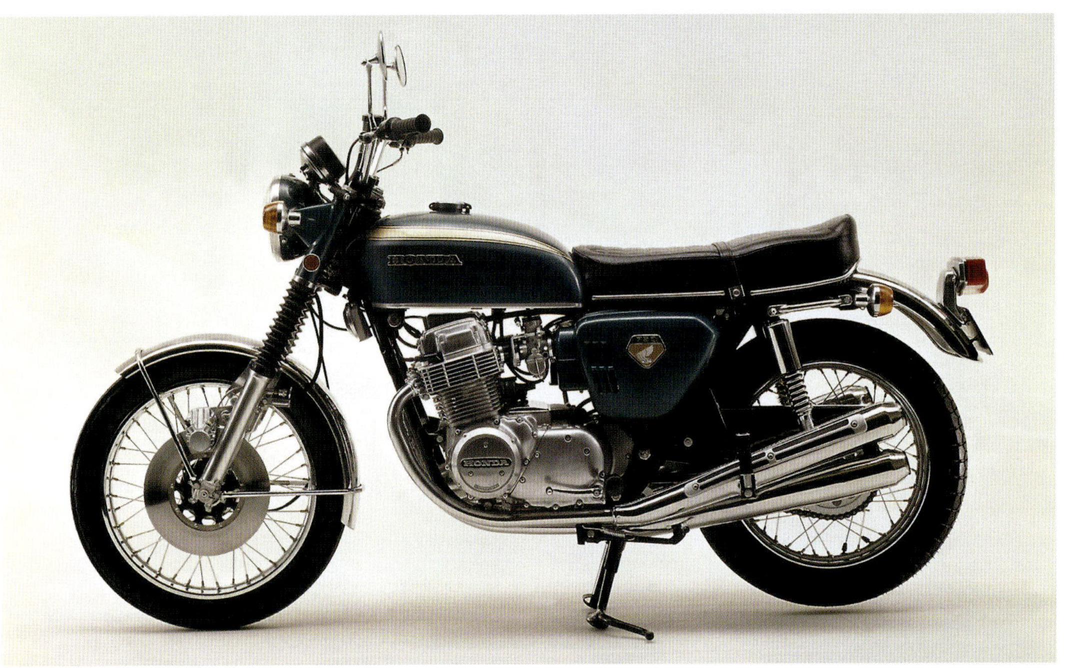

Honda Dream CB750 FOUR

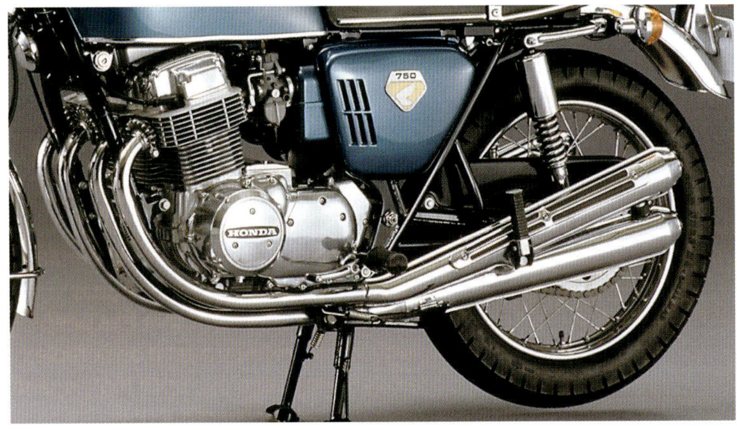

Images provided by Honda Motor Co., Ltd.

Engine and Exhaust
At that time, it was the first mass-produced motorcycle to adopt a parallel four-cylinder engine. The curves of the four shining exhaust pipes protruding from the cylinders add a sense of refinement.

● Four-Wheeled Vehicle (Nissan Fairlady Z)

This sports car was first produced by Nissan Motor Co. in 1969. At the time, Japanese sports cars were seen as copies of Western models, but this design aimed to overturn that conception. The designers crafted the concept highlighting style in addition to performance. As a result, it was enthusiastically received in America, becoming the best-selling sports car in the world.

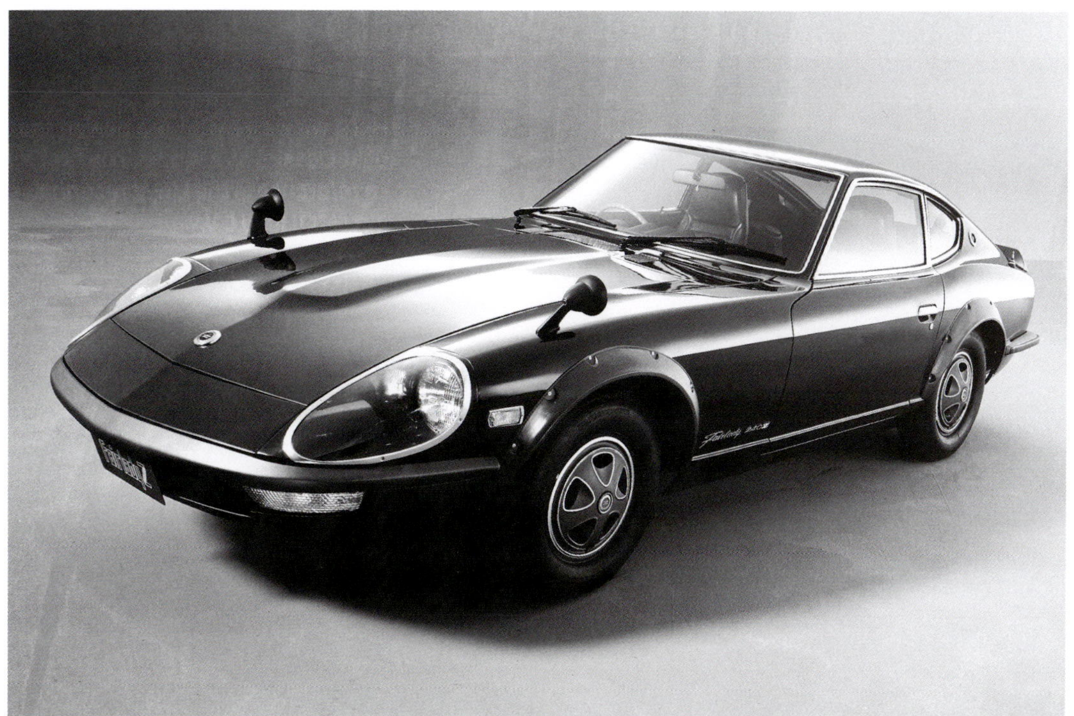

First Generation Nissan Fairlady Z S30

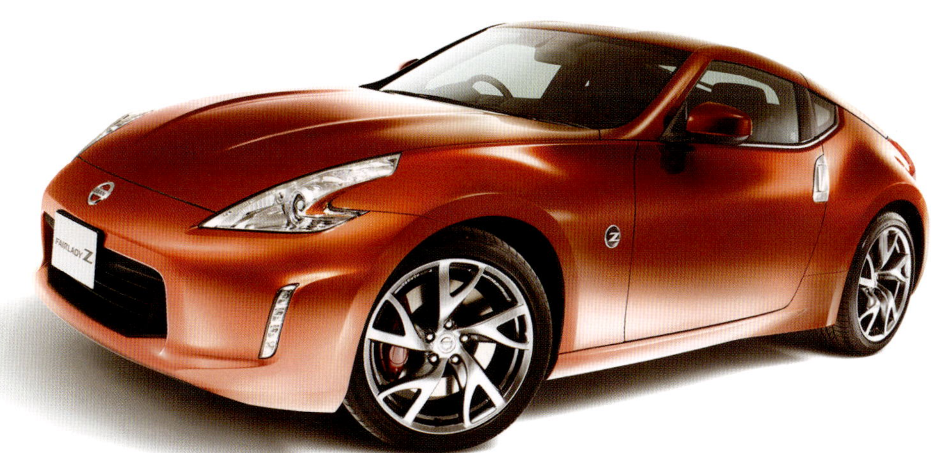

Nissan Fairlady Z Version ST

Images provided by Nissan Motor Co., Ltd.

The Nissan Fairlady Z underwent a full model change in 2008 and continues to evolve today. The rear-heavy proportion feels like a form characteristic of a sports car that has been evolved through the years.

Arranging Standards

When using previous classic designs and as models to inspire and transform your original mecha or sci-fi vehicles, various methods can be employed for referencing the overall form, balance, proportion, parts, detailed features and the specific styles and taste of that era.

Transforming a Biplane into a Fantasy Vehicle

● **Base Biplane**

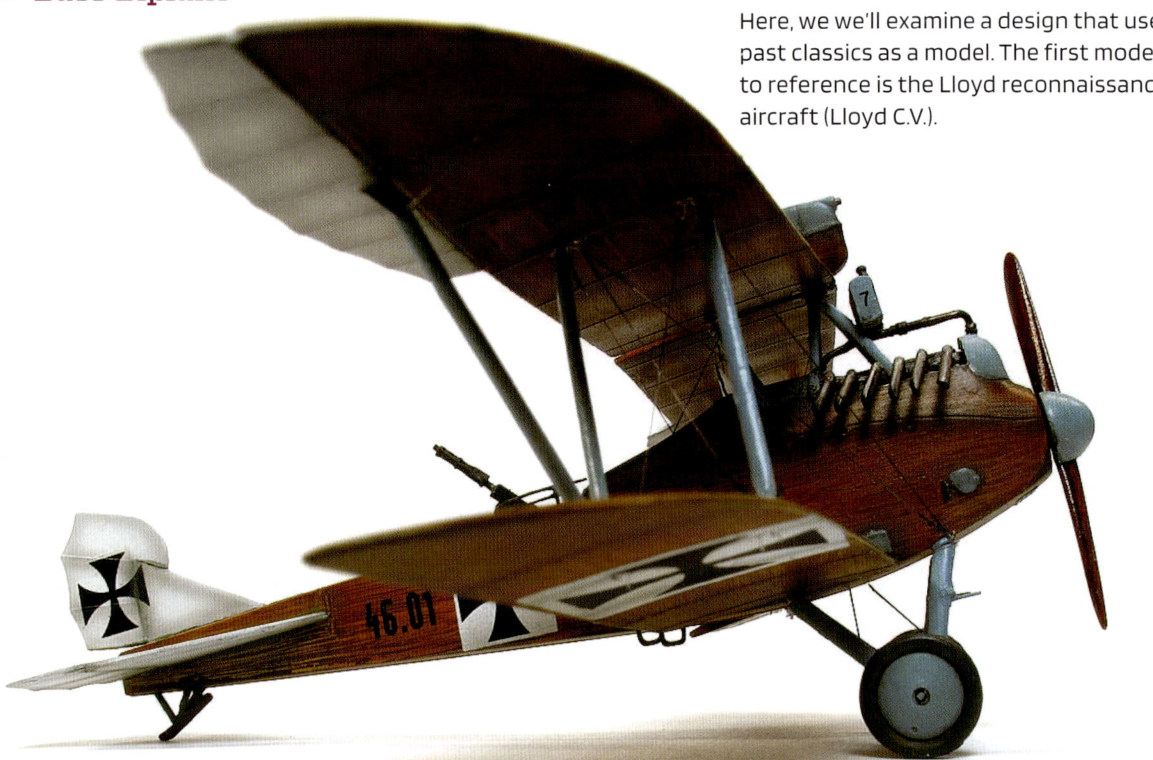

Here, we we'll examine a design that uses past classics as a model. The first model to reference is the Lloyd reconnaissance aircraft (Lloyd C.V.).

Lloyd C.V.
This is a two-seat reconnaissance plane created in 1917 during World War I, produced by the Austro-Hungarian Empire. It has an unusual structure, incorporating the wooden exterior up to the main wing.

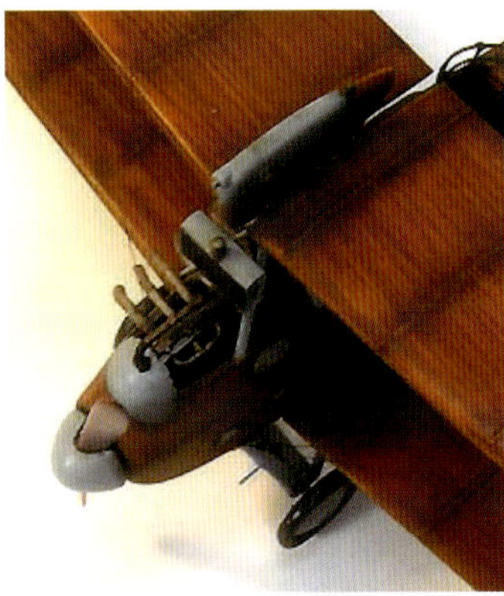

Engine

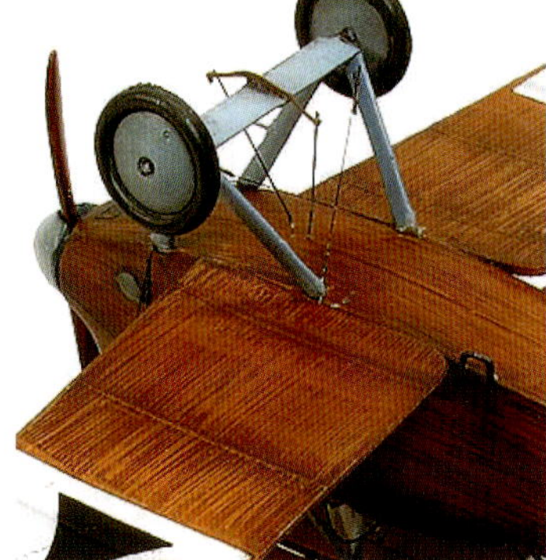

Wheels

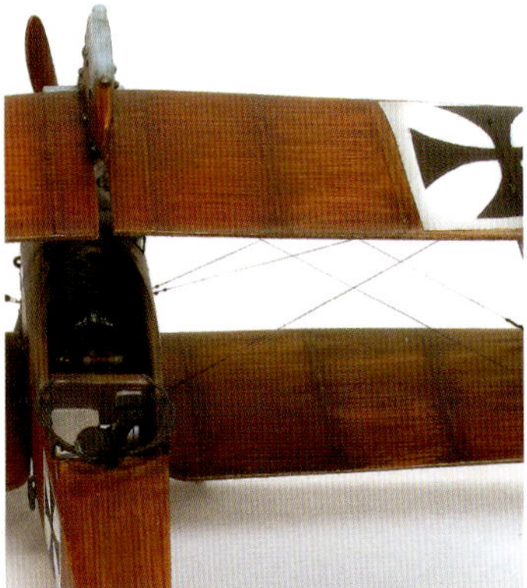

Cockpit

● Proportions of the Lloyd Reconnaissance Aircraft

First, focus on the relationship between the engine, cockpit and the two wings. Plan the shape of the body in the front view and the size of the wings in the top view. The structure resembles a water droplet with a cucumber inserted into the center, formed by the two wings.

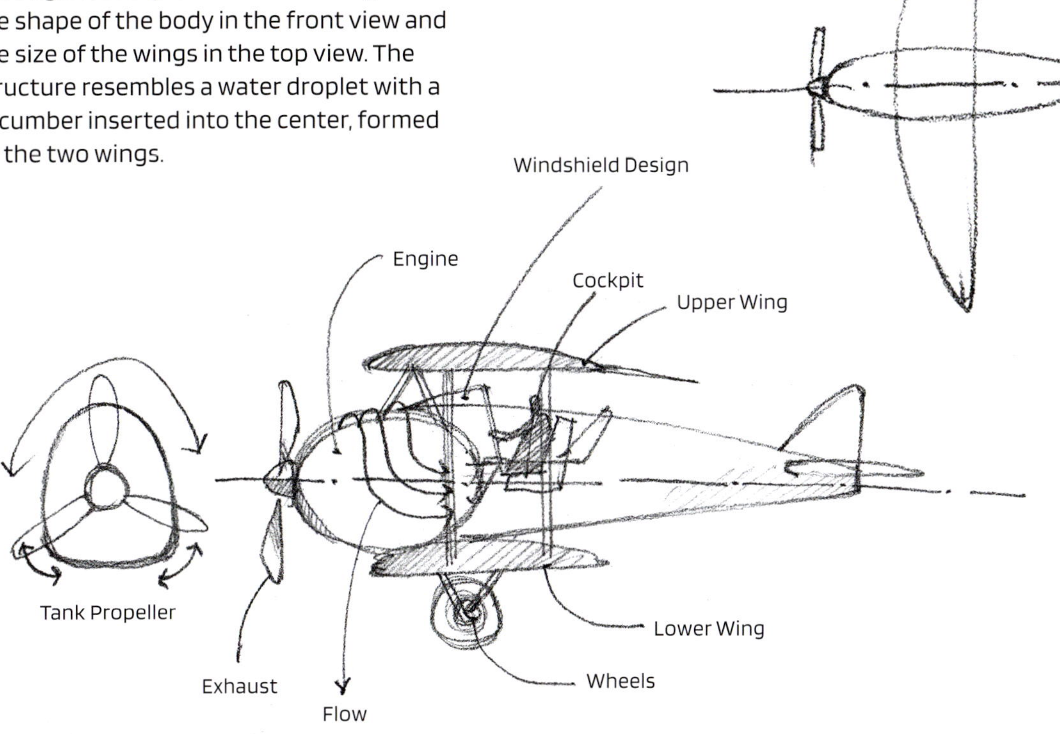

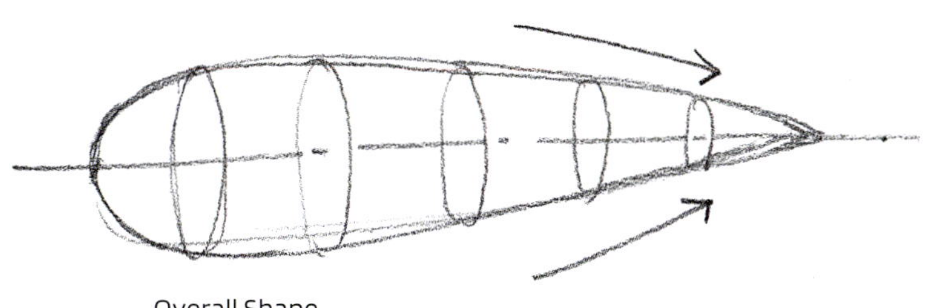

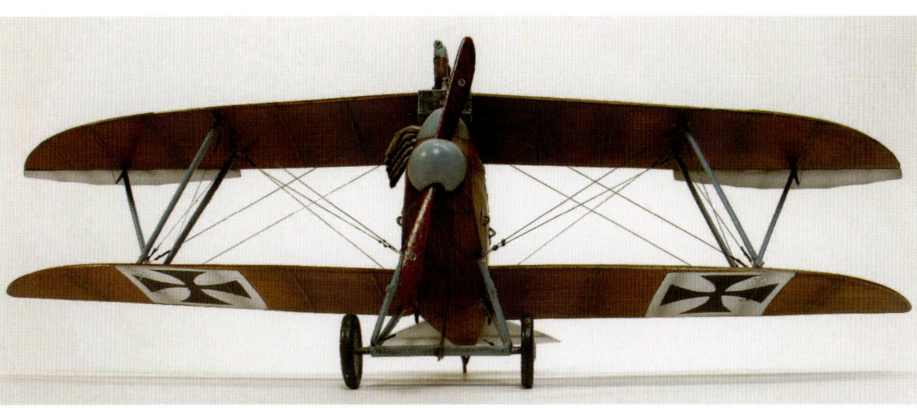

Front View of the Aircraft

● Grasp the structure and arrange the details.

Now we'll create a fantasy-style airplane from the model of the Lloyd reconnaissance aircraft on page 30. The process involves determining the overall structure from a broad perspective, picking out compelling details and further arranging them.

Keep the structure simple!
Don't worry about the details → Decide freely yourself.

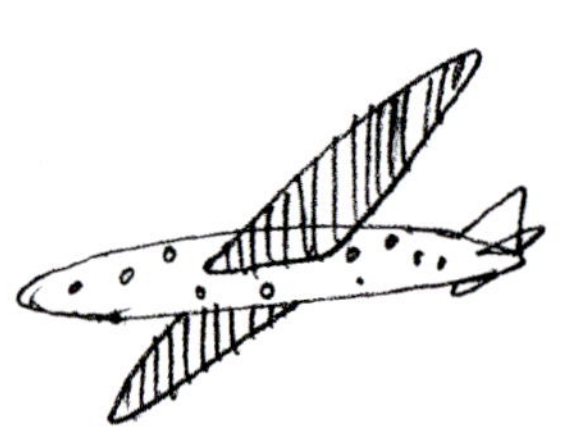

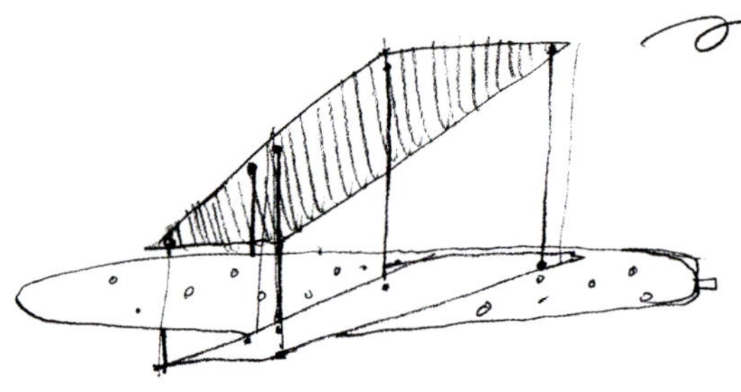

The upper wing is supported from below by the lower wing.

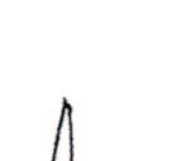

The lower wing is attached to the cylinder shape somewhere (don't worry about the details).

Regular airplane
The wings penetrate the fuselage (Imagine a board stuck into a cucumber).

Biplane
A cucumber is sandwiched between the two boards.

Organize the relationships of each part.

The sturdy legs can be used as they are.

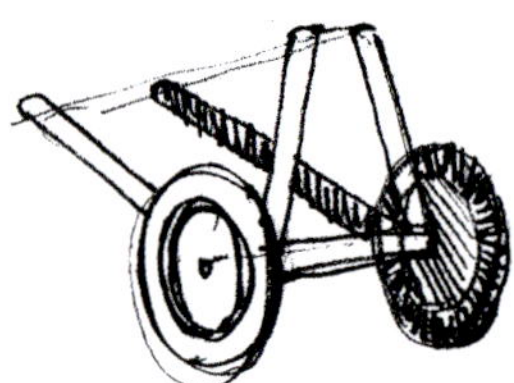

Sturdy legs
Different from modern airplanes
Retro style

Arrange the exhaust.

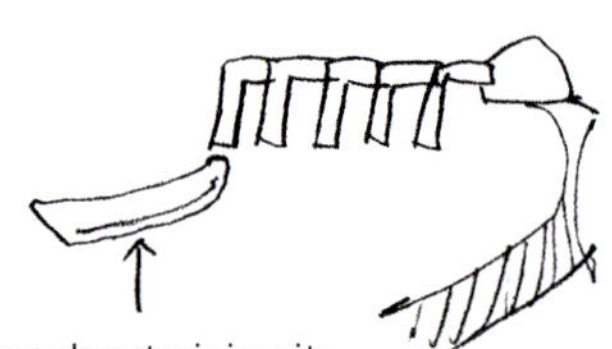

How about giving it a motorcycle style?

The engine's exhaust system is excessive.
Should we organize and shape it in a motorcycle style?

Arrange the wings.

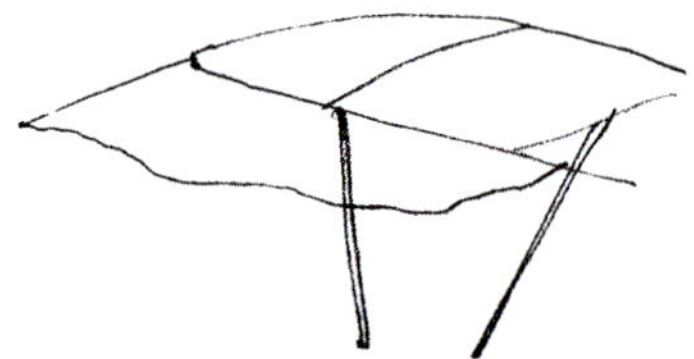

Auxiliary wings with different materials.

What about a bird's wing feather style?

Change the overall image
Wooden → Toy-like tin.

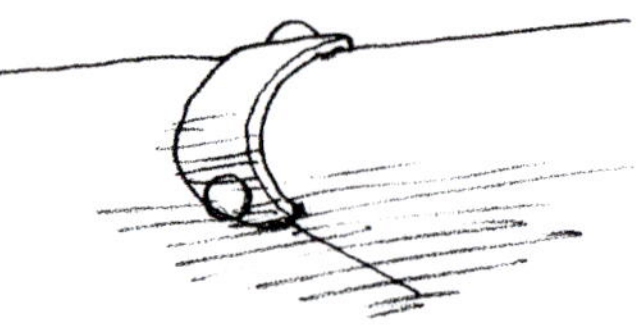

Add auxiliary fittings.

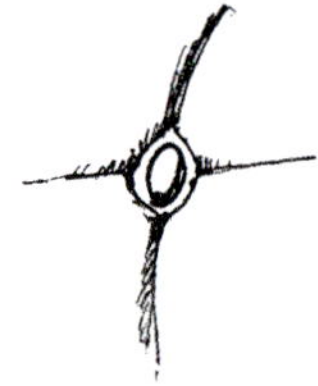

Special details at the intersection.

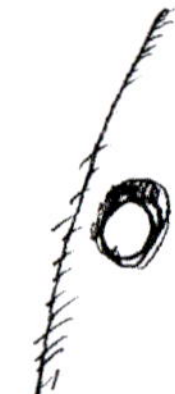

If you drive in nails, the tin will dent.

● Completion

After determining the structure of the wings and fuselage from a broad perspective, we'll add the details considered on the left page. To create a fantasy yet retro biplane, the fuselage has a texture that looks like it's made of tin, and the overall color tone has been unified in a sepia style.

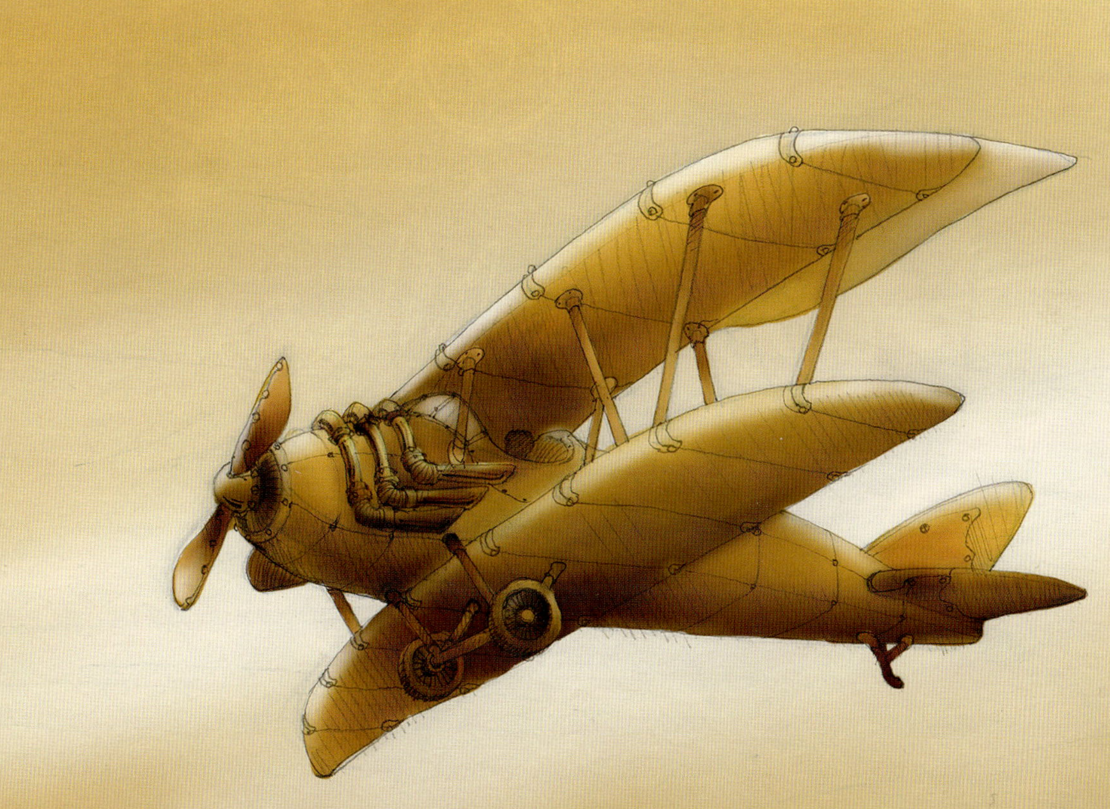

Fantasy-style biplane.

Rearrange the Motorcycle in a Futuristic Style.

Now we'll look at another example of adding a sci-fi twist to a standard vehicle design. The base we're starting with is a large-displacement American motorcycle. Imagine it racing across a desolate desert in a war-ravaged futuristic landscape. When developing rough sketches, keep the image of a wild, chaotic and explosive form in mind.

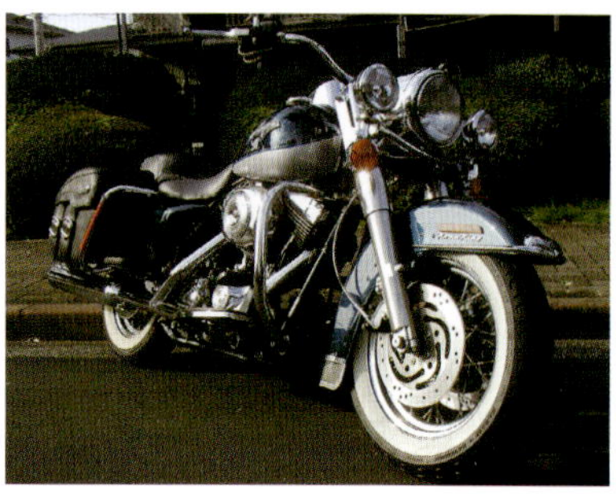

● Form and rough sketches

The basic structure of the motorcycle

When removing external parts like saddle bags

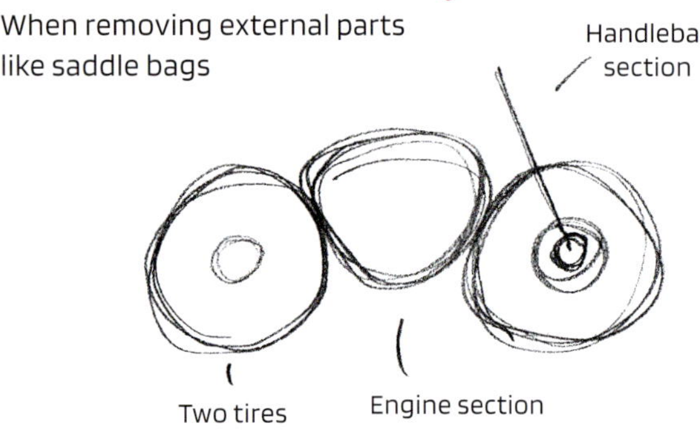

Arrange the silhouette

Change the silhouette to a chopper handlebar style.

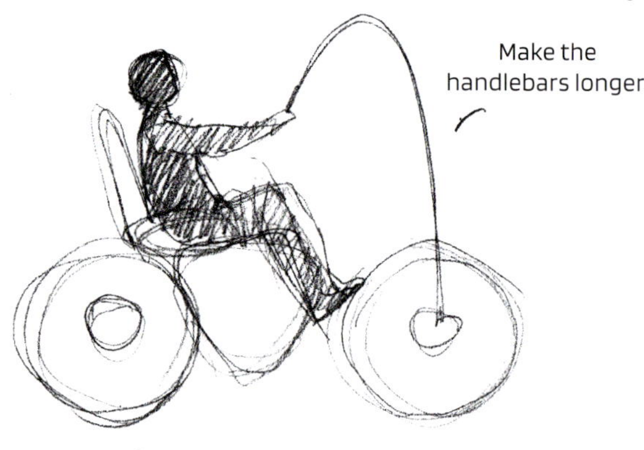

Arrange the exhaust.

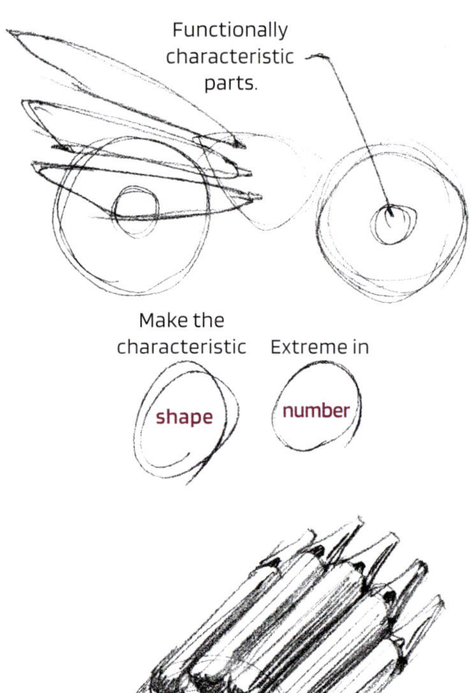

There are lots of exhaust pipes.

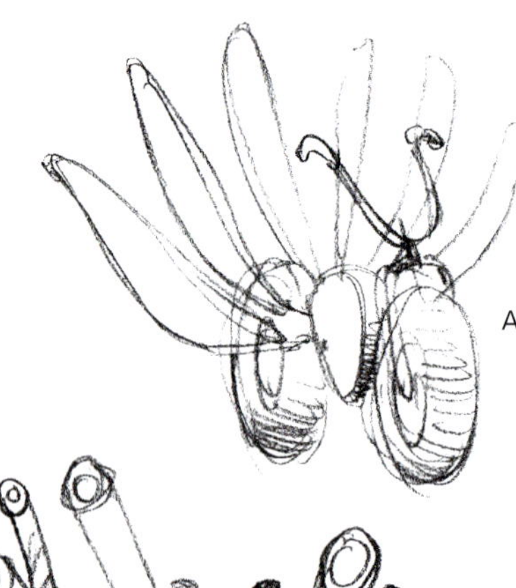

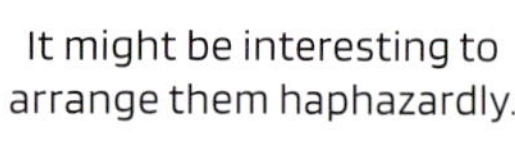

It might be interesting to arrange them haphazardly.

● Finishing the design

Super chopper & extreme exhaust

Exhaust pipes extending
in all directions.

Exhaust pipes
resembling a backrest.

Tilt it dramatically.

● Completion

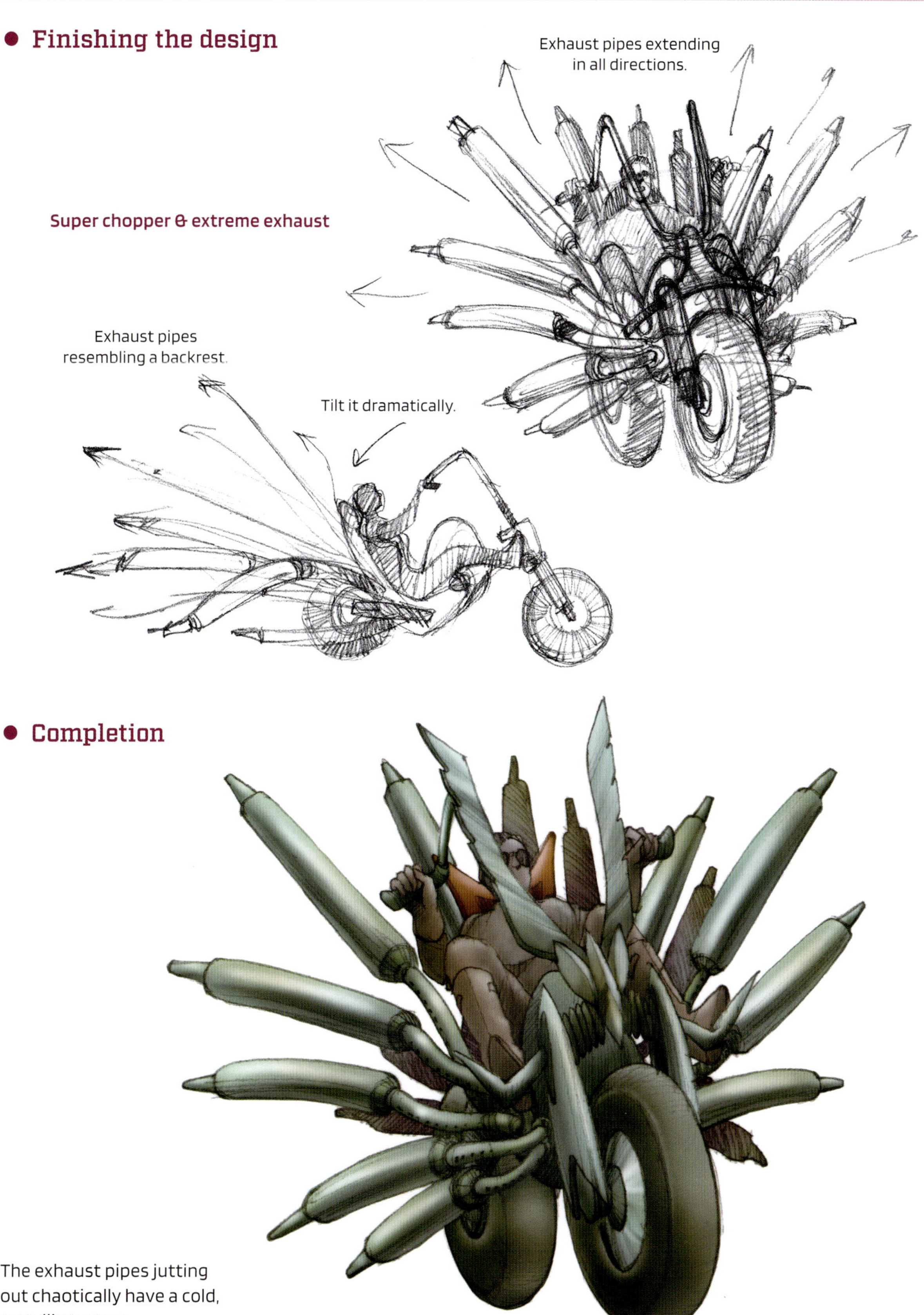

The exhaust pipes jutting
out chaotically have a cold,
metallic texture.

2-2 FINDING A MOTIF

What are some of the ways of searching for elements that serve as design motifs? Many designs are unified in terms of the overall or partial forms, colors and textures as well as by images and concepts expressed visually. So let's look at some of the motifs and keywords that can help determine or shape the direction of your drawings and designs.

Words Associated with Motifs

As representative words that can shape or influence the direction of a design, the table lists some typical examples. Many of these are paired concepts with contrasting meanings. For instance, artificial shapes evoke an image that heavily uses straight lines and ideal geometric forms, while natural shapes, in contrast, suggest the use of complex curves, curved surfaces, and irregular shapes. Additionally, words and concepts associated with motifs include terms that represent styles from specific eras, such as art deco. Past and present trends, like "Lolita," "gothic horror" and "cyberpunk," can be valuable triggers for new and inspired directions in design.

Table 2-1 Keywords for Form Conceptualization

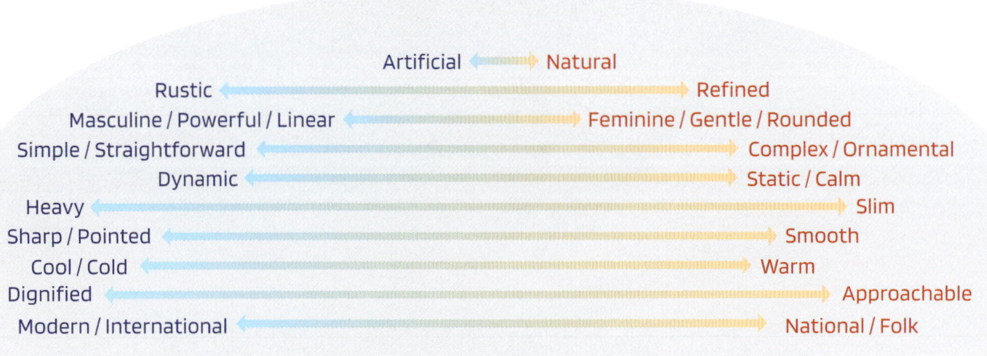

Collecting Motifs

Forms, colors and textures based on words and concepts are common in many design fields, including fashion, interior design and industrial design. To use these as references for concepts in mecha and sci-fi vehicles, observe objects in your daily surroundings and collect examples and design information coordinated to and based on themes. Additionally, deciphering the themes and concepts embedded in design works is also valuable.

● Art-Deco-Style decoration

Art deco is an art movement that flourished and developed in Europe and America from the mid-1910s to the 1930s, following Art Nouveau (page 46). Compared to Art Nouveau, deco designs favored geometric shapes, influenced by Japanese decorative styles, the aesthetics of cubism and Bauhaus, and the advancements of industrial society.

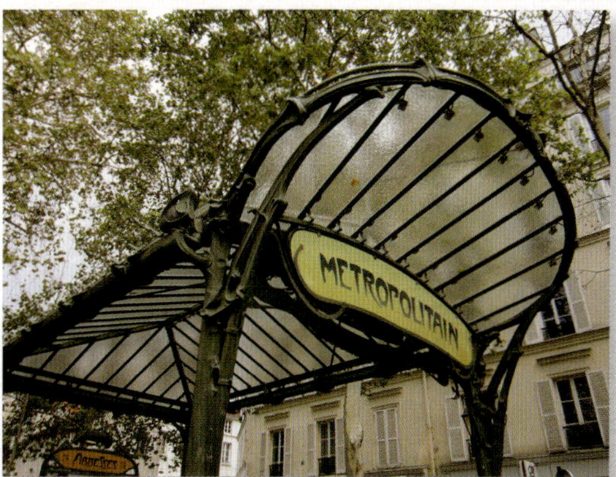

Paris Metro Entrance
This was created for the 1900 Paris Exposition. The design, which heavily utilizes curves based on natural forms, is in the Art Nouveau style and was the cutting edge of fashion at that time.

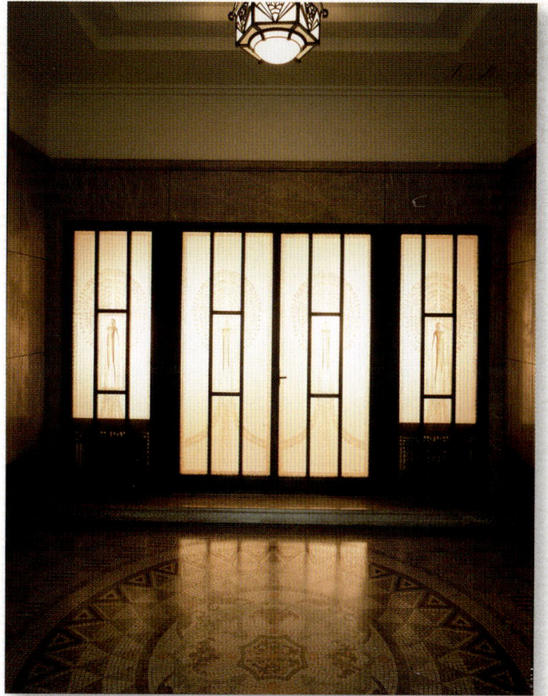

Tokyo Garden Museum Main Entrance
This building (the former Asaka Palace) was completed in 1933, its interior richly adorned with the popular art deco style of the time. The photo shows the glass relief at the main entrance, created by the French artist René Lalique.

Image provided by: Tokyo Metropolitan Foundation for History and Culture Image Archive

● Victorian-Style Design

The ornate style that prevailed during the reign of Queen Victoria in Great Britain (1837-1901), it's used as a term to indicate the general trends in art during that period. At that time, Britain was experiencing a period of prosperity, which invited a blend of various elements, including the fusing of new industrial techniques with medieval and gothic styles. To us, it gives an impression of luxury and elegance as well as extreme formality.

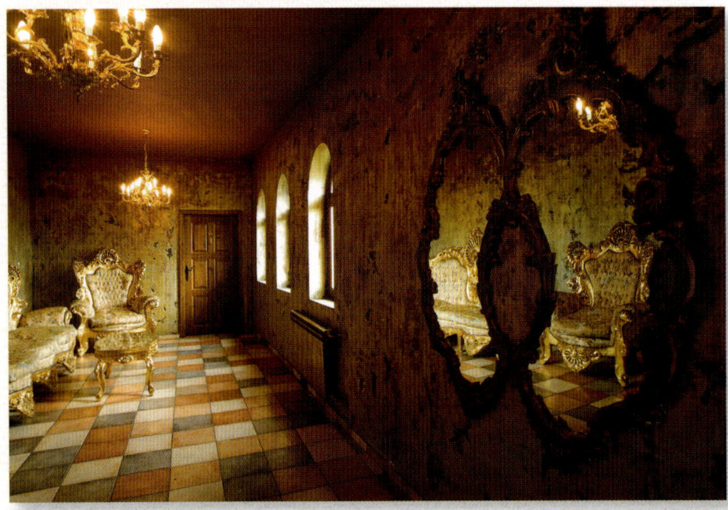

An ornately decorative Victorian-style interior.

● Steampunk

This style emerged from science fiction in the 1980s and has influenced fantasy and historical adaptations and reinterpretations. Many settings are based on the Industrial Revolution, often using Victorian England or the American West during the pioneer era. The fictional machines, known as retro-futurism, are characterized by a fusion of steam engines and Victorian fashion, culture and architecture.

● Cyberpunk

Cyberpunk is a style and movement in science fiction that became popular in the 1980s, completely transforming the concepts of traditional science fiction. The world of the film "Blade Runner" is the most famous example, a harsh-edged industrial lens on mechanized, technology-dominated worlds.

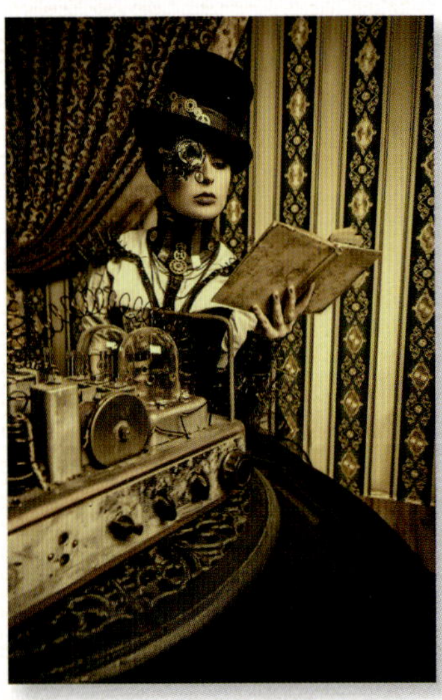

An image that combines Victorian clothing and interior styles with retro technologies like clockwork springs and vacuum tubes.

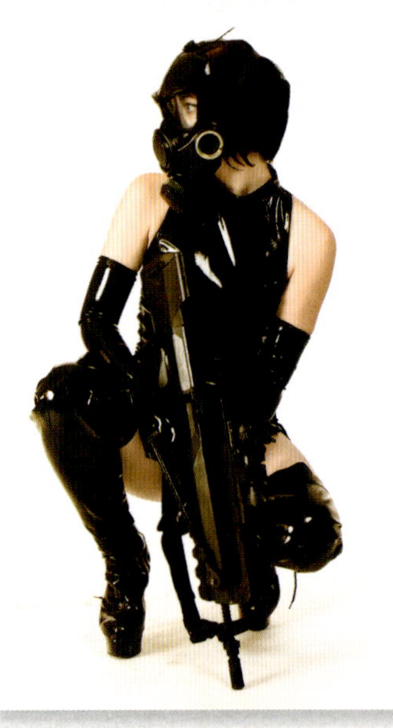

An image of the enhancement and fusion of the human body through mechanics, one of the characteristics of cyberpunk.

● Gothic Fashion

The term "gothic" in Gothic fashion is derived from novels that features eerie plotlines set in dank, spooky European churches, mansions and castles. Works like Bram Stoker's "Dracula," Mary Shelley's "Frankenstein" and Edgar Allan Poe's tales are well-known examples that have given rise to numerous pop culture interpretations. Gothic fashion doesn't precisely re-create the fashion of the era but often fuses elements of 19th-century Victorian dresses with Elizabethan styles.

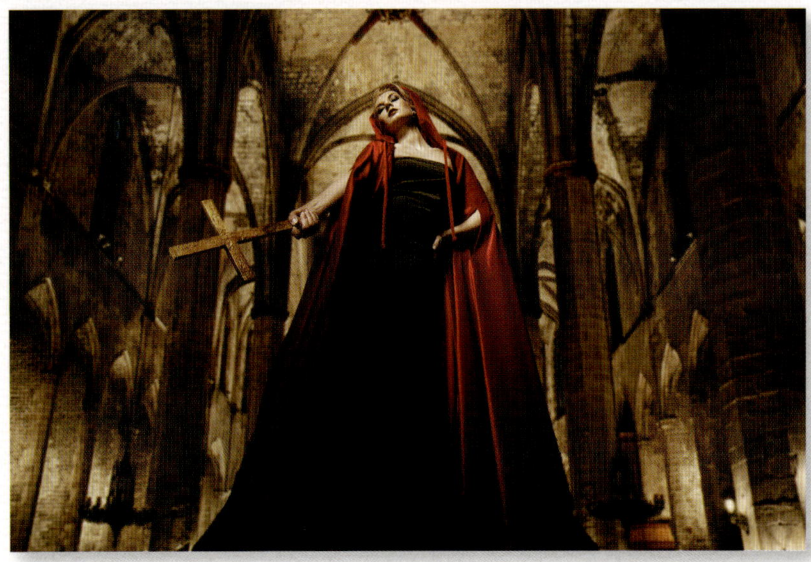

The background features gothic-style architecture, which gave rise to an entire aesthetic movement.

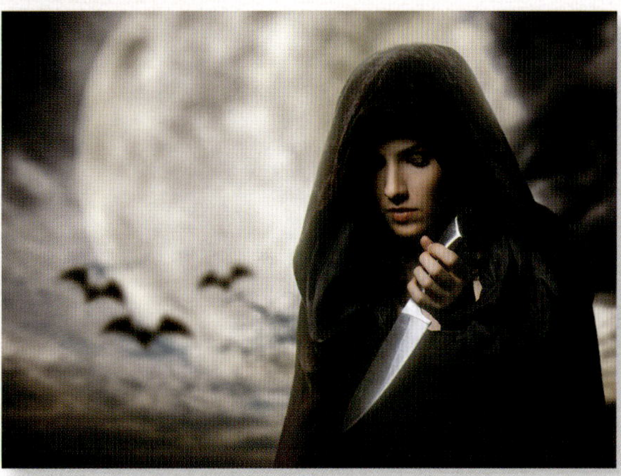

A vampire, as epitomized by Dracula.

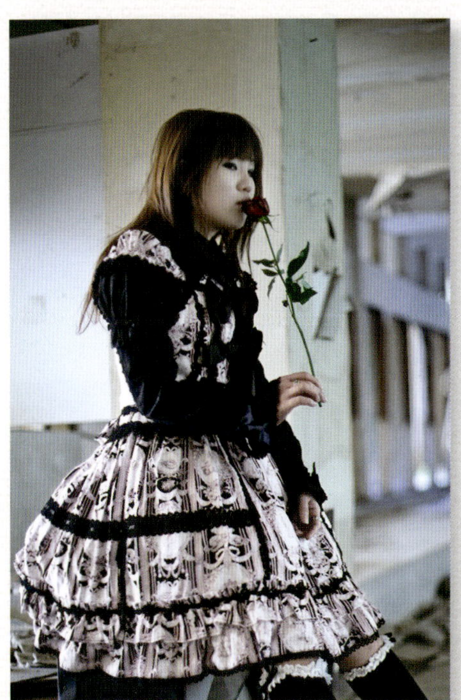

Gothic & Lolita (Gosu Rori)
Abbreviated as "Gosuro," this is a unique fashion style from Japan that combines gothic and girly styles for an offbeat, mismatched look.

Inspired by Motifs

Now let's look at some examples of how to use specific inspirations, and their individual components, to transform and elevate your mecha and fantasy vehicle designs.

Adding a different style to a diesel locomotive

Using the DD51 diesel locomotive as a model, let's develop a form that incorporates elements of steampunk and Victorian styles. The original locomotive is nearly rectangular, so develop a basic form that allows for dynamic decoration.

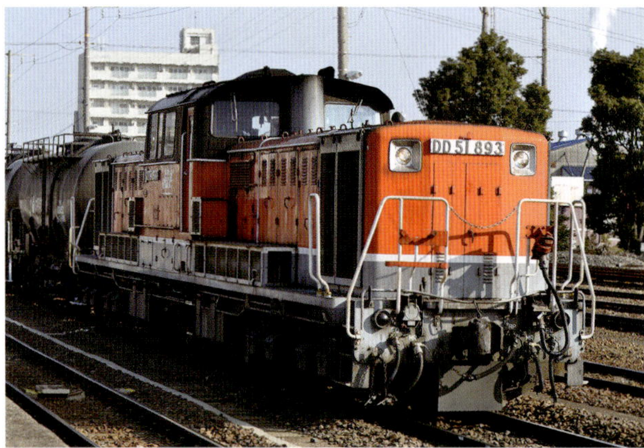

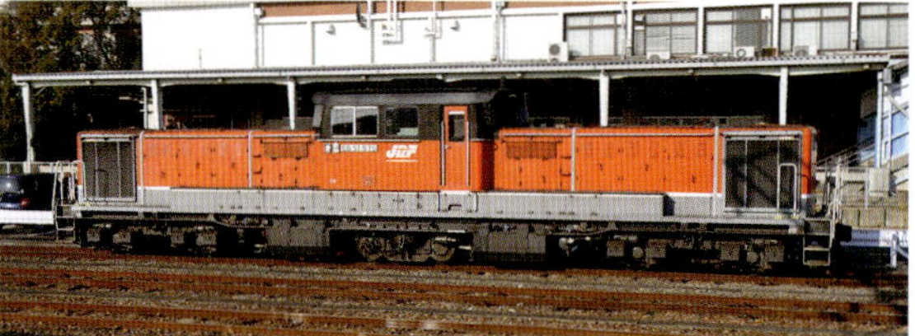

DD51 diesel locomotive

Produced in large quantities since the 1960s to promote "smokeless" operations as a replacement for steam locomotives, the diesel locomotive has played an active role. Although its presence is gradually disappearing with the advancement of electrification, it remains extremely popular among railway enthusiasts.

● Basic Structure of the DD51 Diesel Locomotive

The basic shape consists of a cube sandwiched between two rectangular prisms.

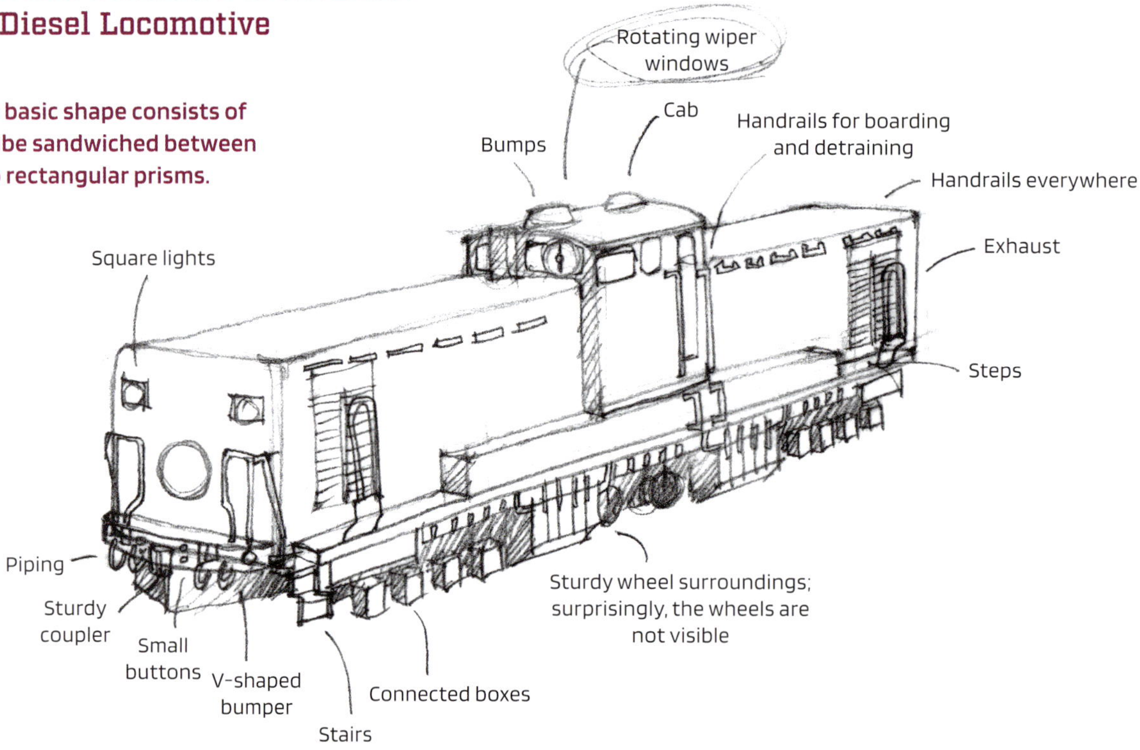

● Let's Arrange the Form

When considering our creation as a sci-fi fantasy vehicle, let's use steam pressure as the power source, giving it a larger scale and weight than conventional steam locomotives. At the front, attach a large snowplow to solidify the form and allow for easier decoration.

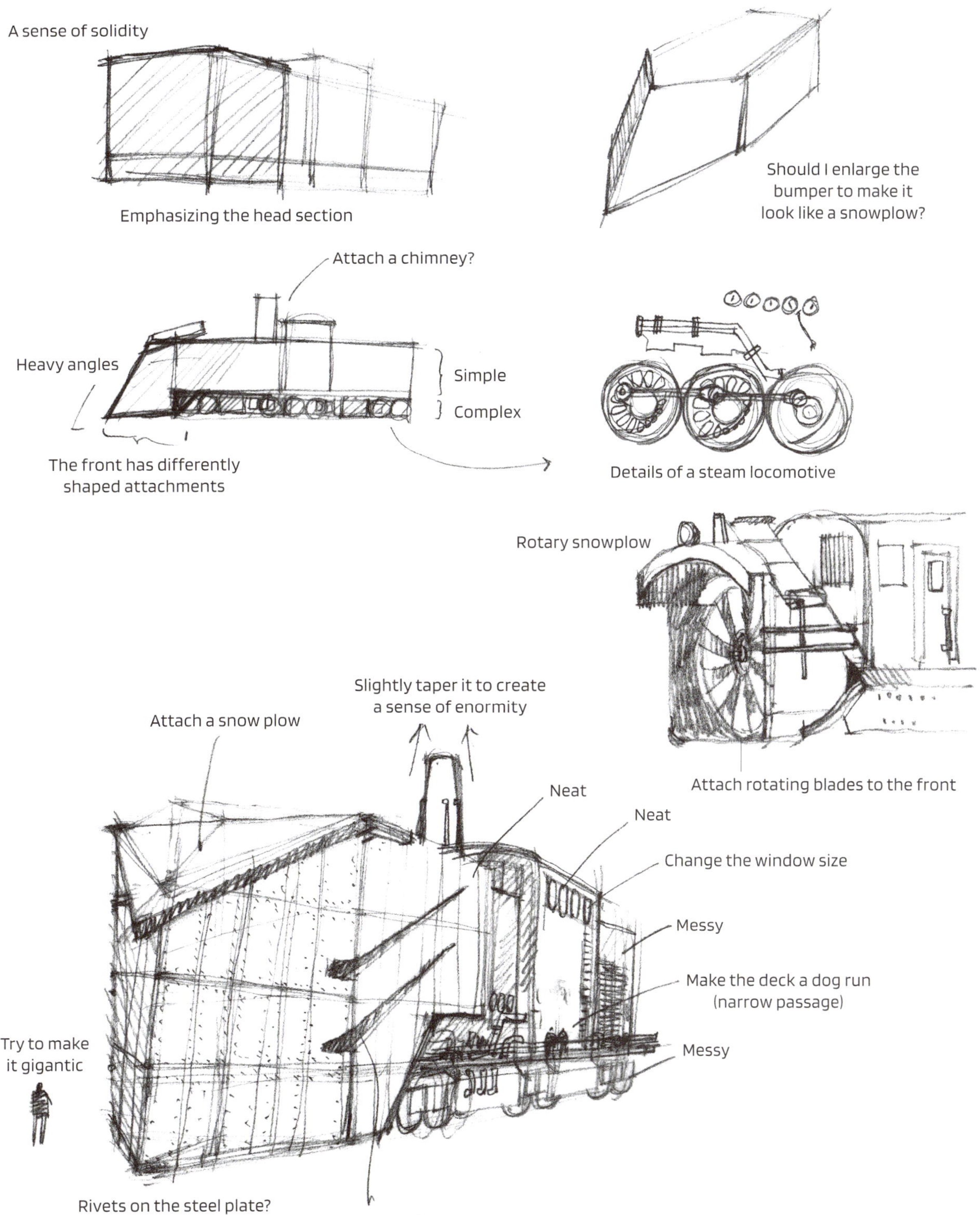

● Gather Decorations and Create Details

Collect shapes and parts that symbolize steampunk and Victorian-style decorative patterns. Here, we'll decide on the details with a retro-futuristic theme as the overall guiding concept.

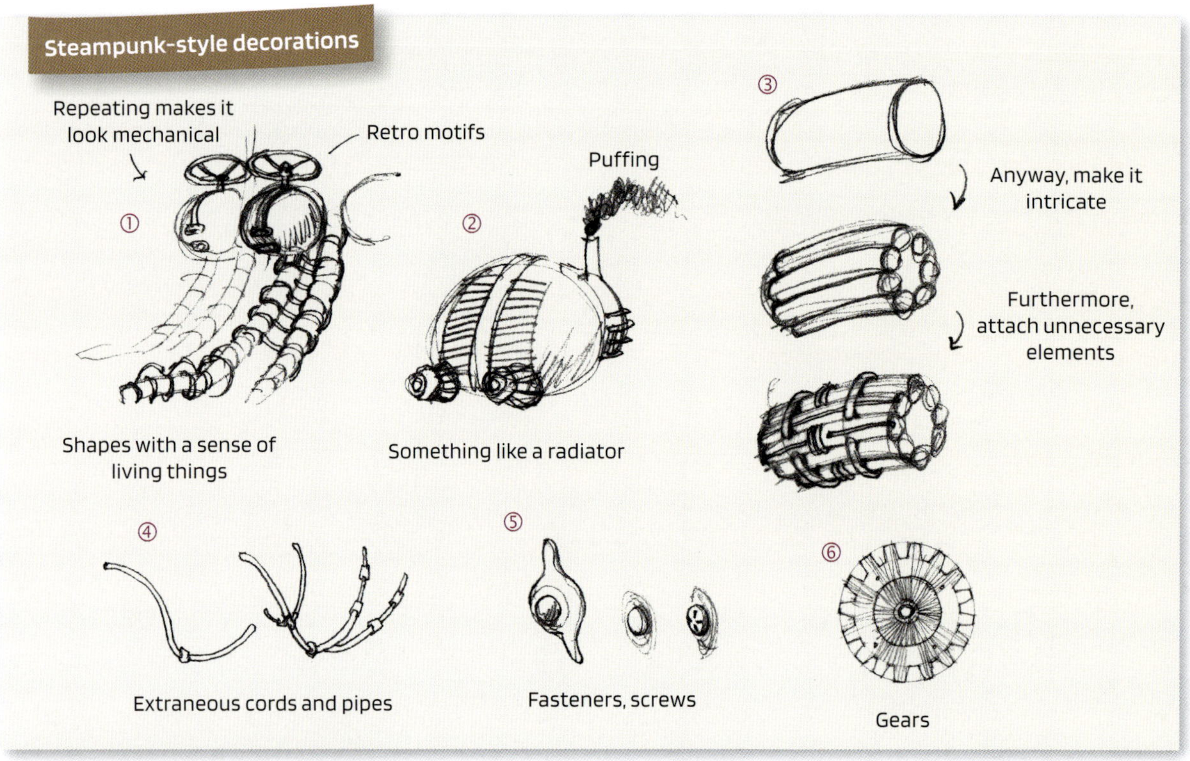

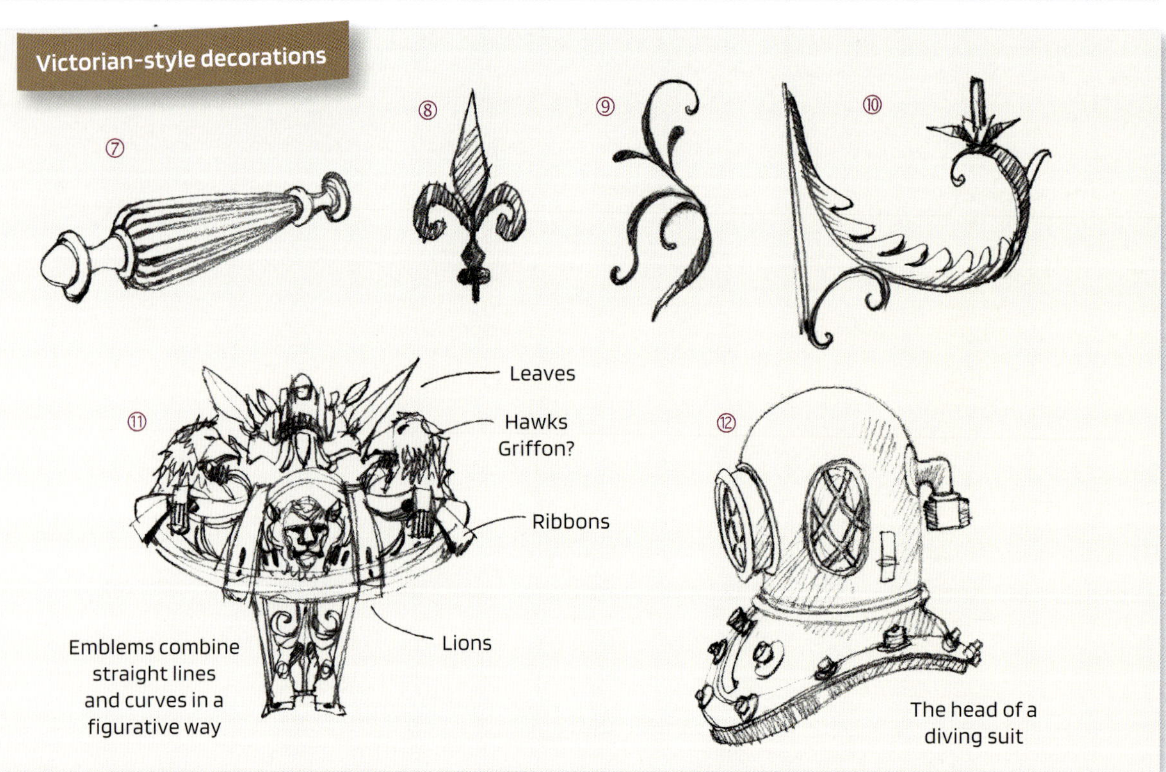

● Completion

Finishing the line drawing

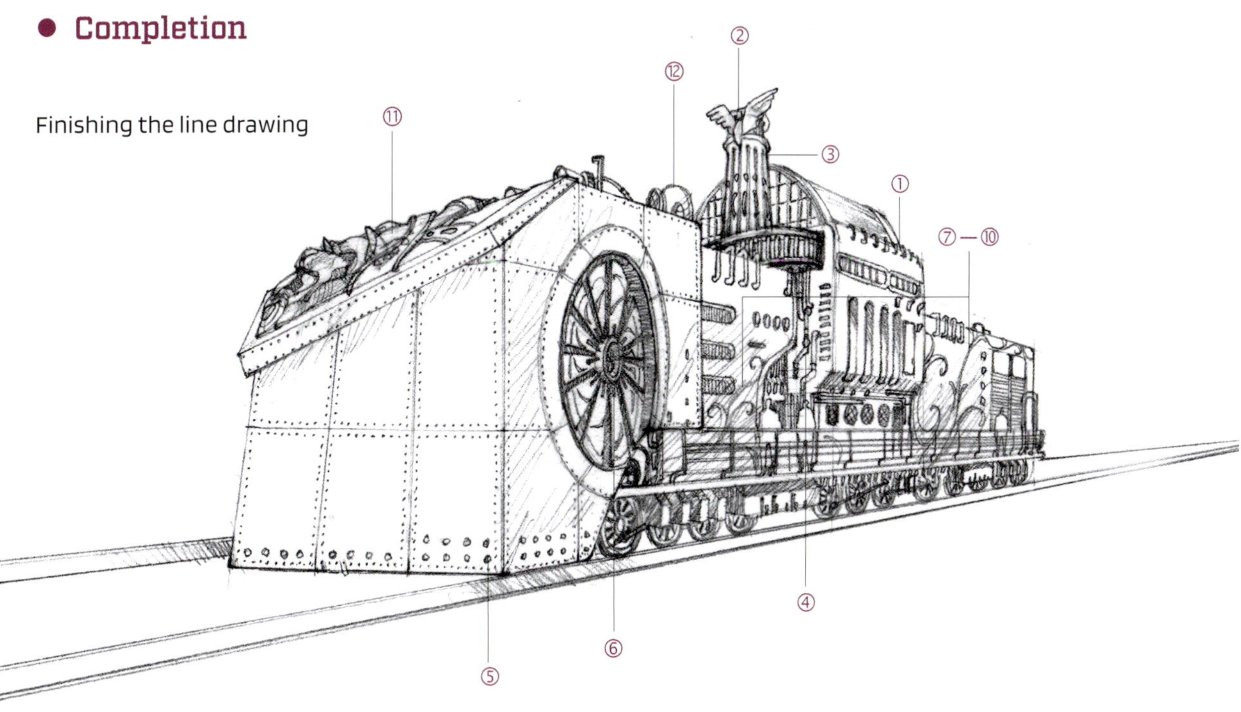

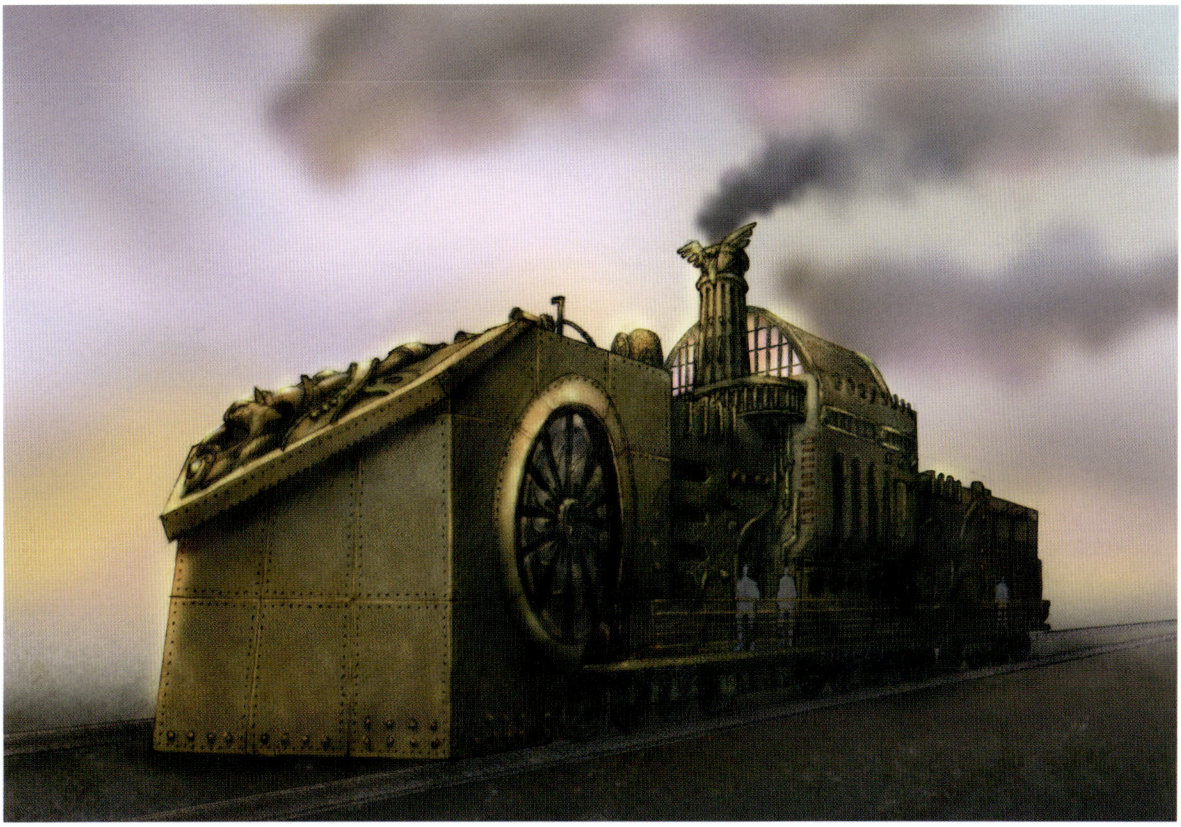

Neo-Victorian Locomotive
The overall color tone is made a dull iron. The highlighted parts are golden, and
the background is a sunset scene.

Unifying Images Through Motifs

Even if the basic forms are the same, introducing various motif inspirations yields different images and designs. by directing them through motifs. For example, how can we represent a concept, such as cute, in visual form? Should the form be complex or simple; sharp, smooth or gently rounded? Maybe warm would be helpful?

So how do you convert words or concepts into forms, while striving for unity and coordination from the whole to the parts? Here, we'll approach a bipedal robot with different motifs as an example.

■ Differentiating from the Basic Form

To create a bipedal robot, include movable parts. First, decide on the basic form. Here we'll consider three types of bipedal robots: sci-fi style, fantasy style and gothic horror style.

● Design Development

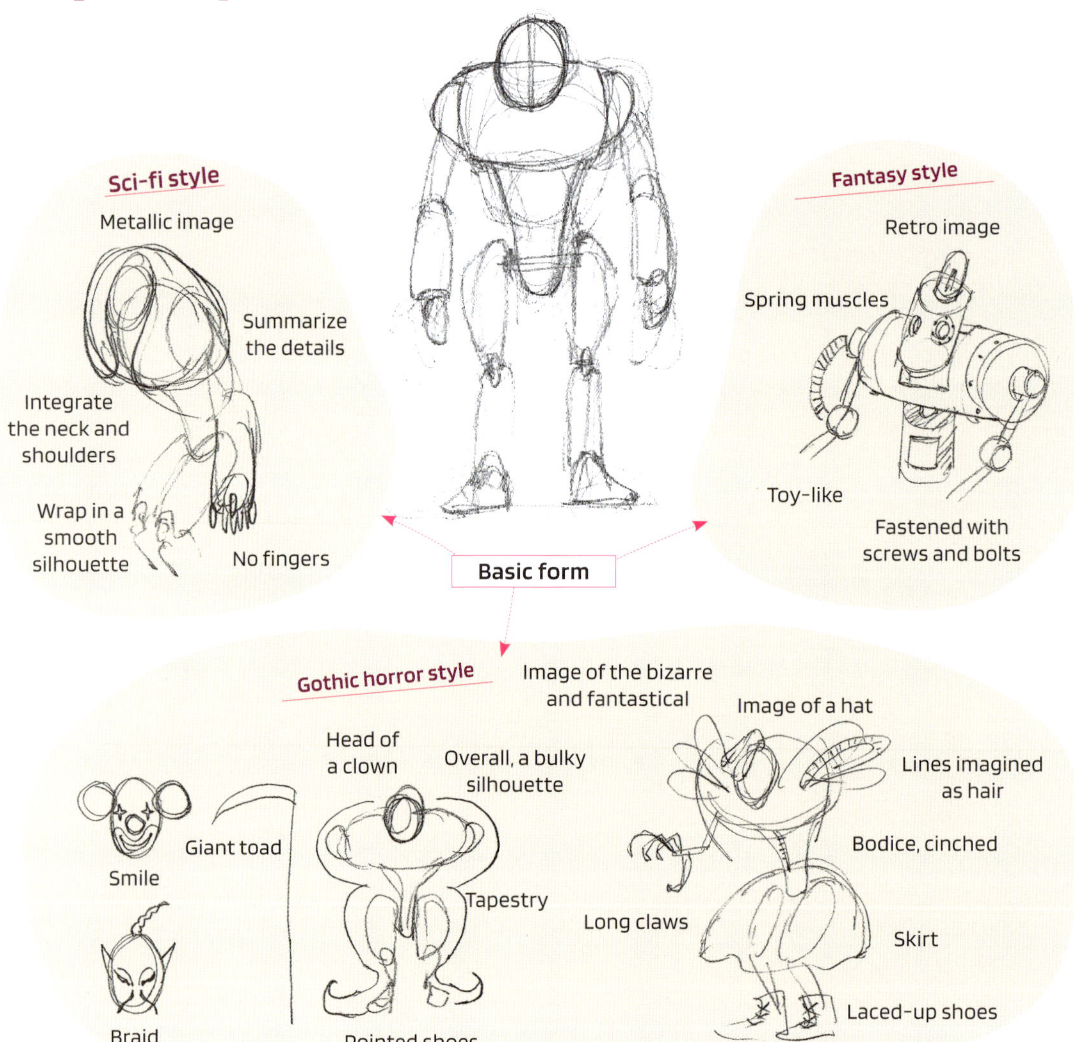

● Sci-Fi Style

The body surface is silver, giving it a glossy appearance. It features smooth curves, and the head and shoulders are integrated into one shape.

● Fantasy Style

Using a retro resource, it's composed of a cylindrical shape with a comical touch that moves mechanically. Parts such as screws, bolts and springs are effectively utilized.

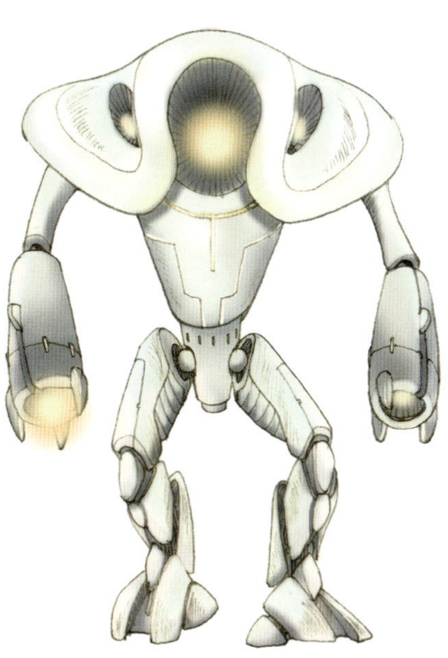

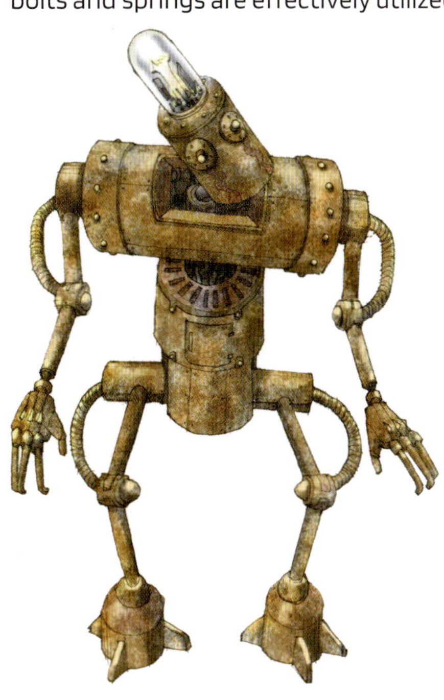

● Gothic Horror style

Using a clown as the starting point for the motif, the transformation combines a baggy style with pants and skirts while incorporating forms and details that evoke a sense of fear.

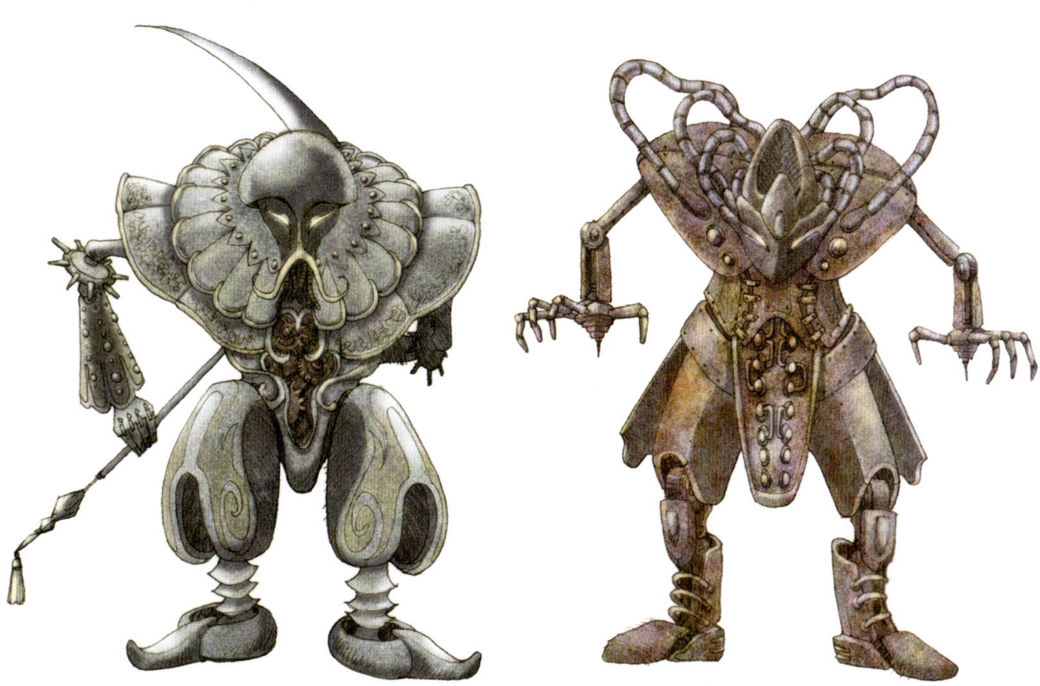

2-3   COPYING AND MODELING

The natural world in all its variety, with its panoply of organic shapes and forms, is an endless source of inspiration. Plants and animals used in their entirety or isolating a single element, pattern or detail be the source of memorable mecha transformations.

What to Look For

While the plant and animal specimens of the natural world can inspire unusual mecha mashups, as laid out in Table 2-2, inorganic creations (human-made letters, shapes and symbols) are also included.

Designs that feature organic motifs like flowers, plants and insects, along with flowing, curved lines offer surprisingly contrasting elements in mechanized, industrial-based vehicles and fantasy modes of transport.

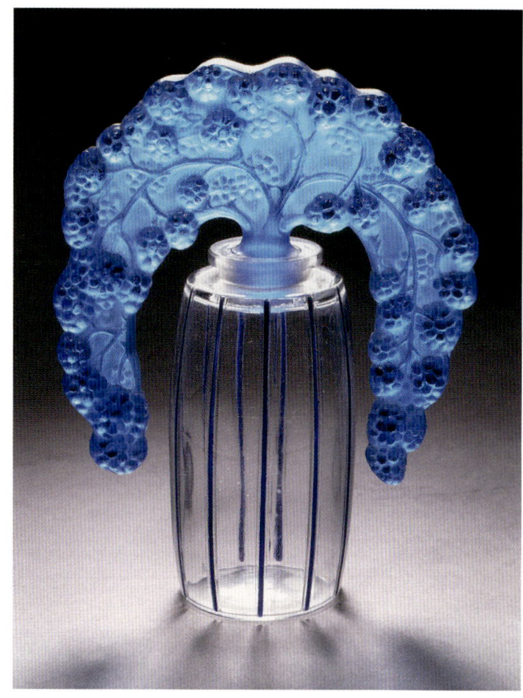

René Lalique's Perfume Bottle
The blue tiara-like stopper is a billowing, willowy shape, creating a beautiful form.

Table 2-2: Mimetic Patterns

Classification	Whole	Parts
Plants	Trees, flowers, mushrooms	Shapes of flowers, fruits, leaves, bark
Insects (Invertebrates)	Beetles, butterflies, bees, cicadas, spiders, crabs, starfish, sea anemones, snails	Mouth, mandibles, legs, antennae, compound eyes, patterns
Animals (Vertebrates)	Fish, birds, mice, rabbits, dogs, wolves, cats, tigers, horses, bears	Legs, claws, fangs, tails, fur patterns
Humans	Humanoid shapes, proportions	Face, eyeballs, ears, hands
Symbols, Others	Crosses, stars, letters, alphabets, symbols	

Metasequoia

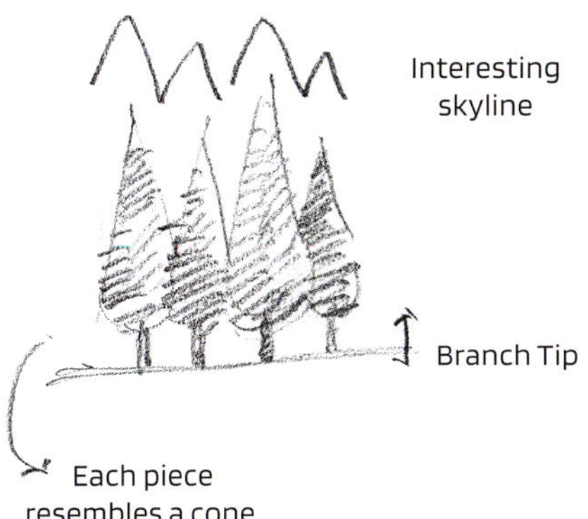

Envisioning a Metasequoia Tree as a Mansion

A futuristic mansion.

● Mimicking Plants

Here are some examples of how to capture the organic form of plants or to focus on integrating certain parts.

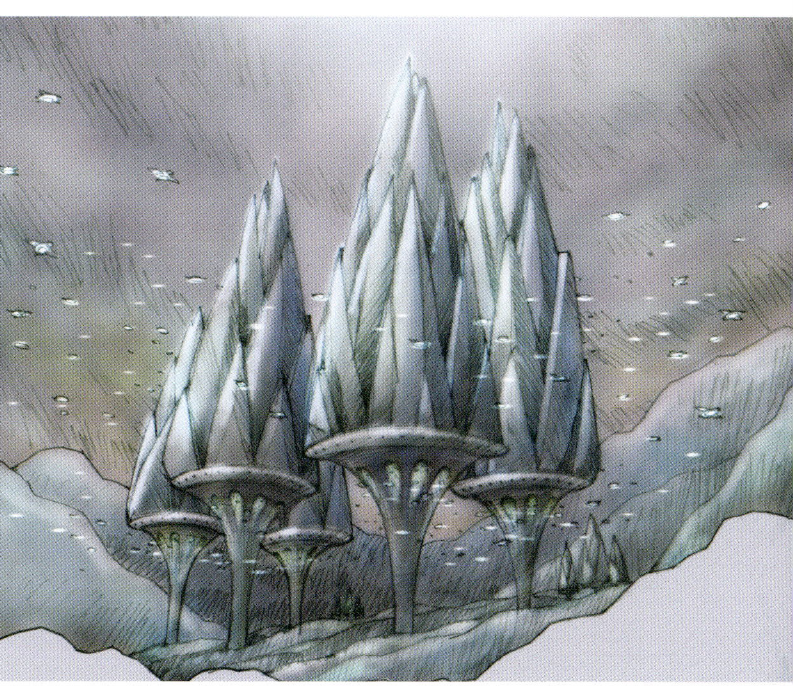

Gallé's Dragonfly Lamp

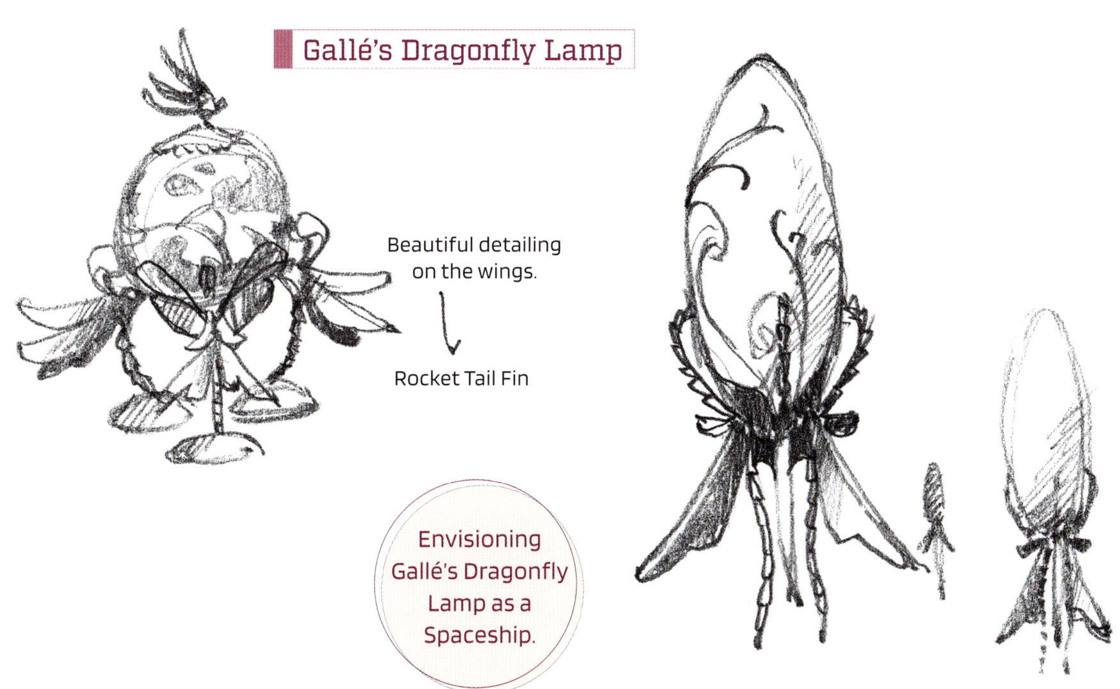

Envisioning Gallé's Dragonfly Lamp as a Spaceship.

Art-Nouveau-Style Spaceship

Asiatic Dayflower

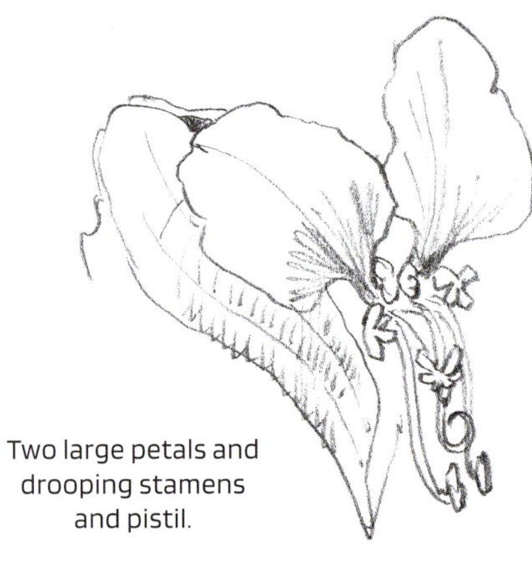

Two large petals and
drooping stamens
and pistil.

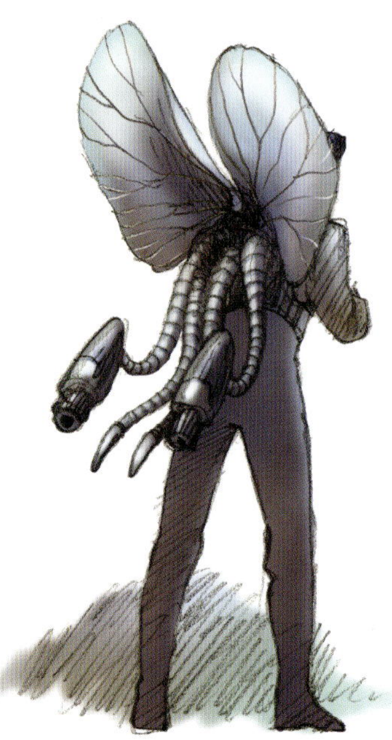

Imagining the
Asiatic Dayflower
as a Flight Pack

Backpack-Style Flight Unit

Rabbit

● Animal-Inspired Designs

When using animals as inspiration, consider its
shape and range of motion. This makes it easier to
conceptualize forms, with additional hints coming
from the skeletal structure of the animal.

Imagining a
Rabbit as a
Bazooka.

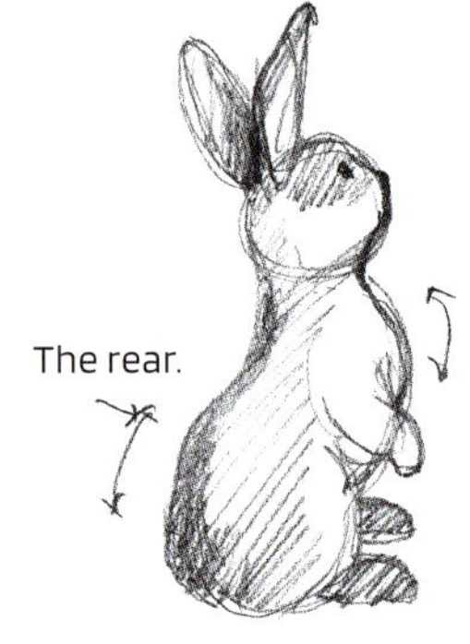

The rear.   chest

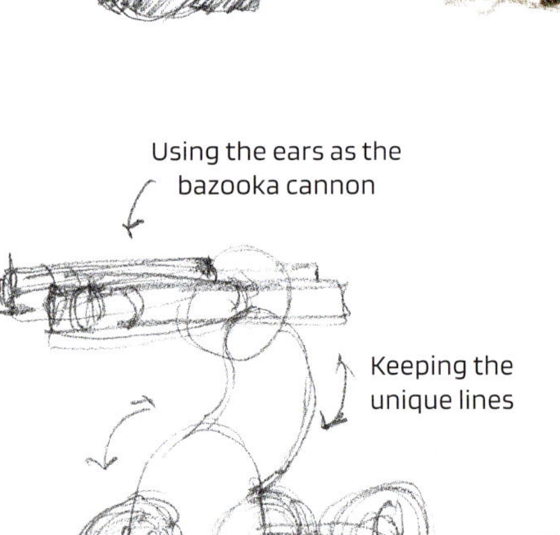

Using the ears as the
bazooka cannon

Keeping the
unique lines

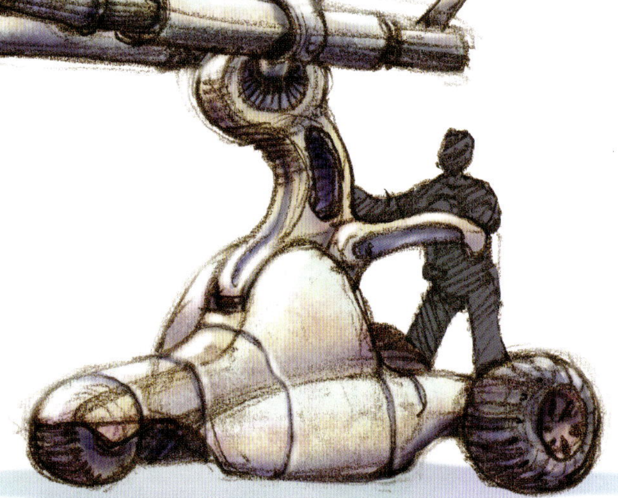

Rabbit Bazooka

Swan

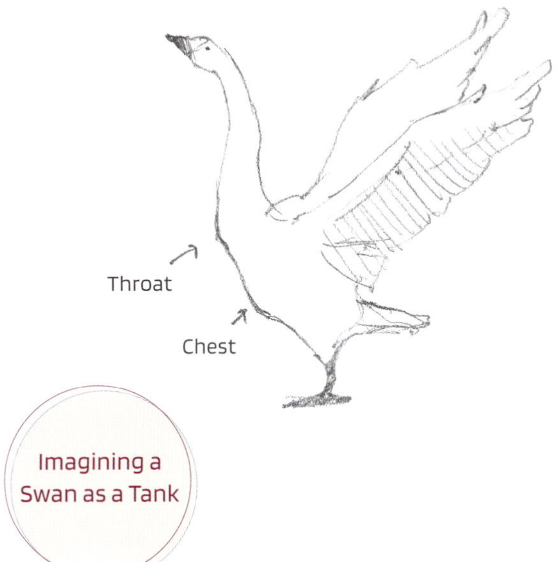

Imagining a Swan as a Tank

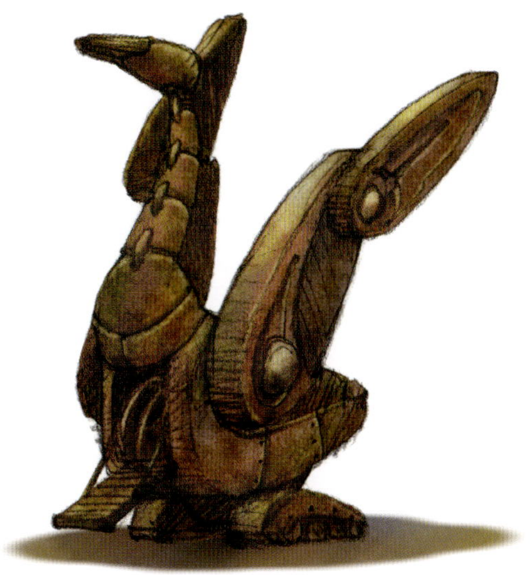

Swan Tank

Sea Anemone

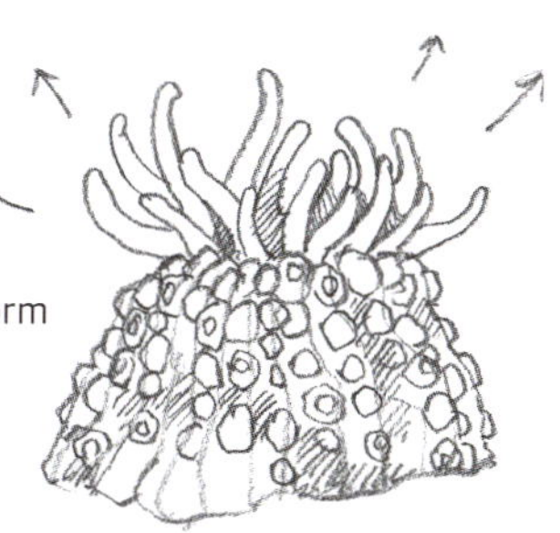

Imagining a Sea Anemone as a Solar Pavilion

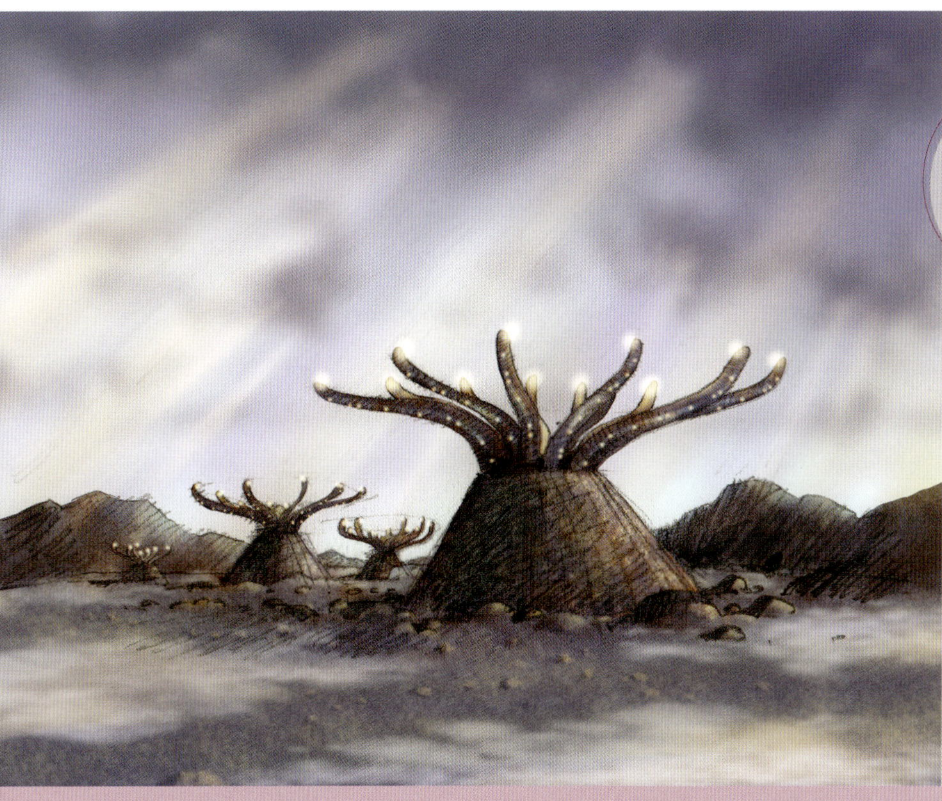

Solar Pavilion

Variations

When applying motifs to a form, you can either appropriate the entire shape or use elements of its structure (its skeleton, parts, details or textures) in different ways. It can be helpful to find and categorize motifs in existing design examples and to gather visual references from inspirations you come across along the way.

● Using a Scorpionfish as a Motif

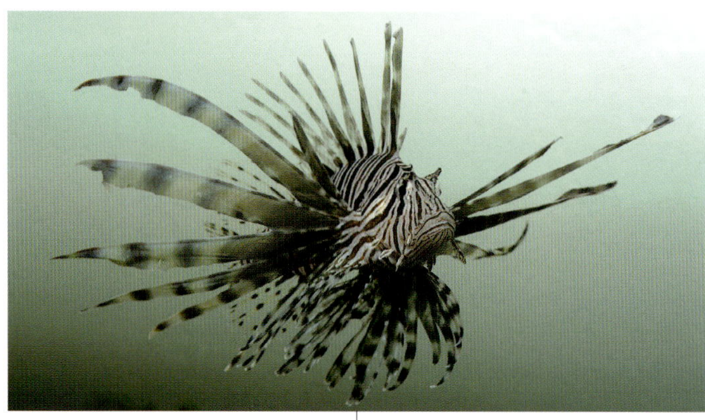

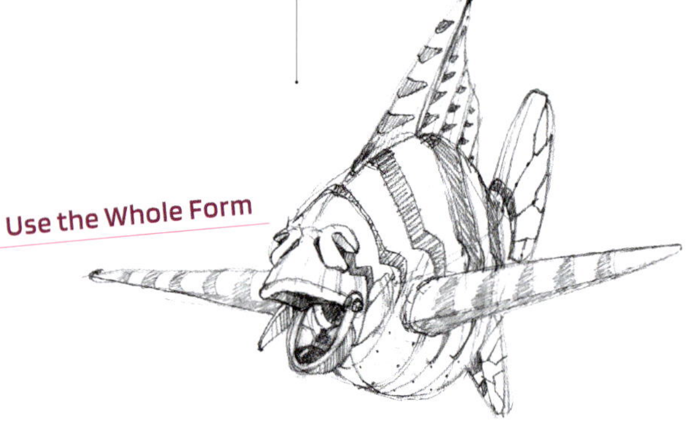

Use the Whole Form

Use the distinctive eyes, fins, mouth and body patterns to create a one-person aircraft with a mechanical design that closely resembles the fish. The open mouth serves as the cockpit.

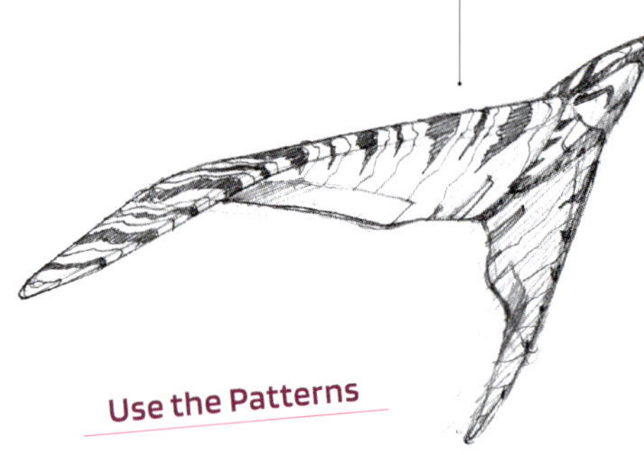

Use the Patterns

Take only the body pattern as a motif. Applying this pattern to an entirely different shape can create an interesting effect.

Use the Fins

Incorporate the structure of the fins. Since these aren't in a typical wing shape, they lend a retro-fantasy aesthetic.

● Using a Dragonfly as a Motif

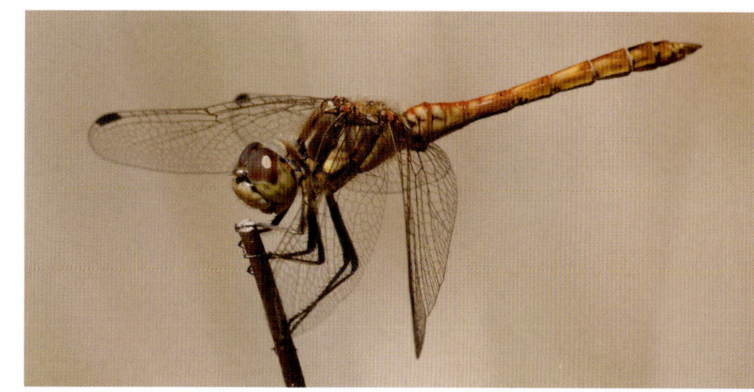

Head

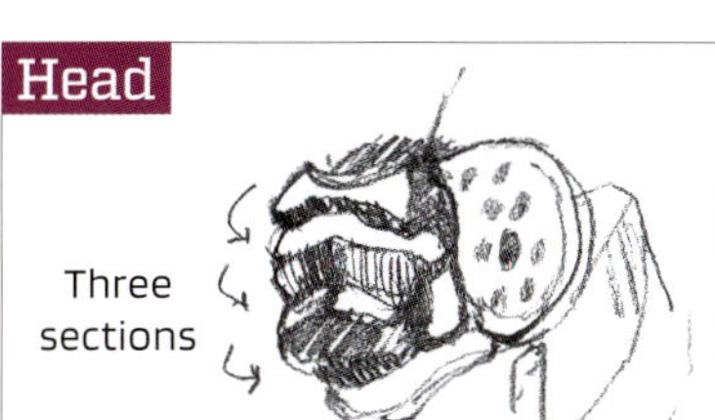

The face has a rather structured appearance. Imagine the head as the cockpit.

Dragonfly-Style Manned Interceptor

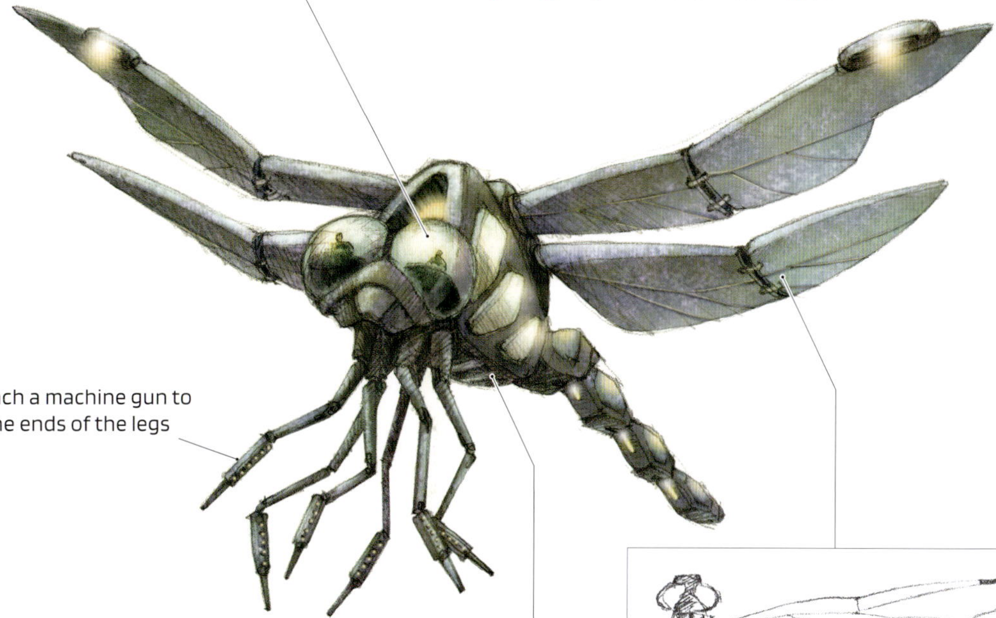

Attach a machine gun to the ends of the legs

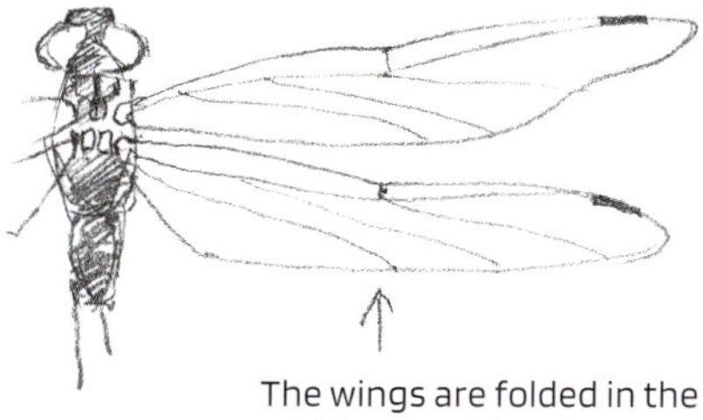

The wings are folded in the middle. Use this structure directly in the wing design.

Wings

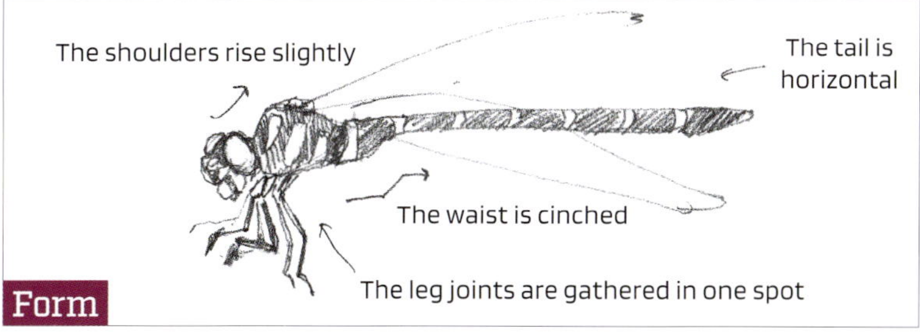

Form

Techniques

In sci-fi and fantasy worlds, various types of mecha and vehicles appear that are direct referents to the natural world. Here, we'll look at an example of a spacecraft modeled after an insect.

● Create a Mecha Design Based on a Beetle

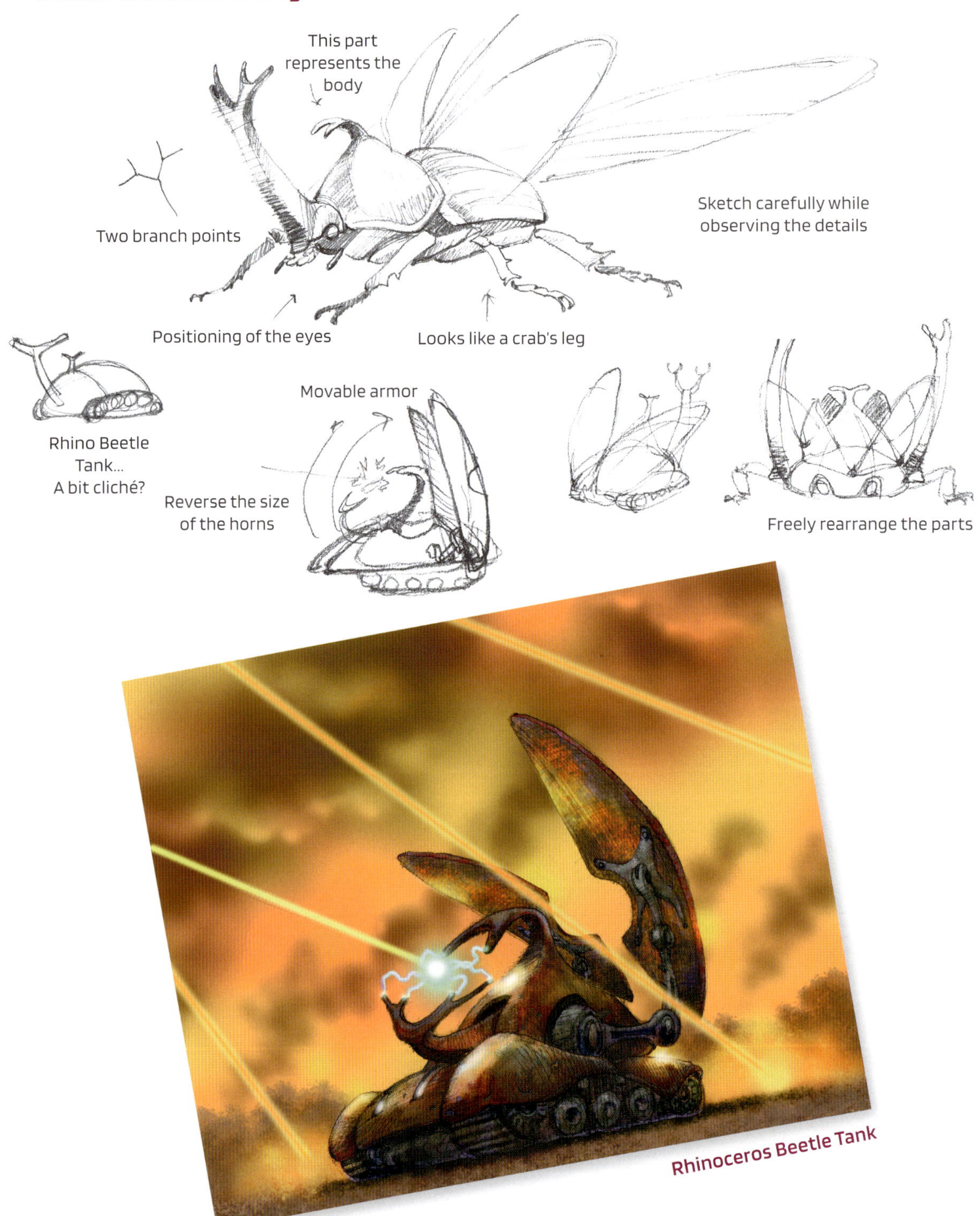

Rhinoceros Beetle Tank

● Create a Vehicle Based on a Bee

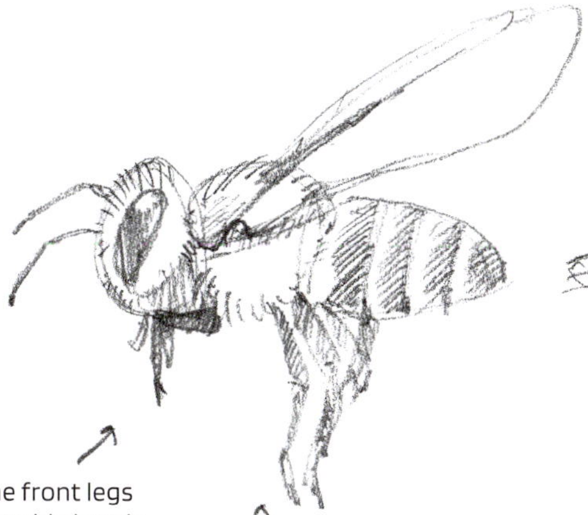

The front legs
resemble hands

The hind legs are
positioned quite far back

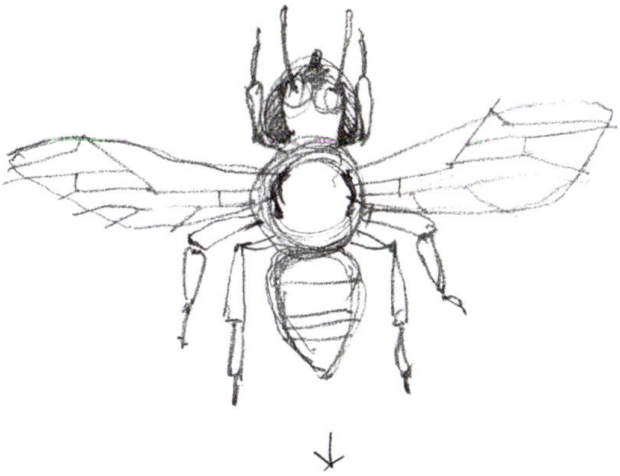

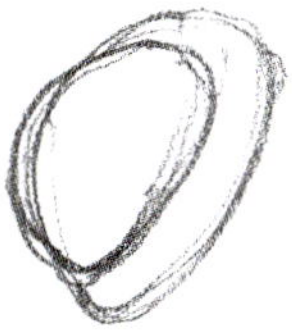

Large eyes
↓
Combine into one
as the cockpit

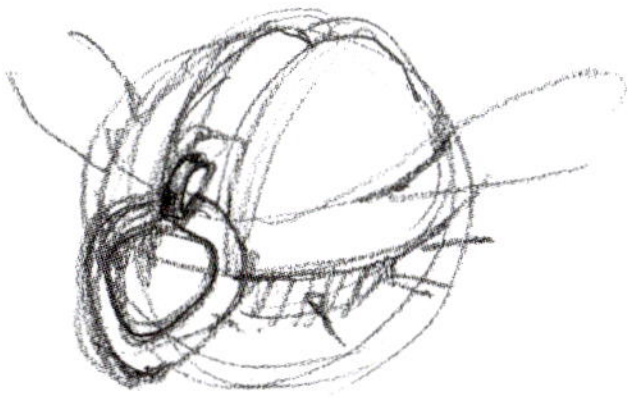

Consider how the head
(the cockpit) attaches

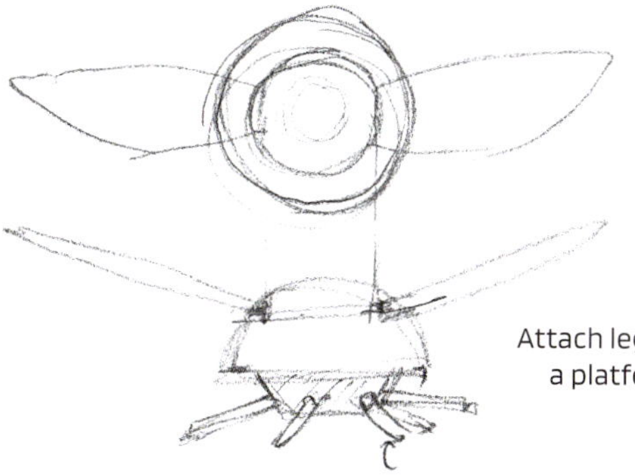

Attach legs and
a platform

Maybe make the legs
radiate outward...

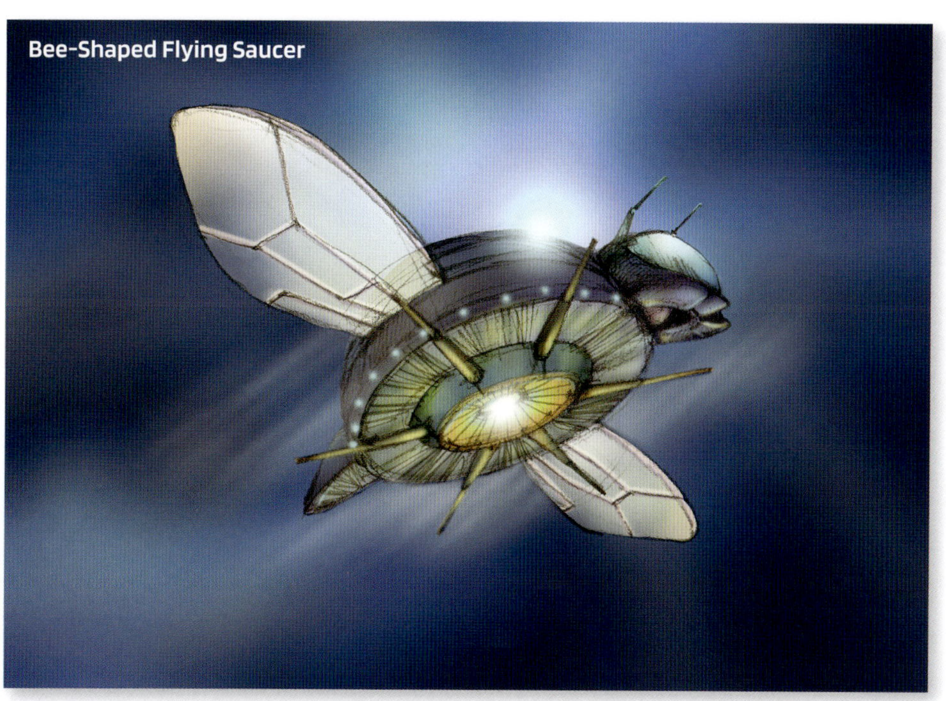

2-4 COMBINATIONS

A final approach to consider is creating entirely new designs by combining different or similar elements. In the worlds of sci-fi and fantasy, many machines and vehicles appear that are hybrids of creative freedom. Think of the rich source material that serves as inspiration: the chimera of Greek mythology has a lion's head, a goat's body and a serpent's tail. The mechanized version of that would be a sight to behold.

Elements and Methods of Combination

Before organizing the elements and methods of combined forms, first consult Table 2-3. Elements include basic and applied shapes from the previous section, as well as the classic designs, motifs and imitations discussed in this chapter. Methods range from simply attaching or linking elements to more complex approaches, like blending or completely fusing them.

Table 2-3: Elements and Methods of Combination

Elements	Selection	Method
Basic and applied shapes, standards and classics, motifs, imitation	Heterogeneous or similar items	Attach/link, blend

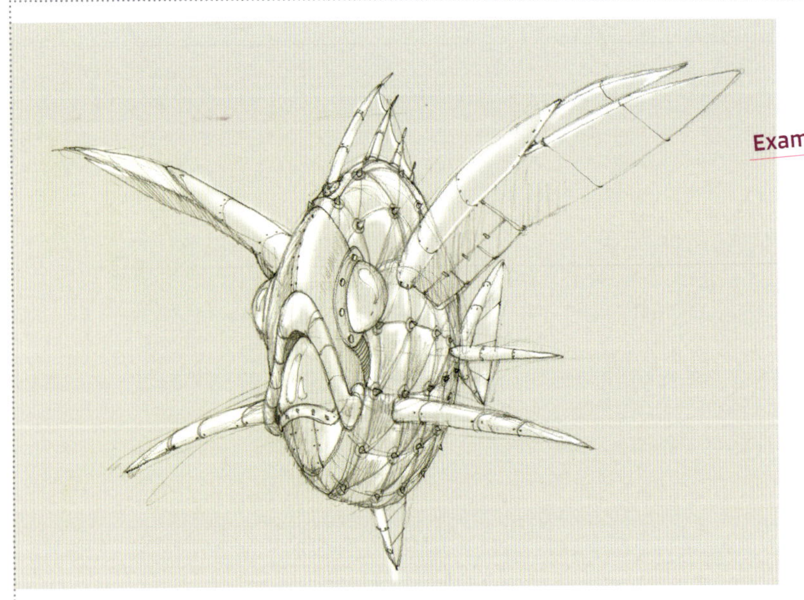

● **Attach**

Wings were added to a fish. Structurally, it would make more sense to replace the front fins with wings if they were to expand; but here wings are deliberately attached to the back, ignoring skeletal structure. This results in a fantastical look, so a tin-aircraft-like detail was added.

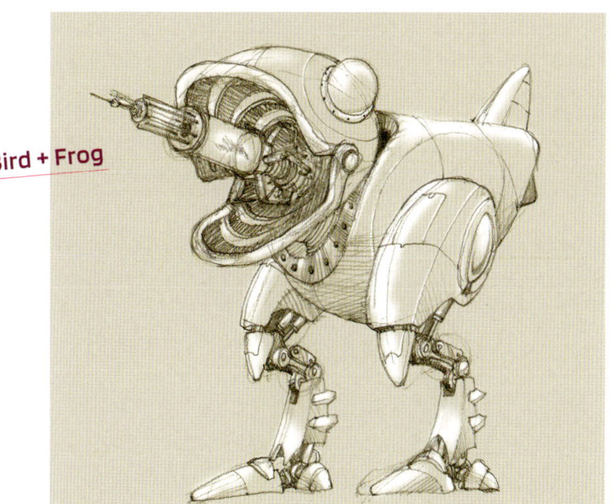

● Link

A frog's head was attached halfway to a bird's legs. Taking inspiration from a frog's long, extendable tongue, a laser cannon was added emerging from the throat. A mechanism for extension and retraction was drawn in the throat, and by observing the unique joint structure of birds, the form stands apart from humanoid robots.

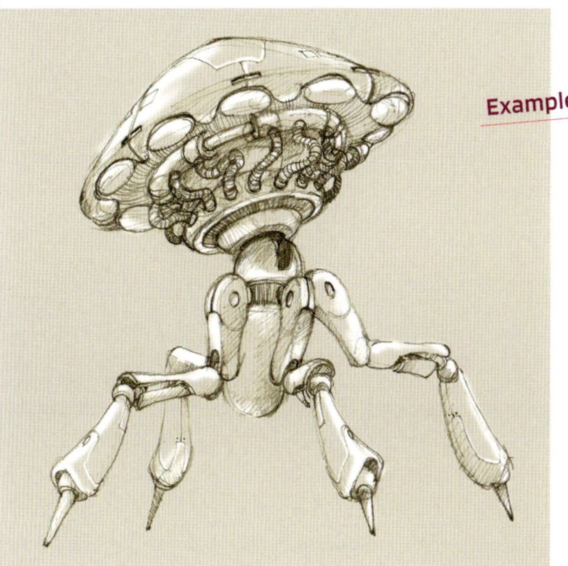

● Blend

This surveillance robot combines an insect and a mushroom. It has cameras around the edge of the mushroom cap resembling insect compound eyes, allowing 360° monitoring. The legs are simply mushroom stems attached to insect legs, while the cap detail blends insect and mushroom characteristics.

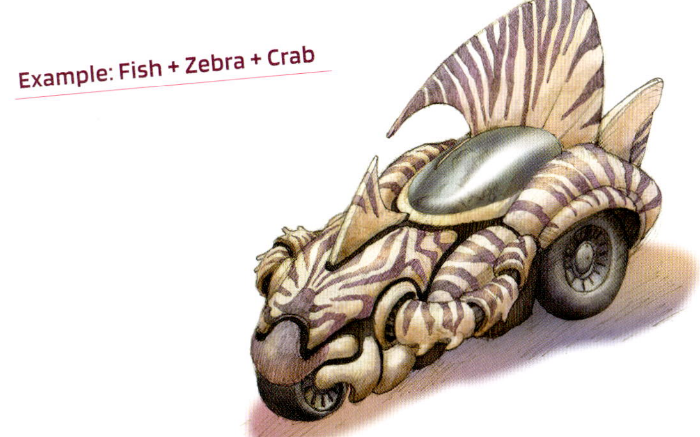

● Fuse Completely

The overall form is that of a fish with a zebra pattern added to its surface. Details throughout incorporate crablike elements.

Combination Techniques

As an example of creativity through the combination of forms, we draw a self-propelled exploration camera by combining the lens part of the camera with a tortoise. The point is not to simply mount the camera on the animal, but to connect the two different elements by adding the form of the seagull's wings.

● Camera Lens + Tortoise + Seagull Feathers

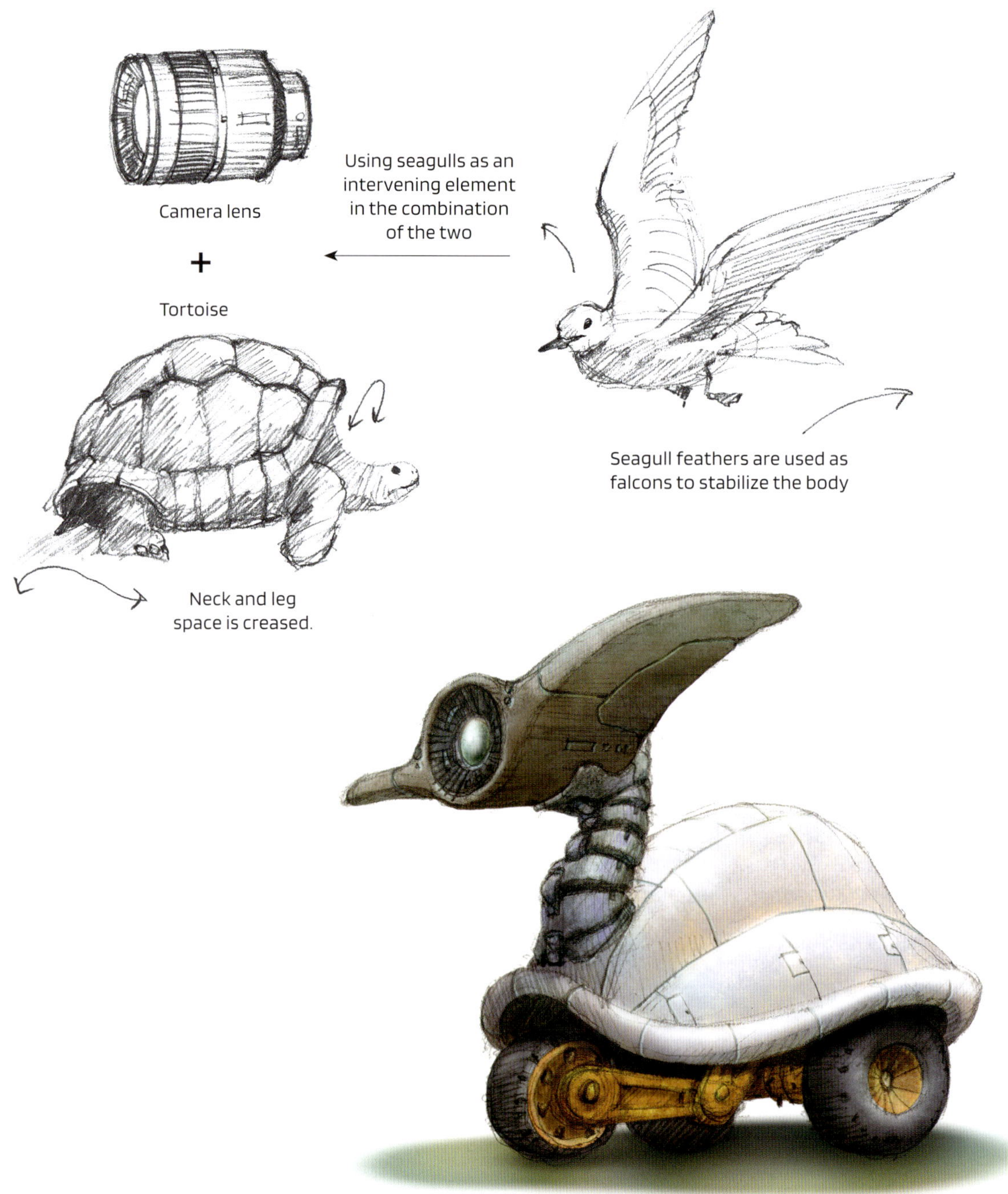

Self-Propelled Terrestrial Search Camera

 | # Fusing Terrestrial and Flying Objects

Here we've combined a car and an airplane. Since airplanes already have wheels, maybe we'll just put wings on a car. But how the idea be further refined and elevated? Here we have tried to fill in the hybrid design a bit more.

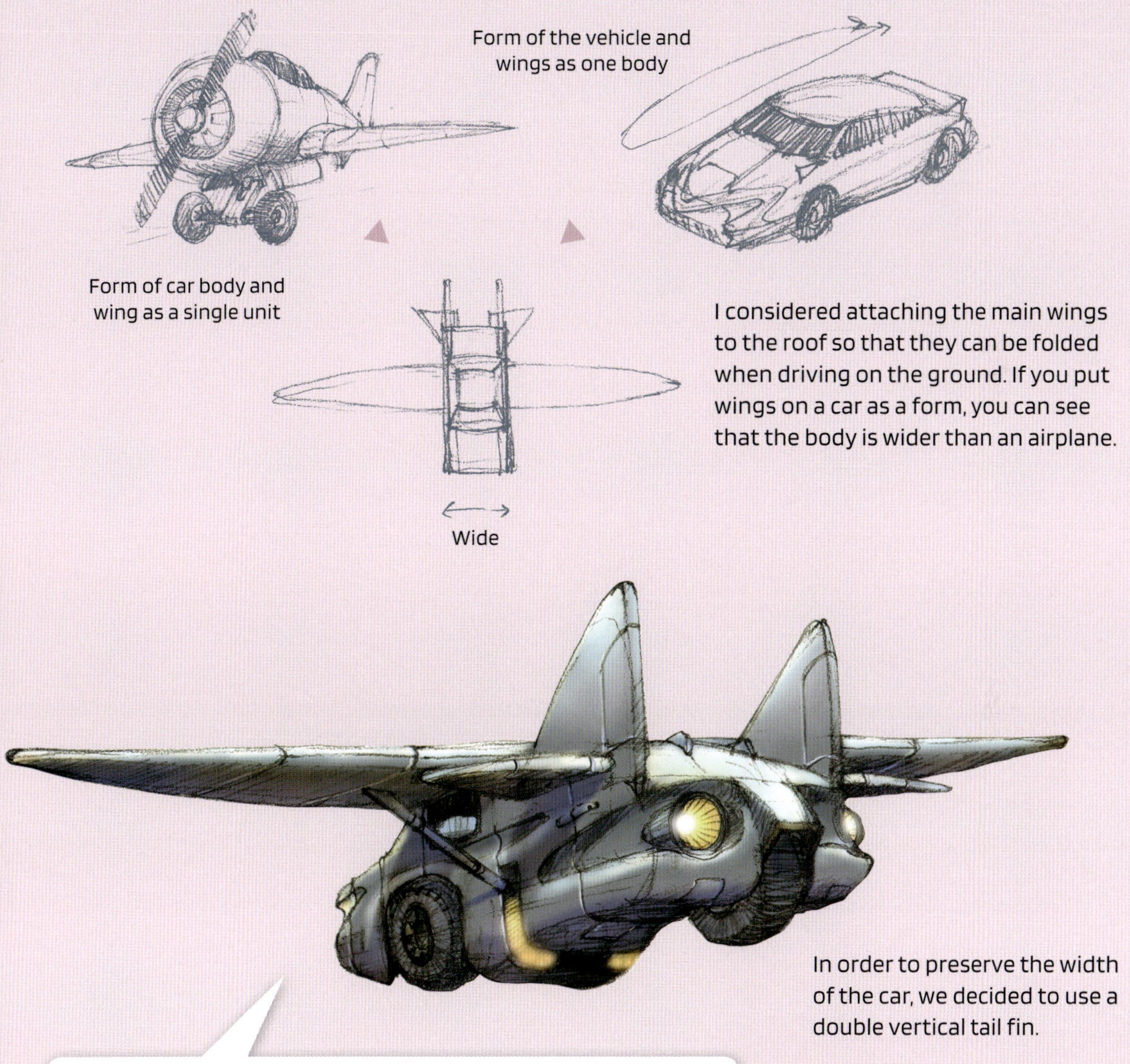

I considered attaching the main wings to the roof so that they can be folded when driving on the ground. If you put wings on a car as a form, you can see that the body is wider than an airplane.

In order to preserve the width of the car, we decided to use a double vertical tail fin.

DID YOU KNOW?

The entire body of the vehicle is fitted into a form resembling the cross-section of a wing, highlighting the aircraft aspects of the silhouette rather than that of a car. The tire section is shaped to fit into the lines of the body, and the rear sports a single wheel.

TAKE A CLOSER LOOK | Chibi-Style Effects

Cartoonish, exaggerated or caricature-style effects are commonly used in Western painting and illustration. Ancient cave paintings and Aboriginal artworks are examples of the different ways people of the past have perceived and represented the world around them. The unconventionally shaped human bodies in cubist paintings are yet another expression of a new way of viewing and perceiving form.

A clear example of caricature in Western painting is the portrayal of the human figure. In order to emphasize the character and features of an individual, parts of the face and body are exaggerated, as are movements and motions. This technique is still used today in portraits and manga. In recent years, in the world of animation, the approach is pushed to a new extreme with characters represented with two heads.

In this way, caricature and chibi-style effects are not only an expression of satire or critique, but can be broadly defined as the exaggeration or accentuation of form with a certain intent. Cartoonish styles are also effective in the expression of mechanisms and vehicles to highlight their distinctive functions, forms and designs.

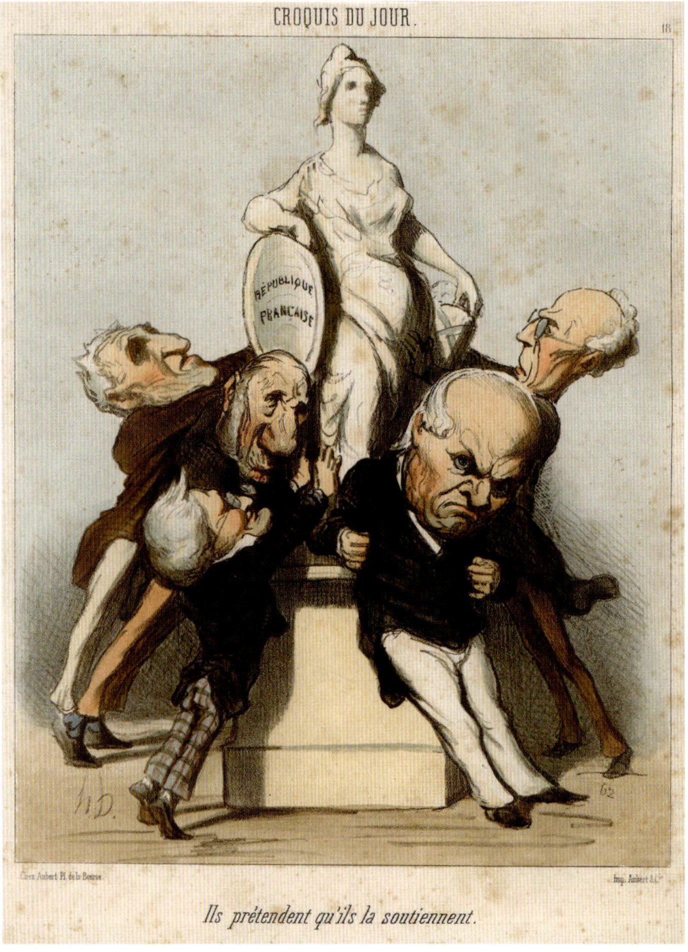

Honoré Daumier, "The French Republic, Their Support Is False,"
19th-century color lithograph

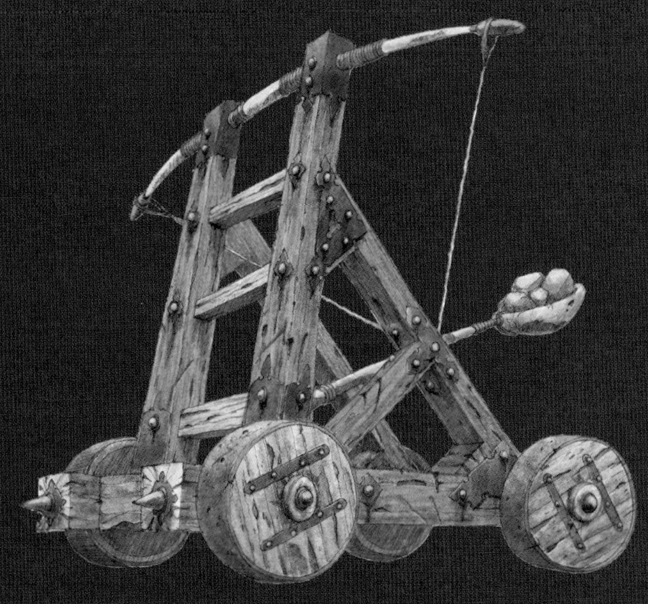

Part 3
ILLUSTRATION TECHNIQUES

Now that we've learned the basics, it's time to get
to the hard and fun work of actual creation. Here,
we'll take those 3D and drafting essentials and
transform them into mindblowing mecha, learning
how to draw and design original sci-fi vehicles.

3-1   LINEAR APPLICATIONS

Line drawing, the most basic of all techniques. Drawing fluid, functional lines is so fundamental that you can tell a lot about an artist's expressive ability just by looking at a single drawn line. To be able to create your own futuristic designs, the only way is to learn the basics and then practice them repeatedly.

Touch

In line drawing, there's no such thing as an inorganic line, because the lines are touches, or lines that reflect and suggest the artist's intention and aim. Line drawing is often called freehand, as opposed to lines drawn with a ruler. Expressive touch is created by the thickness, type, strength and rhythm of the lines. Their combination is probably nearly infinite, and is created by the movement (or strokes) of the fingers, hands and arms.

Figure 3-1 Line Drawing Representation

Thickness

Changes due to hardness or pressure of pencil.

Type

Changes due to jagged or broken lines.

Speed Rhythm

Changes due to the speed of drawing and the rhythm of brush pressure.

● Creating a Sketch

Lines drawn quickly can be dynamic and express a sense of speed, but on the other hand, they typically add up to a rough image, a draft. Slowly drawn lines are static and stable and create a more polished, finished image, but they also give less of an impression of life and dynamism.

Fast Sketch

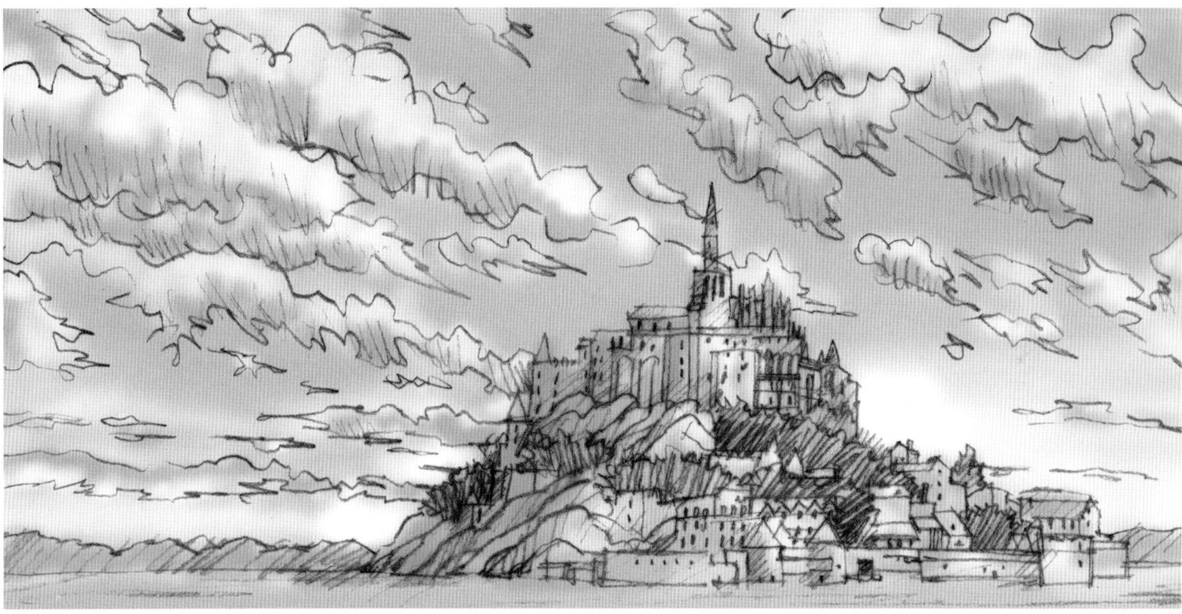

Slow Sketch

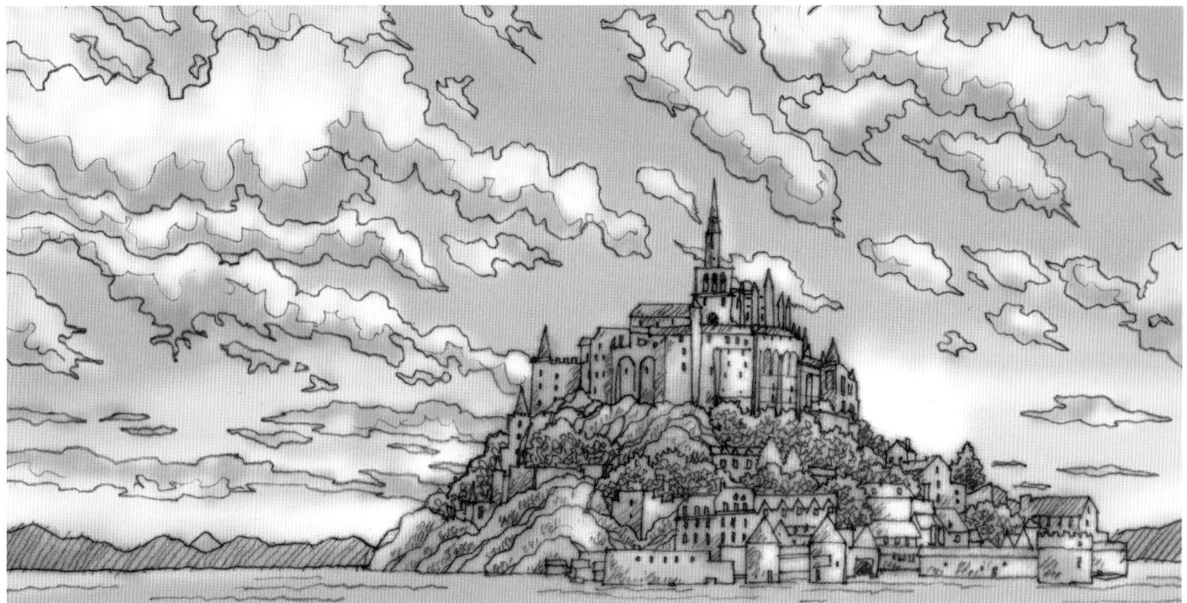

Outlines

The boundary between an object and the surrounding space (its silhouette) or the borders of
its surfaces are depicted with outlines. They replace the contact points of a three-dimensional
object and its surrounding space with a boundary line. It's important to understand that
they have neither thickness nor weight and blend into the space. Be aware that outlines can
sometimes clarify the object's form, but other times they may interfere.

■ Outline of a Cube and Cylinder

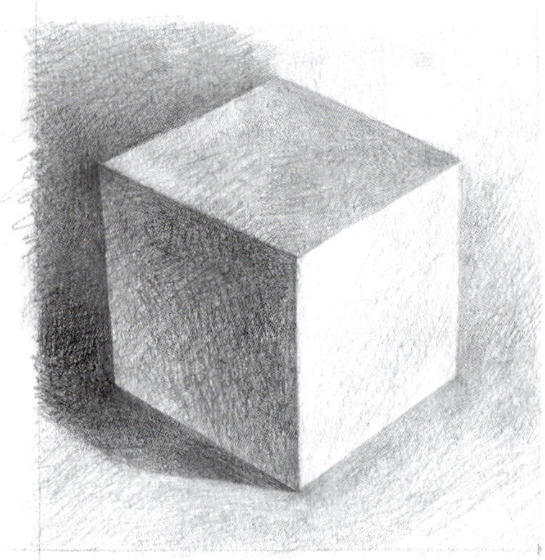

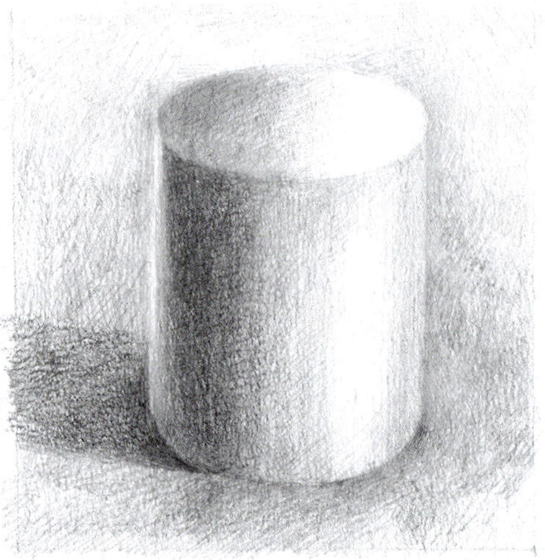

[Clearly Defined Outline]
The three surfaces of a cube are distinctly present
in space, making it easy to draw its outline.

[Side Outline Blending with Space]
For a cylinder, the only distinctly present surfaces
are the top and bottom circles, with no definable
side surfaces, so the boundary lines blend into the
surrounding space.

※ As shown in the figure above, when an edge between a three-dimensional object
   and the background is curved, it's essential to understand that the outline is a
   boundary line that merges into the space.

● Differentiating Outlines

Let's consider outlines with a more complex example. Below is a four-legged robot modeled after a turtle. Here, the edges of the legs and the shell are curved surfaces, so these outlines should blend into the space. However, outlines are being used selectively here to emphasize the depth of the object. The outlines in the foreground are drawn clearly, while in the background, outlines are omitted as much as possible to create a sense of definition and presence.

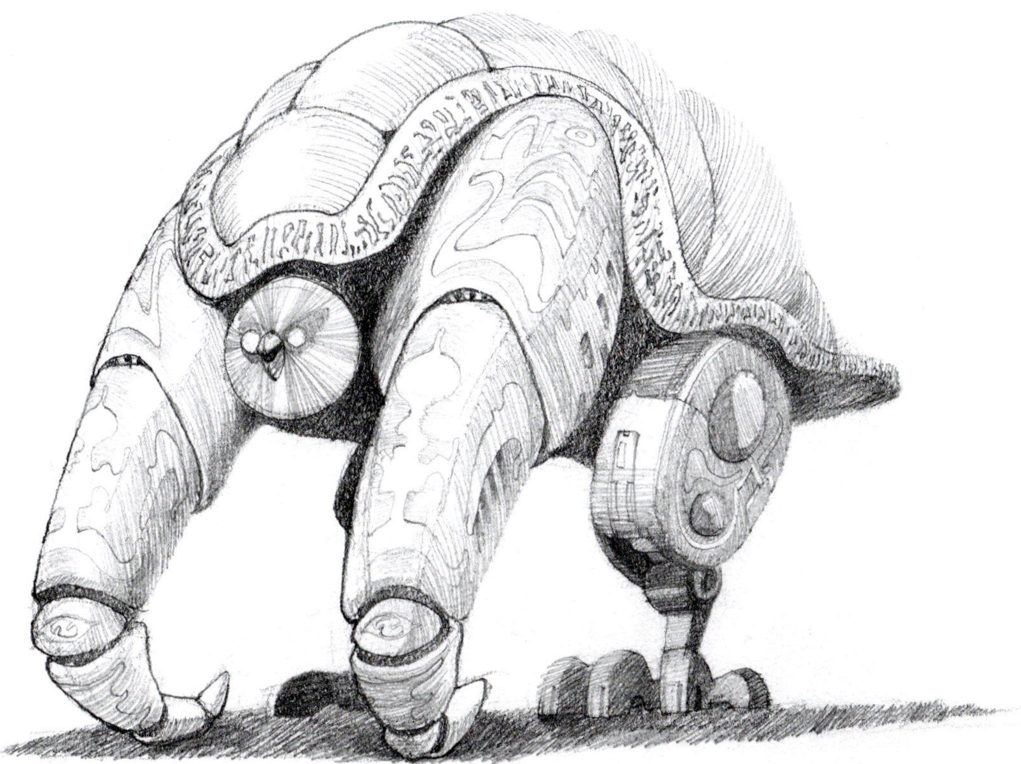

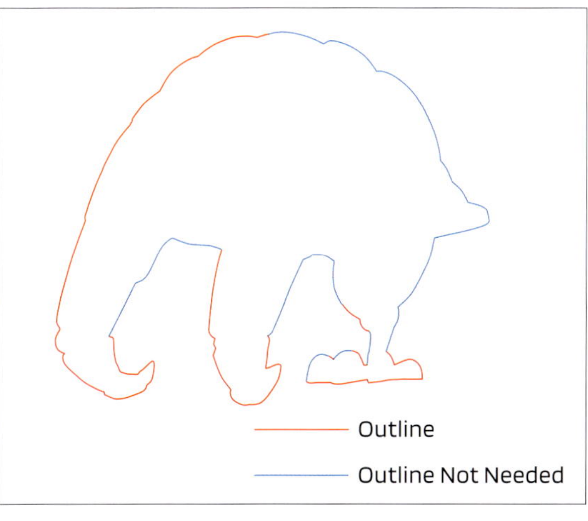

The red lines show where the outlines are clearly drawn. Conversely, the blue lines indicate areas where lines are minimized to blend into the surrounding space.

Depth Expression

When designing three-dimensional objects such as mecha and sci-fi fantasy vehicles, creating a sense of depth is essential. Depth can generally be divided into three stages: far, middle and near, in order of the distance from the viewer or screen. The fundamental technique for depicting depth is to include more detail in objects that are closer to the viewer and to draw them with strong, clear lines. As objects recede into the distance, details are omitted, and they're expressed using softer, less defined lines. Generally, the more detail is included in an area of a drawing, the more expressive and defined it becomes, making it appear to protrude into the foreground.

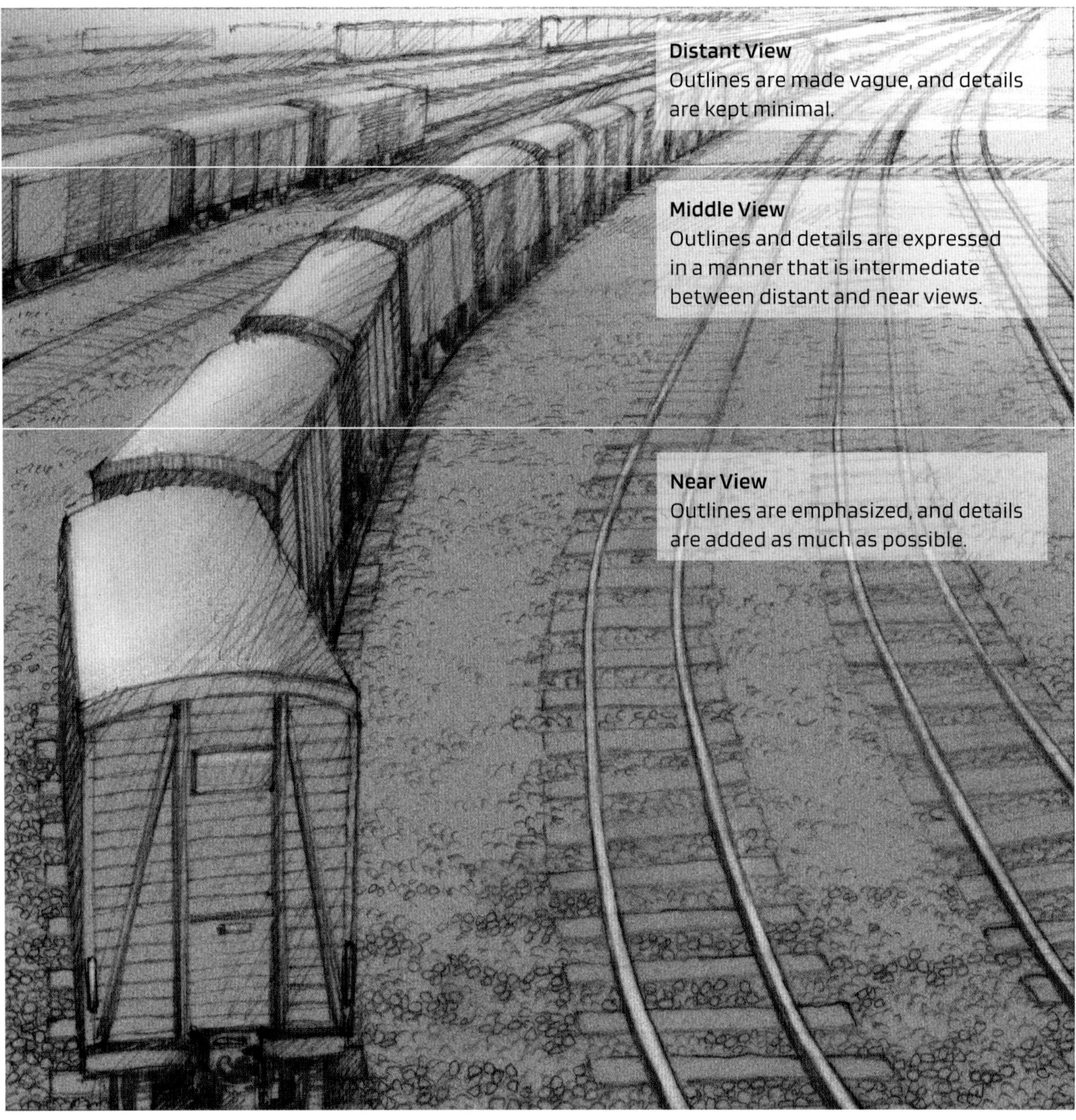

● Vehicles Captured from a Long Angle in the Depth Direction

In cases like the submersible shown below, where the dimensions in the depth direction are elongated, drawing all outlines with the same tone can be effective in expressing size and weight. The outlines of the parts closest to the viewer should be strong and clear, while they should become weaker and more simplified as they move away from the viewer, creating a sense of contrast.

[When Depth Expression Is Not Used]

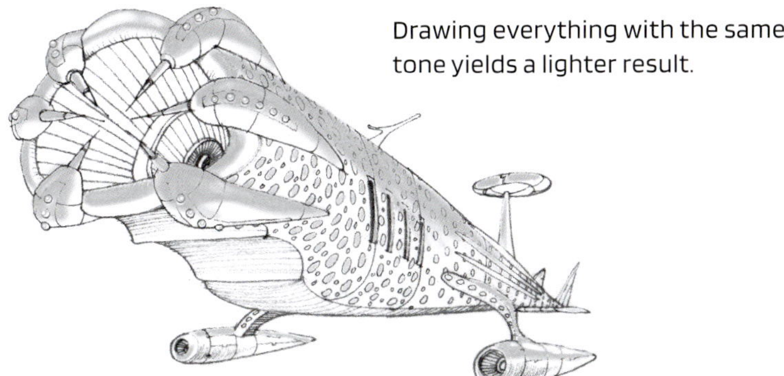

Drawing everything with the same tone yields a lighter result.

[When Depth Expression is Used]

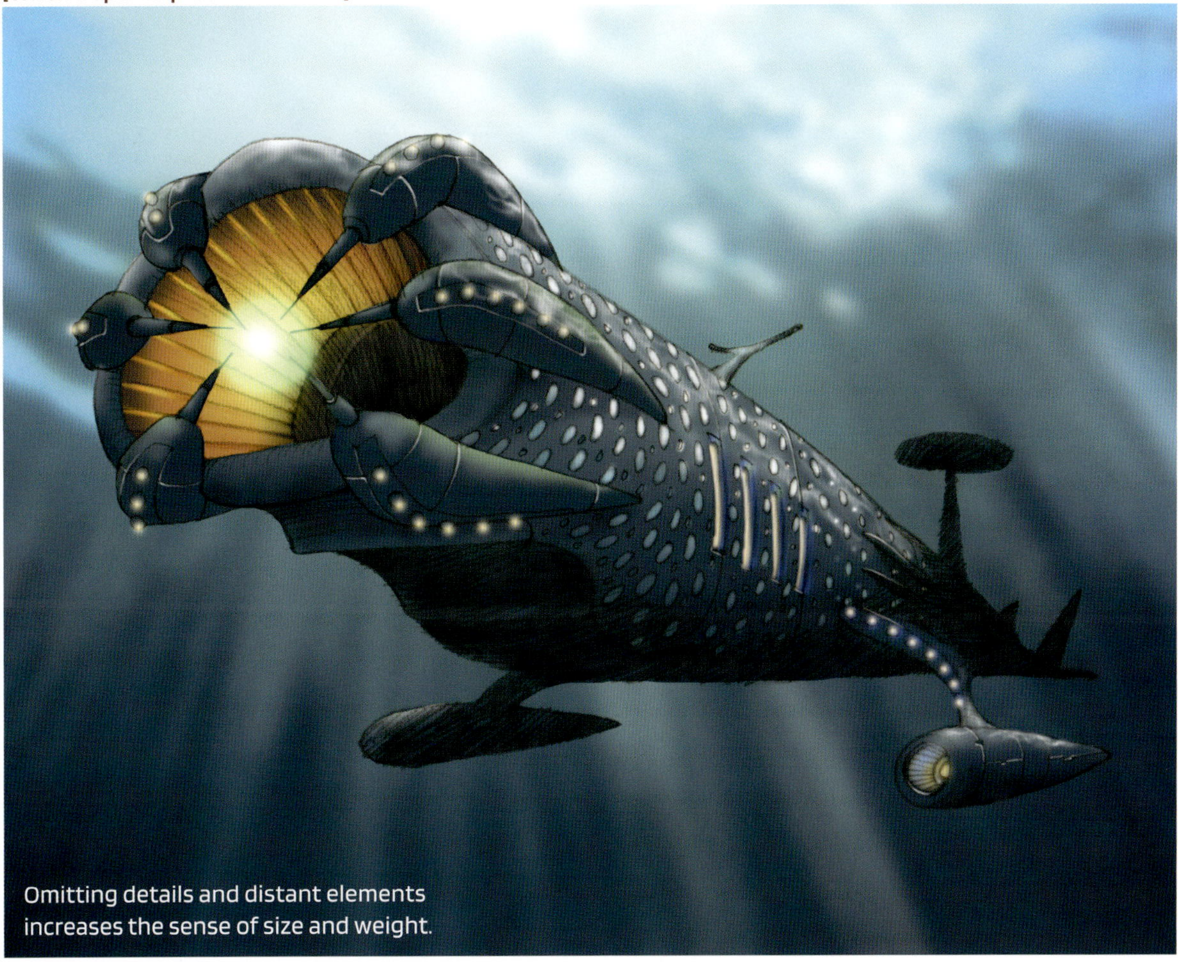

Omitting details and distant elements increases the sense of size and weight.

Whale Shark (Dimensional Submersible Modeled after a Whale Shark)

3-2 APPLYING SHADING

Shading and shadows add depth, drama, dimension and definition. These key highlights heighten the realism of your drawing in identifying the light source illuminating your mecha mashup or sci-fi vehicle design.

Shades and Shadows

The light we see can be divided into two types: natural light or sunlight. These two types of light have the property that when they strike an object, the same object may appear to have slightly different colors, with sunlight generally appearing more natural to humans. The most significant difference between natural and artificial light is the direction in which the light travels. Natural light travels in parallel waves due to the distance from the sun, while most artificial light radiates outward in all directions.

When light hits a three-dimensional object, bright and dark areas are created. The darkened areas are called shade. When light hits an object, it casts a shadow on the opposite side. While shade and shadow are both darkened areas, it's important to remember that they aren't necessarily black.

Figure 3-2 Shadows and the Direction of Light

The areas of light and dark are the shade, while the shadows created by the object are the shadow. Shadows created by natural light are drawn parallel, while those created by artificial light are drawn radially from the light source.

● Differences in Shadows Based on the Direction of Light

The light coming from slightly above and to the left, as shown in the upper diagram, is a commonly used angle that provides a clear balance of shadows that reveal the shapes of the entire object or its parts. On the other hand, the middle and lower diagrams make use of backlighting. The area occupied by shadows becomes larger, and some three-dimensionality may become unclear, but this can add a dramatic effect to the image.

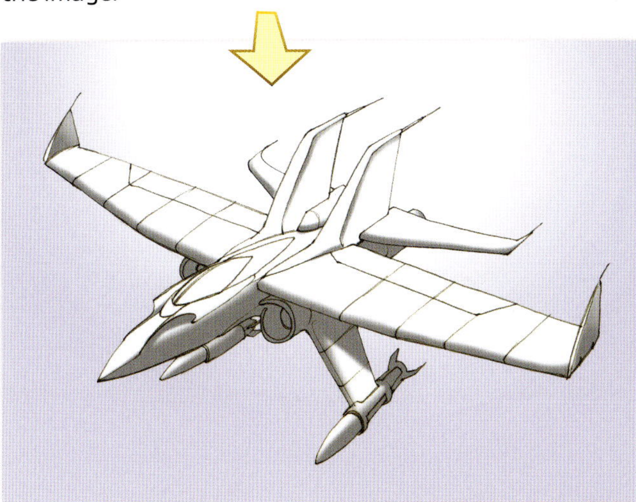

Light coming from slightly above and to the left of the object.

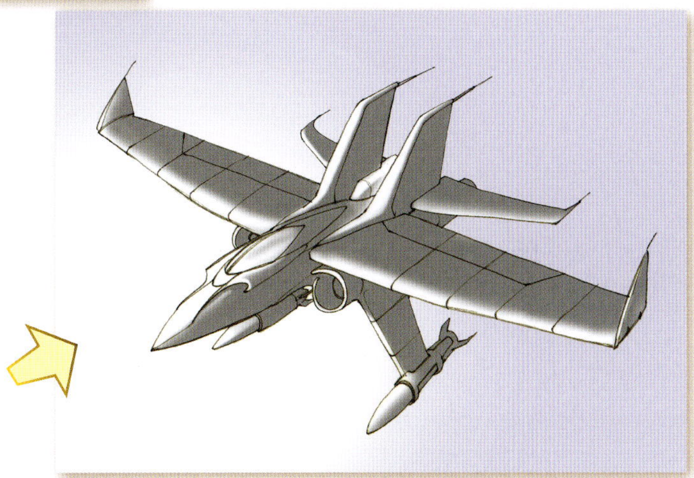

Light coming from slightly below and to the left of the object.

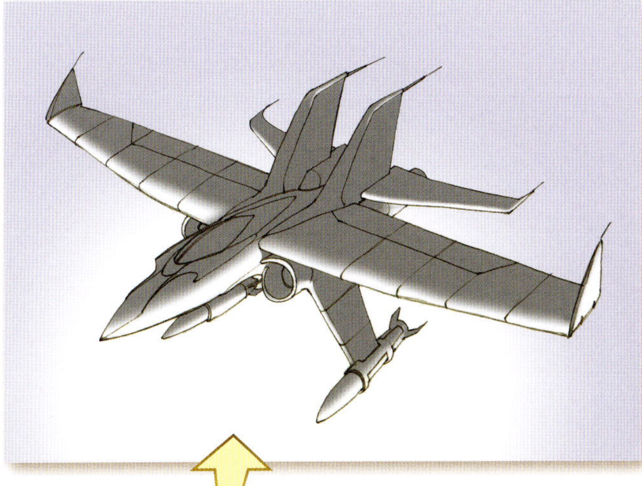

Light coming almost directly from below the object.

The Law of Gradients

An object's shaded or shadowed parts are not simply black. Upon closer observation, you can see a continuous range from the brightest areas to the darkest. This range is called tone, and the continuous change is referred to as gradation.

The tones in the shadows of a three-dimensional object can be broadly divided into three categories: light, medium and dark, with reflections added in. These three tones and reflections occur according to a basic law, which applies to even the smallest surfaces and details. The reflective parts are qualitatively different from the other tones. This difference arises because the colors of nearby objects are reflected.

With this gradation of the three tones and reflections, a strong transition will always appear at the boundary between the bright and dark surfaces and the reflective tone.

● Monochrome Tones and Reflections

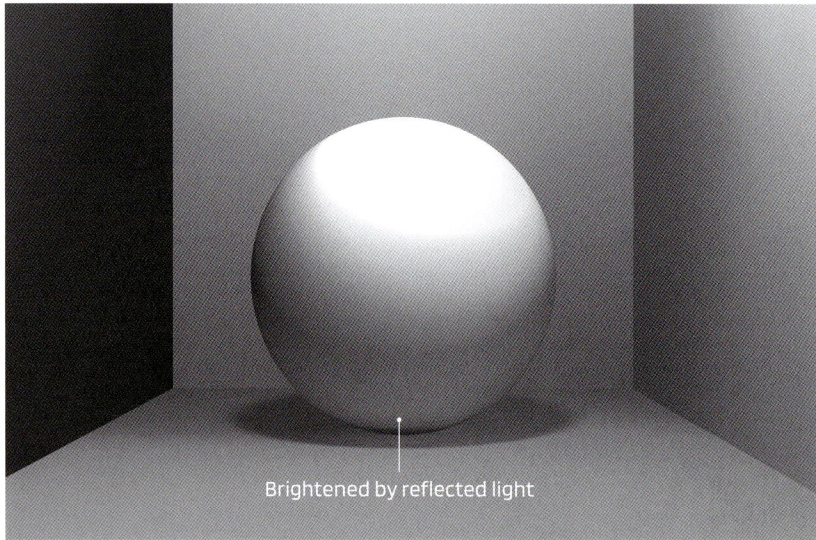

From the lit areas, there will be tones with gradation. When shifting focus to the dark tones, you can see that some areas are brightened by the reflected light from the ground.

● Color Tones and Reflections

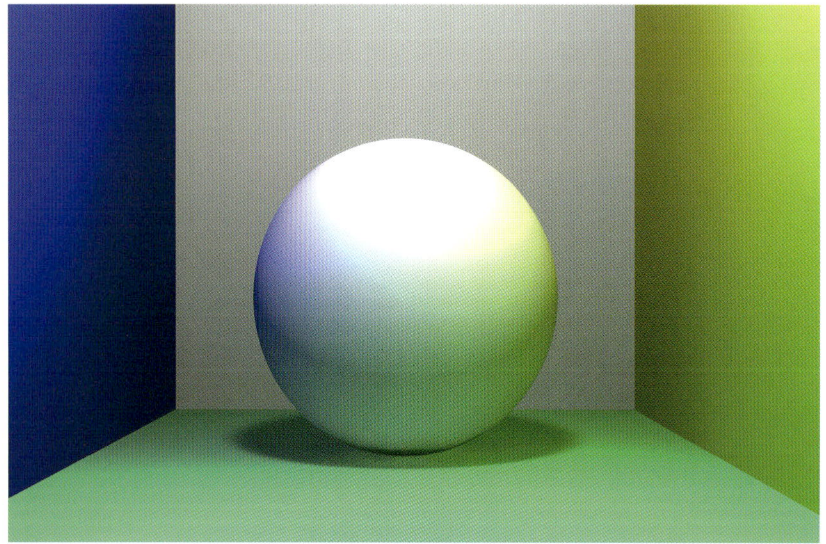

When the colors of the sides and ground are reflected on a white sphere, you can see the extent of their effect.

● Drawing Tones and Reflections

Spheres, cylinders and curved surfaces can be made to appear three-dimensional by adding the light, medium and dark tones along with reflections to the contour lines. Rather than simply transitioning from light to dark areas, try drawing while imagining the reflections from the ground and between parts. The key is to apply the same effects when drawing even the fine details.

● Humanoid Robot Riding a Motorcycle

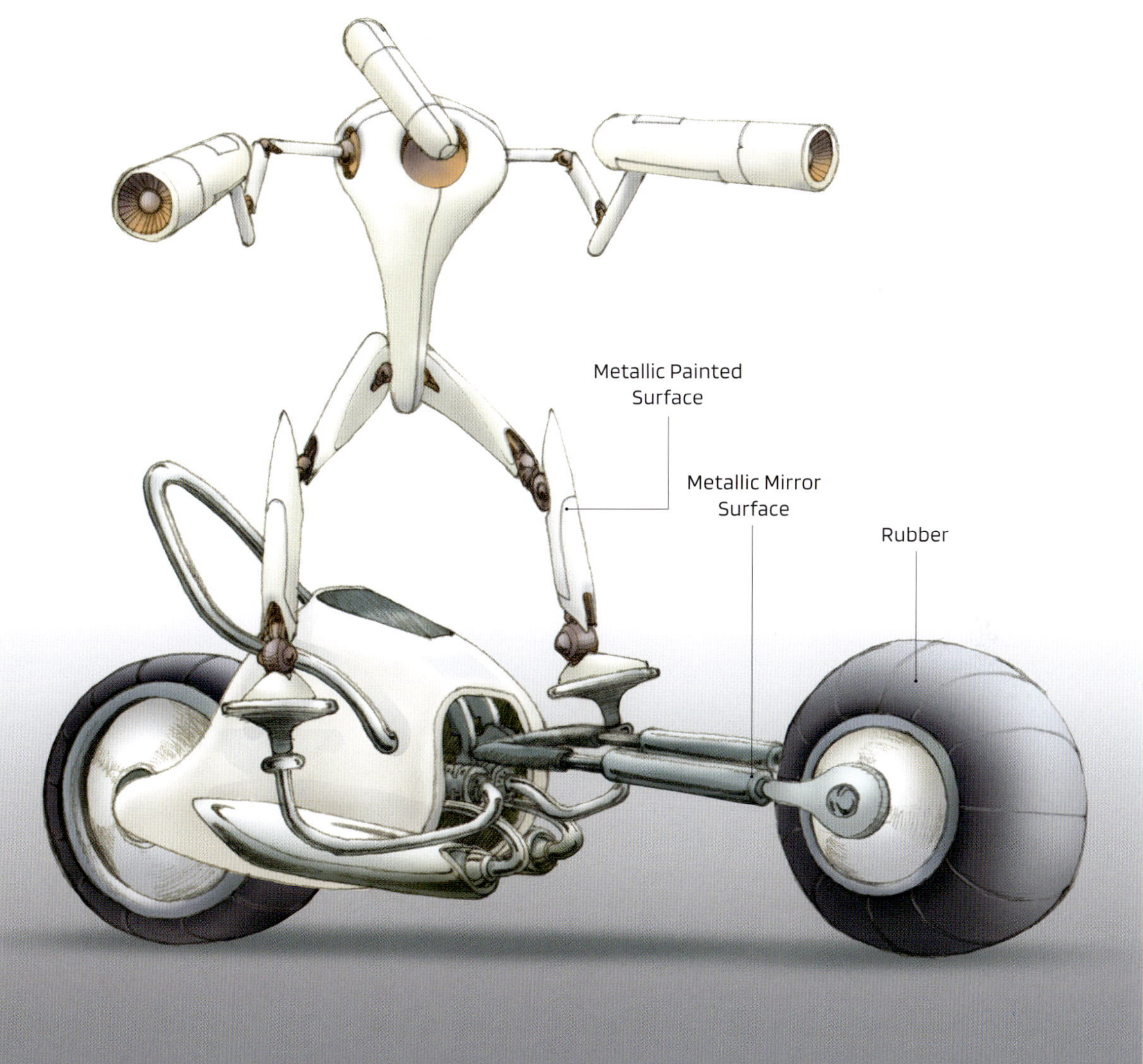

Here, the changes in the three tones of light, medium and dark increase in the order of rubber < metallic painted surface < metallic mirror surface. In particular, the metallic mirror surface enhances the contrast of the reflected scenery and can be effectively distorted to express texture. Furthermore, the metallic painted surface has slight reflections of its own shape, while rubber reflects almost nothing.

The Law of Shadows

To accurately depict the shapes of shadows created by light, one needs to understand perspective drawing techniques need to be applied:

①The shape and length of a shadow change depending on the direction and angle of the light.

②Shadows change shape according to the surface they fall on or strikes.

The first law can be explained through the differences in shadow lengths at noon and in the evening. The length of the shadow can represent a time of day. The second law will be explained using the illustration on the right page.

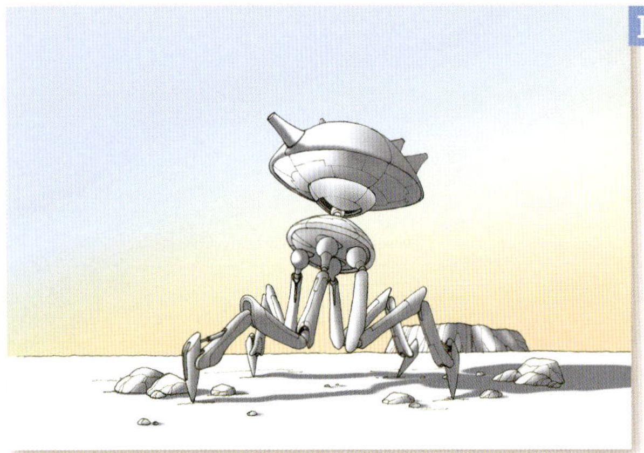

The shape and length of shadows change with the direction and angle of light.

Morning or evening shadows when the sun is low in the sky.

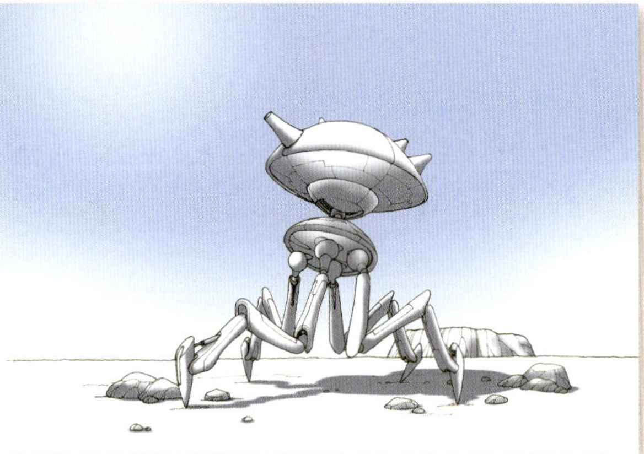

Noon shadows when the sun is high in the sky.

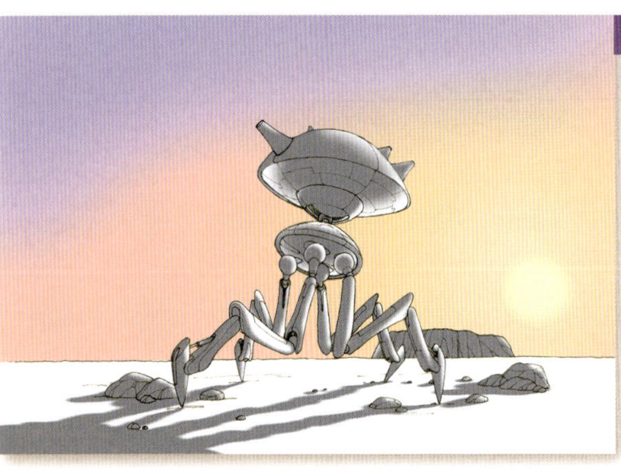

Shadows created by backlighting.

● How Shadows Fall

When drawing shadows, you may feel limited if you always add them to flat surfaces. There will be scenes you're working on where there are walls or steps behind three-dimensional objects, or where objects are floating in the air. In such cases, let's explore how these shadows fall.

A: Shadows formed along the back of a three-dimensional object. The part hitting the wall creates a shadow along the wall.

B: Shadows created by stepped three-dimensional objects. The shadow rises along the shape of the stairs.

C: Shadows of elevated objects. They're almost the same shape as the flat surface; if they move away, the shadow is slightly reduced.

D: Shadows formed on concave surfaces. The flat shape shifts, similar to military projection.

> Shadows change shape according to the surfaces they fall on or strike.

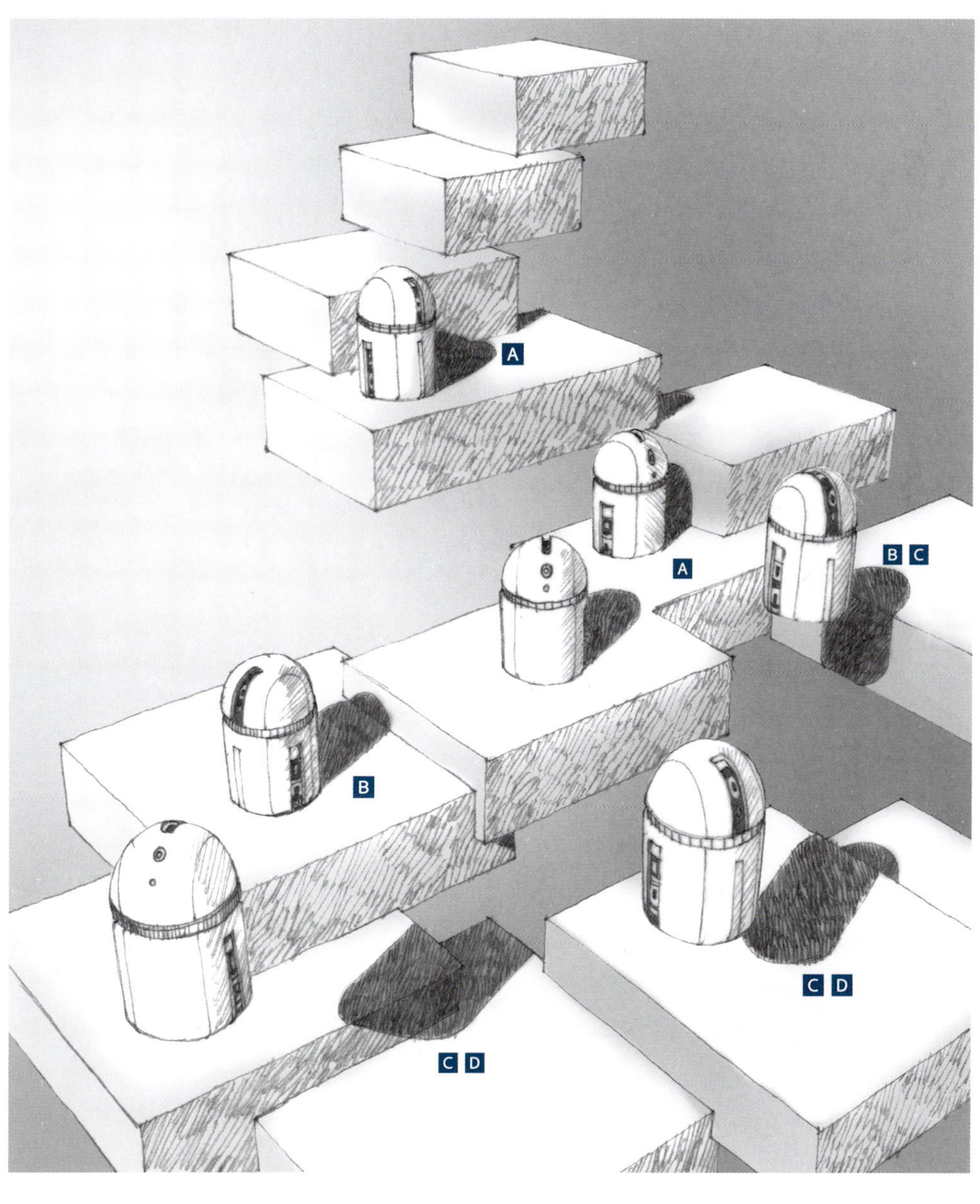

3-3 MATTER AND MATERIALS

By carefully observing the state of light hitting a three-dimensional object, you can capture, suggest and express the texture of materials, their density, gloss and the transparency of the object's surface. Here, we'll learn tips on how to represent and differentiate varying types of surfaces.

Surface Aspects

The surface of an object varies depending on the material, such as metal, stone, wood or plastic. We judge the differences in material texture to some extent based on the visual information presented on the surface. This visual information includes surface density (rough, bumpy, smooth, etc.), gloss, shine and transparency, effects that arise from the material's color and how light strikes it.

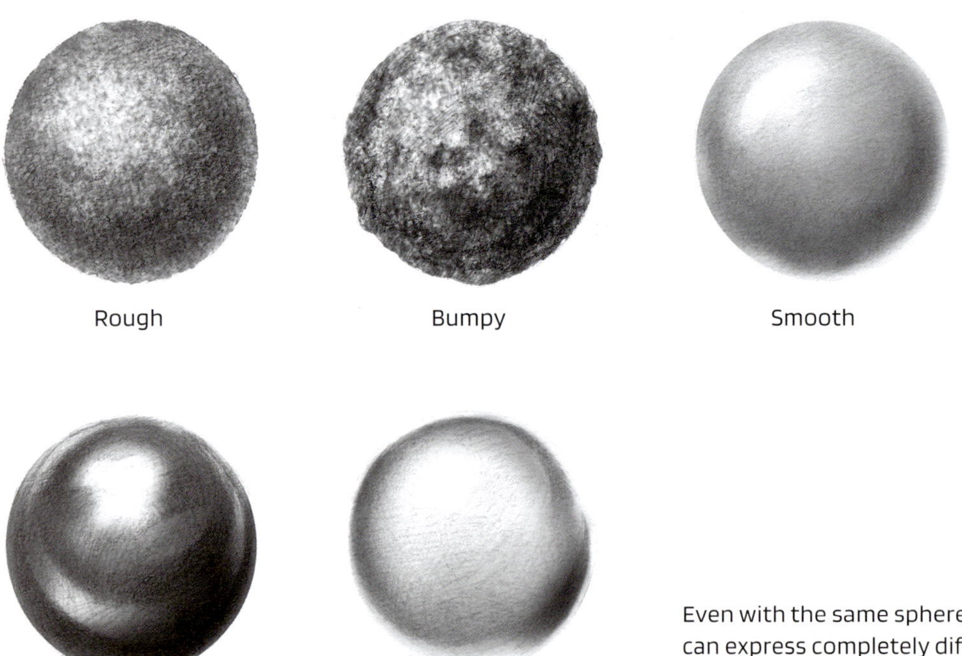

Rough   Bumpy   Smooth

Shiny   Transparent

Even with the same sphere, you can express completely different materials by differentiating the surface appearance.

Illustrating Material Textures

Here, we give examples of representations for a range of materials: wood, stone, metal, glass and concrete. Rather than detailed depictions, each can be differentiated by a style that emphasizes simplification or symbolized expression through the use of repetitive patterns.

● Material Texture Representations

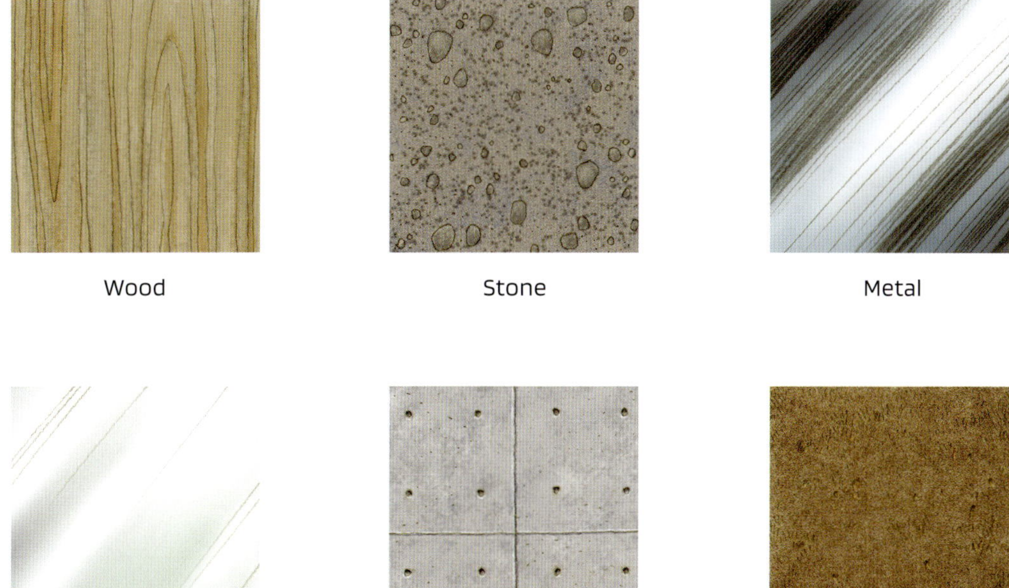

| Wood | Stone | Metal |
| Glass | Concrete | Non-glossy metal |

HINT Symbolized Representation

In material texture representation, if wood grain or growth rings are drawn on the surface, naturally it suggests wood; if there's a pattern resembling sand or pebbles, it identifies stone. Similarly, randomly angled shadows or stripes give the impression of a glass surface, and if you emphasize the shading in those stripes, it can look like a glossy metal surface. For concrete, drawing formwork marks from when it was poured makes it look realistic. Thus, while observing actual objects is key, it's also helpful to know commonly recognized manga-style representations.

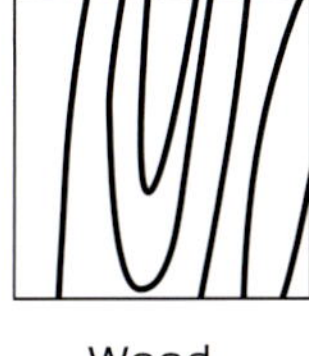

Wood

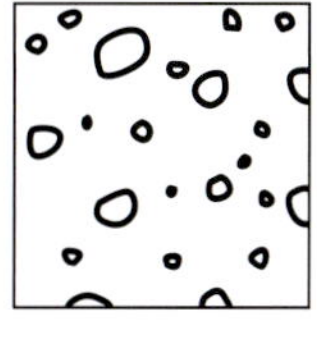

Stone

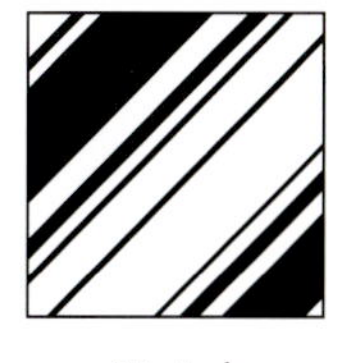

Metal

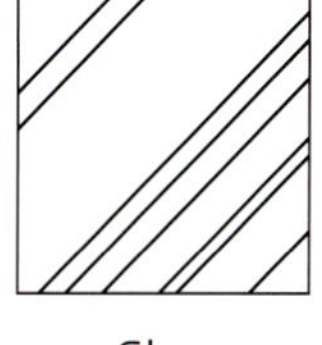

Glass

● Using Light to Enhance Material Texture

By learning patterns of how light hits and reflects from surfaces, you can better express and capture the material texture of three-dimensional objects. By conveying material texture, you can more realistically evoke the weight, surface temperature and tactile qualities of a vehicle.

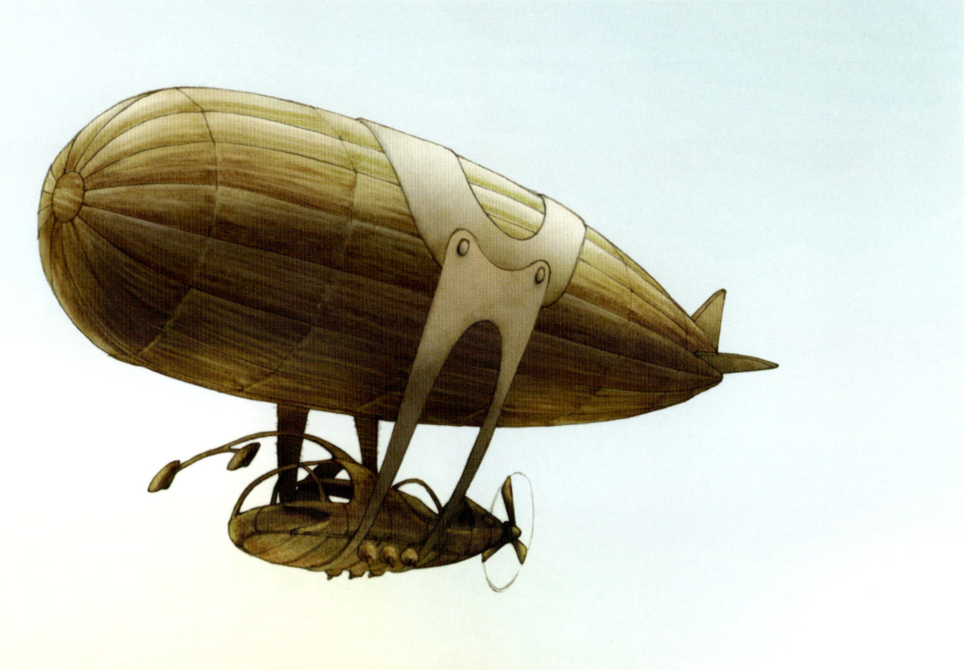

Wooden Airship (Fantasy Style)

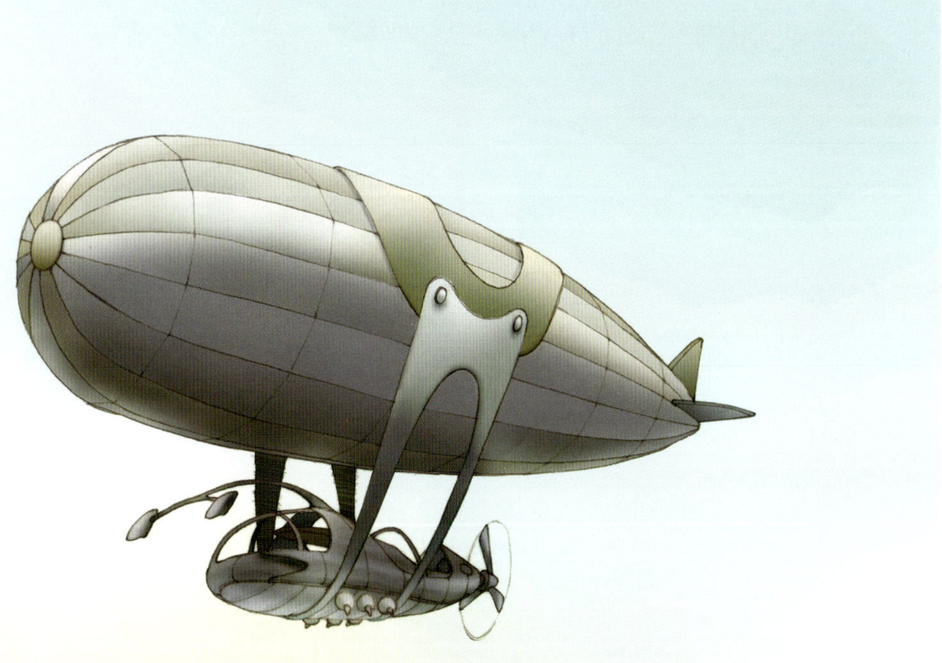

Metal Airship (Sci-Fi Style)

Staining and Surface Effects

The final technique is aging, which involves adding signs of wear and degradation to the material texture. Material aging varies by type—such as cracks, chips, scratches and stains—and adding these elements can create a more realistic design, suggest character and convey the passage of time.

● Without aging effects

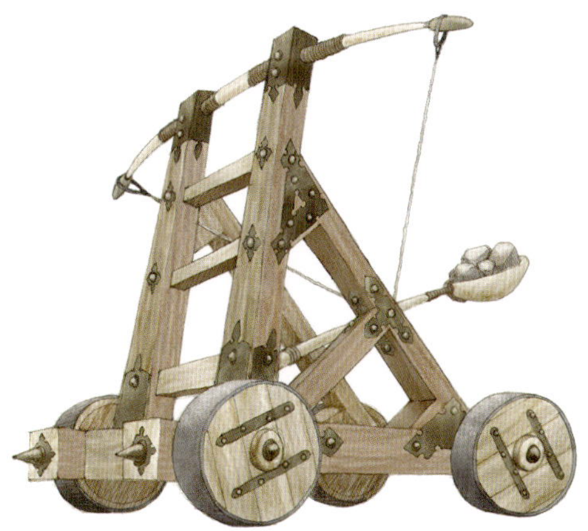

● With aging effects

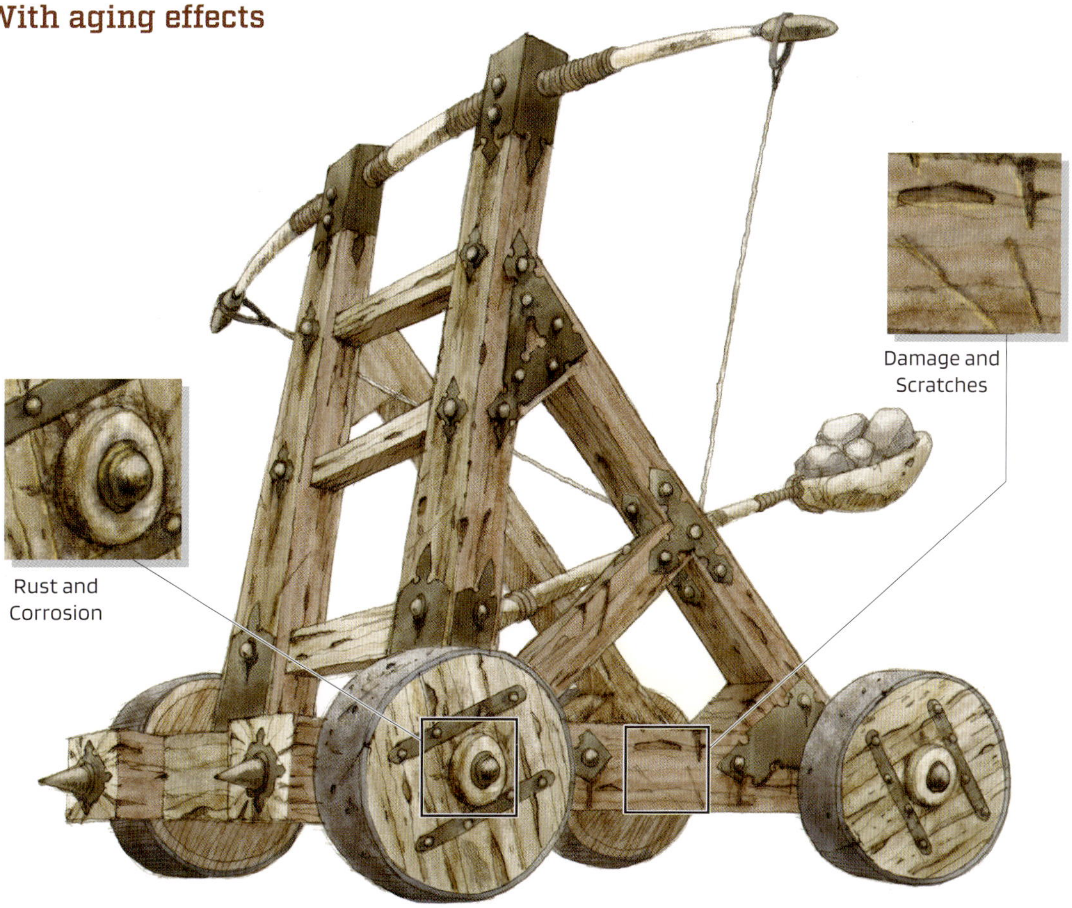

Rust and
Corrosion

Damage and
Scratches

TAKE A CLOSER LOOK | Intrinsic Color and Background

We see light reflected off objects. Usually, we can only perceive an object's color through light. Sunlight comprises the rainbow's seven colors, with longer wavelengths appearing red, shorter ones blue, and the middle wavelengths green. An object that reflects red wavelengths appears red, one that reflects all wavelengths appears white, and one that absorbs all wavelengths appears black. Naturally, the perceived color changes depending on the light source and conditions. Daylight gives the most natural color appearance, though sunlight changes in hue with the time of day. At dawn or dusk, when the sun is low and only long wavelengths penetrate the thick atmosphere, the light appears reddish. On cloudy days, when short wavelengths scatter more easily, light takes on a blueish hue. At night, artificial light shifts hues because artificial lights have different wavelength ranges than sunlight.

Let's now consider the background colors in a drawing. First, assume the basic, standard setting: outdoors on a clear day, and the object is illuminated by daylight. In this case, the colors of the object and background don't interact much; only slight reflections of the background color appear in shaded areas. This setting is ideal for expressing individual colors, but for the overall composition of a drawing, you need to carefully select background elements to avoid a lack of color harmony.

A commonly used technique is to coordinate the background color with the inherent color of the main subject. In other words, by minimizing the contrast between the local colors of the subject and the background, you can create a balanced, unified composition. This approach can give the artwork a cohesive look, as if under an evening or morning sky. The sky at these times is dominated by long-wavelength red, making it easier to achieve a unified color scheme.

Another technique, if you want to emphasize the subject's local color, is to use analogous or complementary colors for the background, creating a sense of color harmony. This results in a reflected-light effect, where the main subject appears seamlessly integrated with the background, resulting in a cohesive composition.

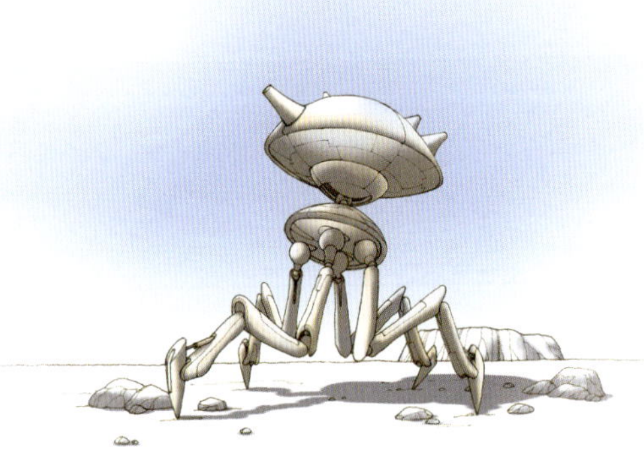

Local Color in Daylight

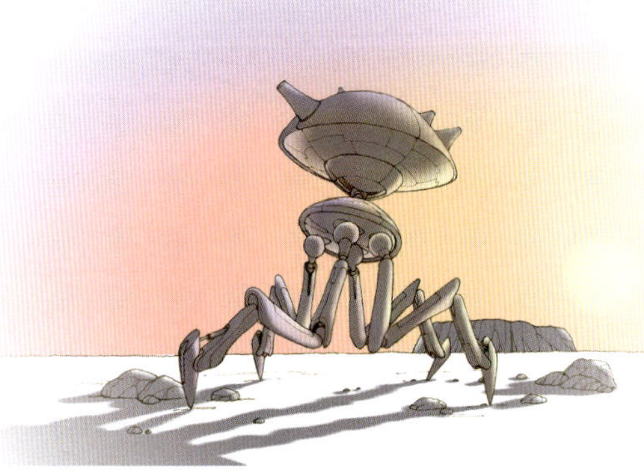

Local Color Changing in Evening

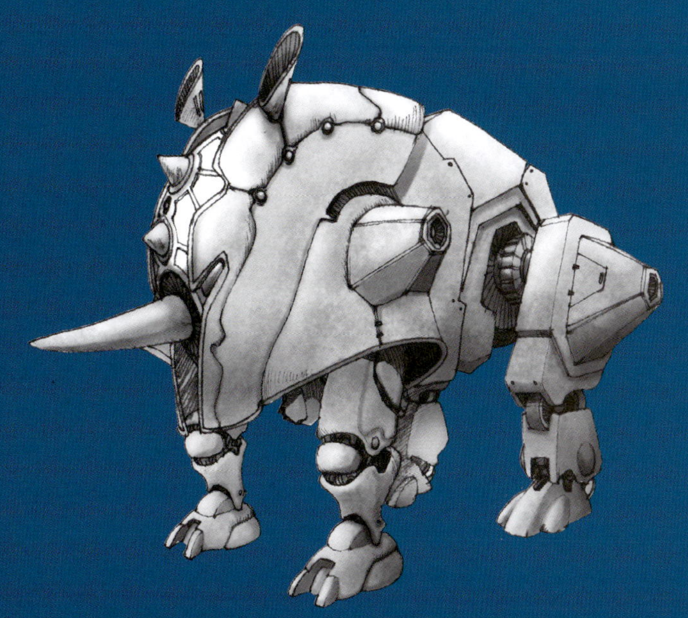

Part 4
PRACTICAL ASSESSMENTS

Now it's time to put into practice the various
methods, perspectives and expression techniques
we've learned so far. Refer to the process and
drawing steps until your design is just right, and
incorporate them into your creations.

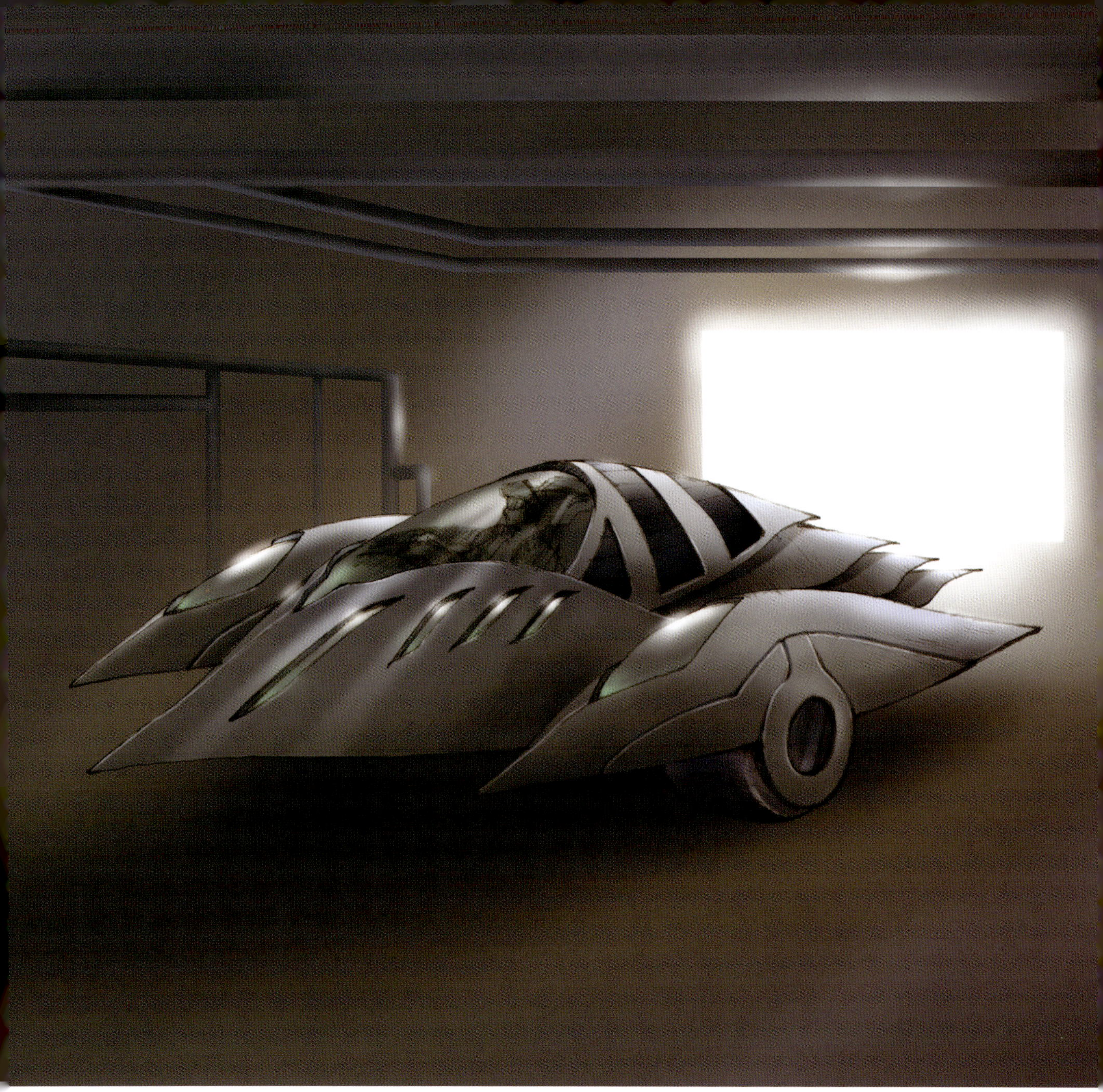

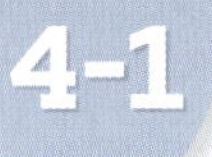

4-1　FUTURISTIC AUTOMOBILE

This is a racecar inspired by a combination of a near-futuristic car design with elements of a medieval knight's armored plating. It's solar-powered, so equipped with solar panels. The design is centered on a triangular form to convey a sense of speed.

Developing Your Ideas

To emphasize speed, round forms are minimized, with most shapes made pointed. Therefore, the design will be expressed as a combination of triangles and pyramids.

Drawing a Cool Car

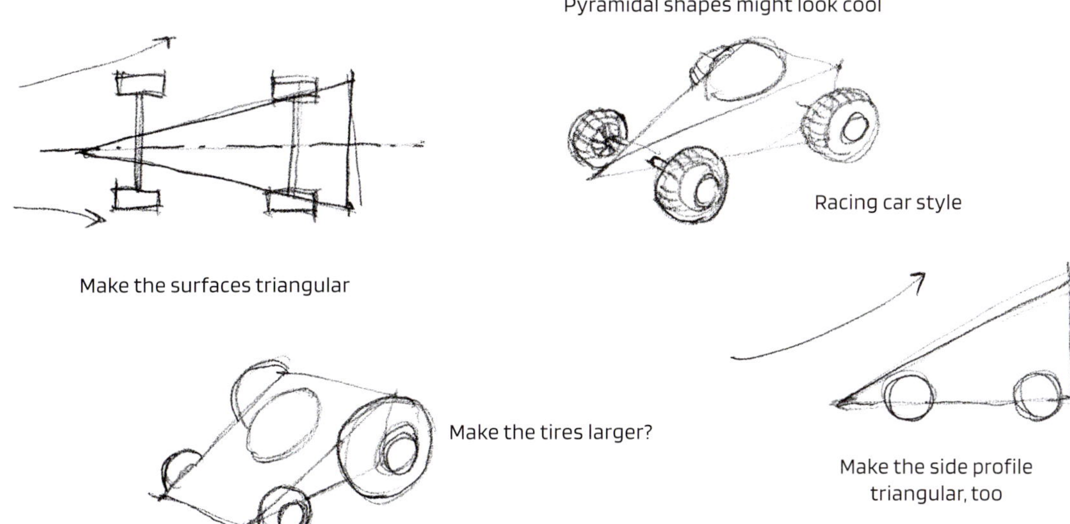

I want more speed

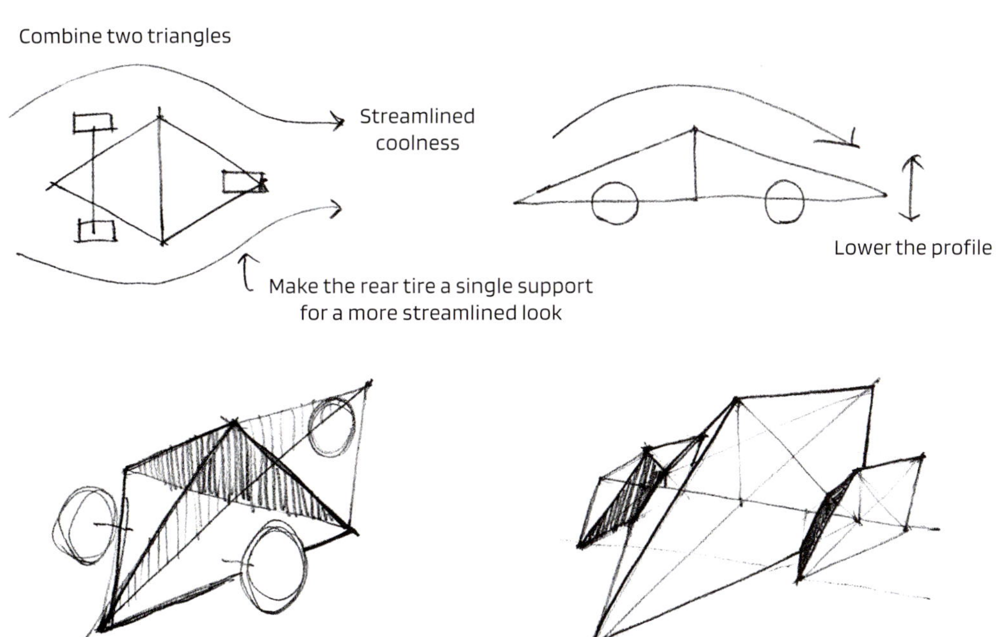

Refining Details

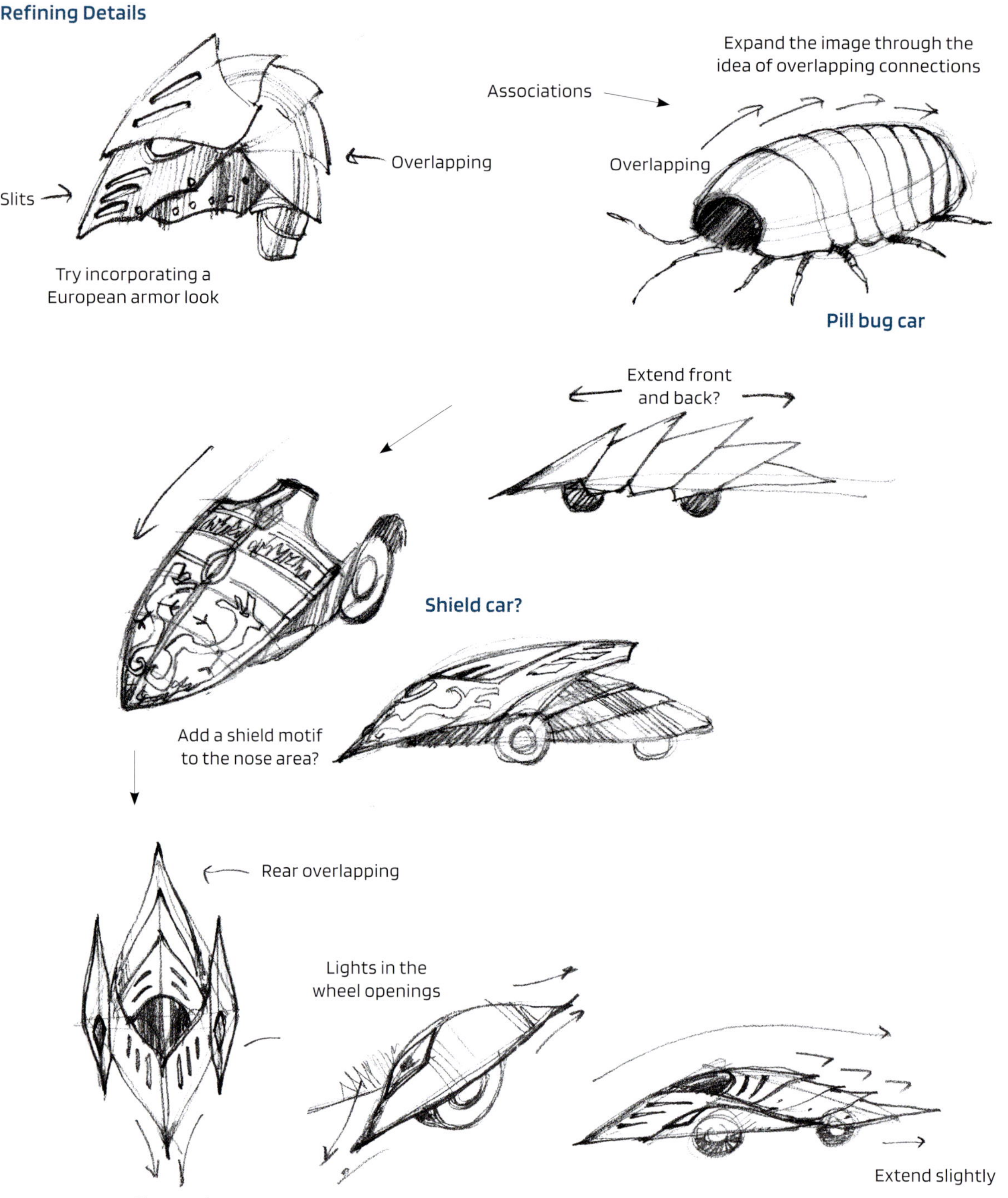

Forms and Rough Sketches

While refining the details, I thought about adding an exoskeleton. This led to a decorative style inspired by medieval Western armor. I focused on the visor slits in the head section and layered shapes at the moving parts. The goal is to achieve a form that doesn't seem too weighed down by the armor's mass.

Structures and Basic Figures

Once the rough sketch is broadly organized, we move on to creating a three-view drawing. Imagine how the motif would appear from the front, side, and top, and use a grid to verify the shape. At first, simplify the shapes. As you become more familiar with the process, you can subdivide the grid to create more complex forms.

Roughly confirm the shape and add guide lines for the three-dimensional perspective grid.

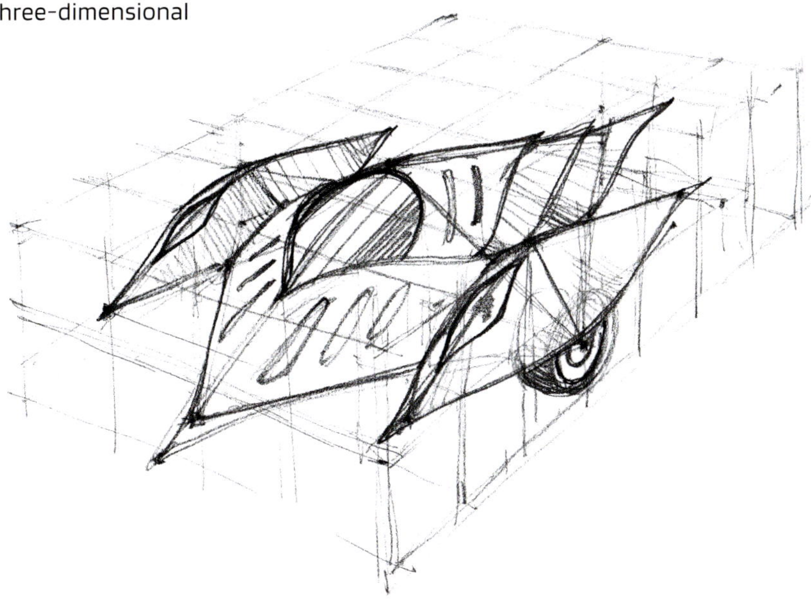

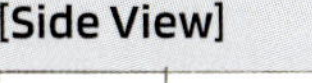

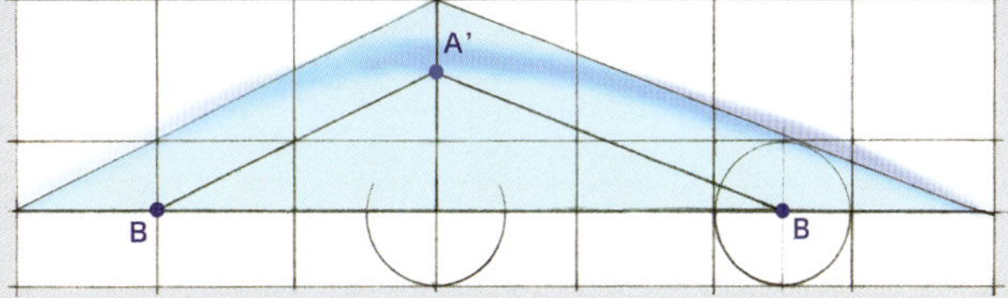

The shape of the wheel cover in the top view is also triangular. In the front view, determine point A. For easier construction, position it in the center of the square grid. The point A' in the side view is the projection of A. Draw a line parallel to the body from A' to determine B. In the top view, B' is also set to ½ of a grid square.

The entire form fits within a grid that's 4 units wide, 7 units deep and 2 units high.

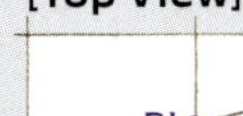

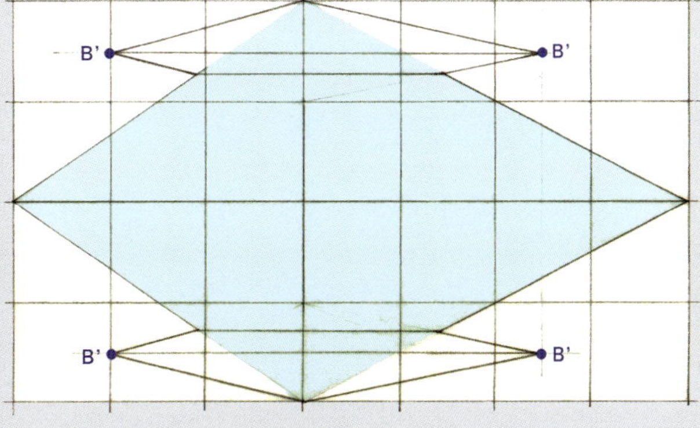

Drawing Steps

Preparing the Grid
Create the grid
based on page 132.

Blue lines: grid from page 132
Black lines: grid to be used this time

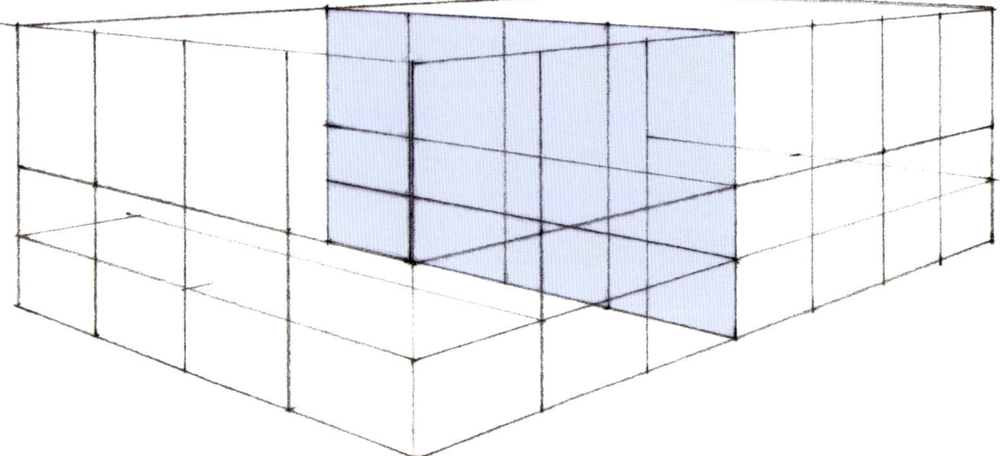

1　Creating the Perspective Grid
Create a three-dimensional perspective grid with
width 4, depth 7 and height 2. Pre-divide the surfaces
for both wheel cover tops (blue areas) into halves.

2　Plotting the Basic Shapes
Mark the main body vertices (the red points).
The blue points will be the vertices for the wheels.

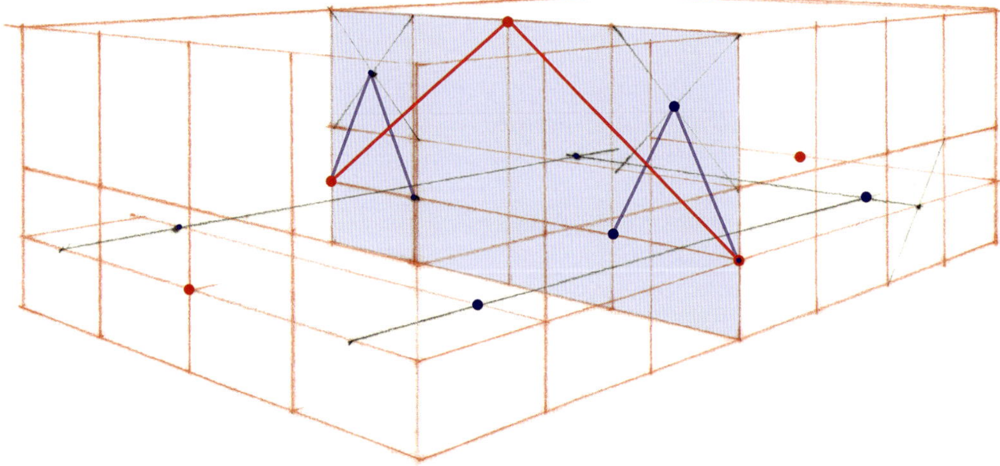

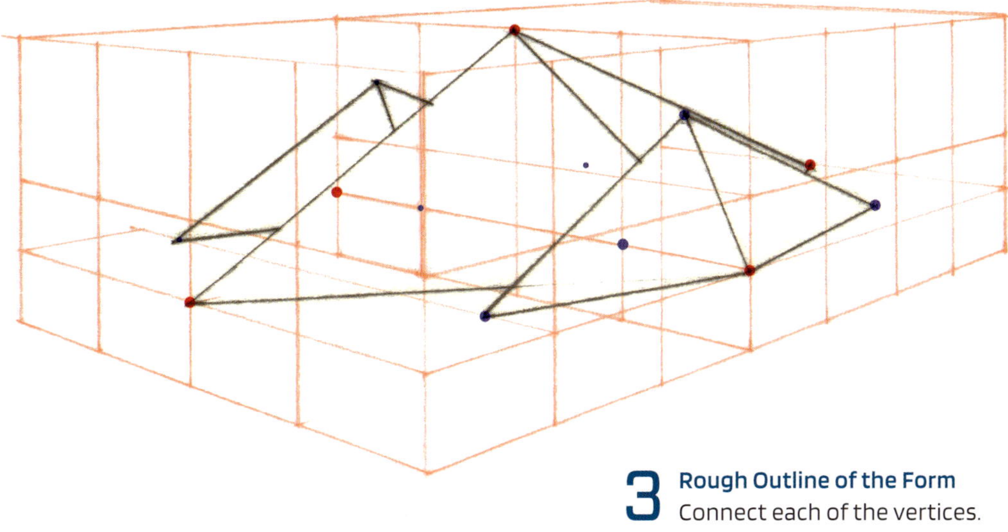

3 **Rough Outline of the Form**
Connect each of the vertices.

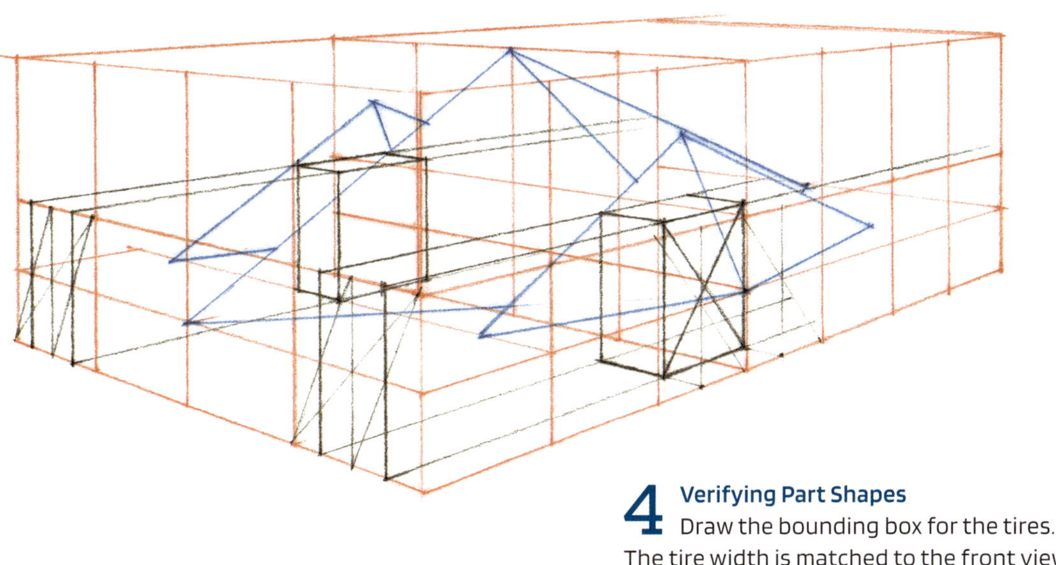

4 **Verifying Part Shapes**
Draw the bounding box for the tires.
The tire width is matched to the front view.

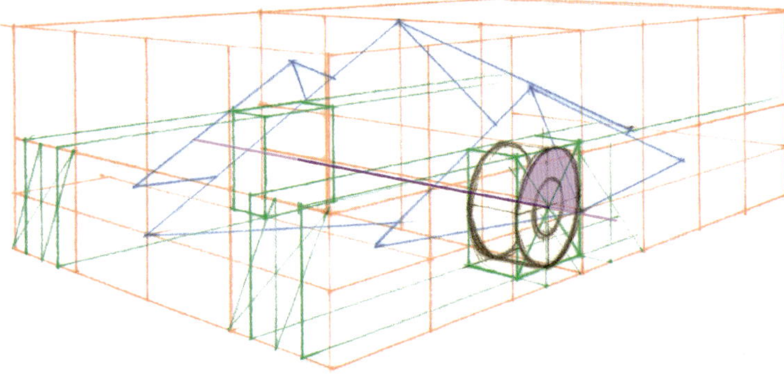

5 Drawing Ellipses
While considering the axis for both wheels, draw the angled tires.

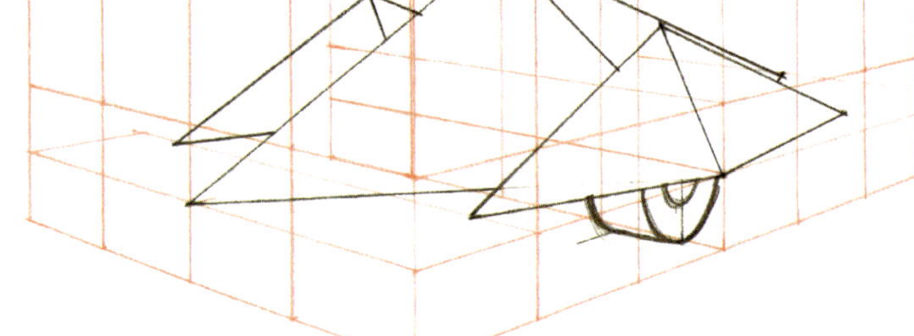

6 Refining the Basic Form
Organize the lines drawn so far.

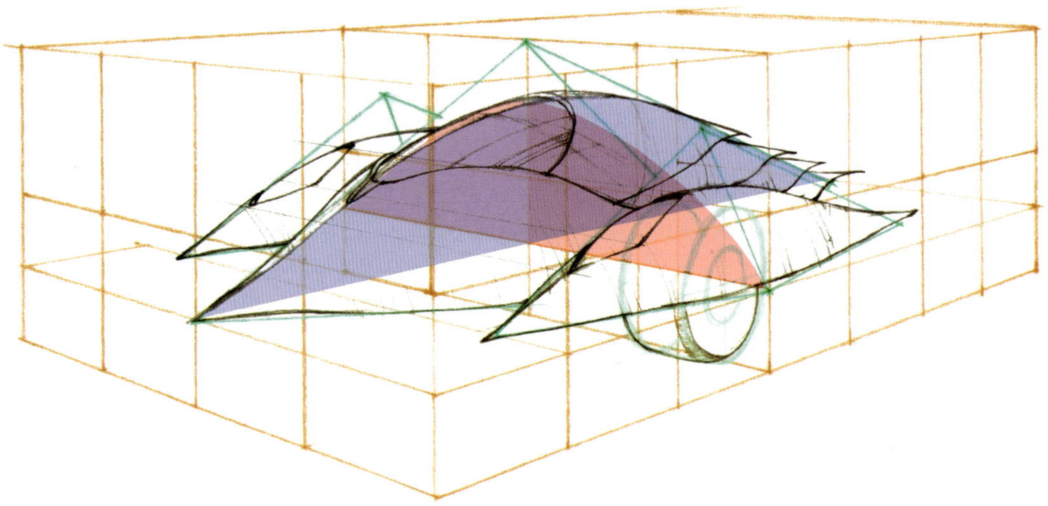

7 Solidifying the Overall Form
Referencing the front and side views, draw the body curves with an awareness of the wrapping shapes. The light red fill represents the front view, and the light blue fill represents the side view.

8 Finishing the Line Art

Begin the detailing. Since the plane inclinations vary continuously, draw with an awareness of the grid and the cross-sections.

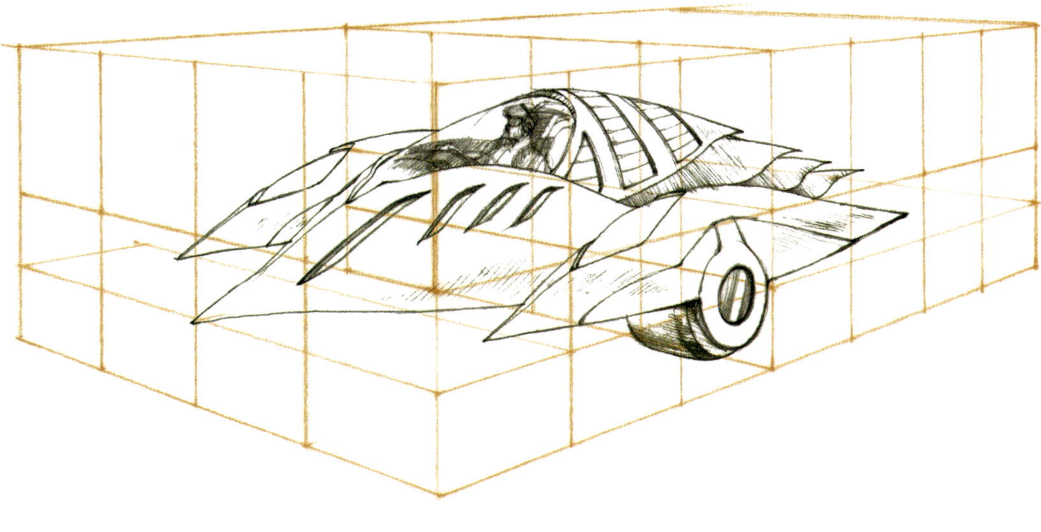

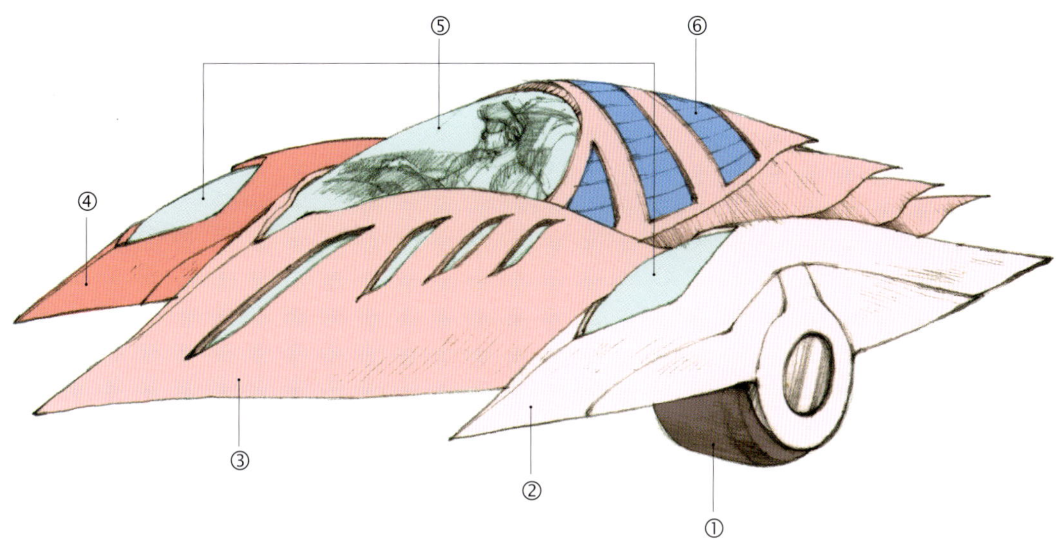

9 Layer Separation Before Coloring

Separate each part into layers from ① to ⑥. In this case:

① Tire section
② Foreground wheel cover
③ Body
④ Background wheel cover
⑤ Glass
⑥ Solar panel

The layers are distinguished by clearly identifiable colors.

※ The line art is scanned, and coloring is done using Photoshop.

10 Adding Tone

Add basic light and shadow with gray.
The light source is assumed to be behind the body.

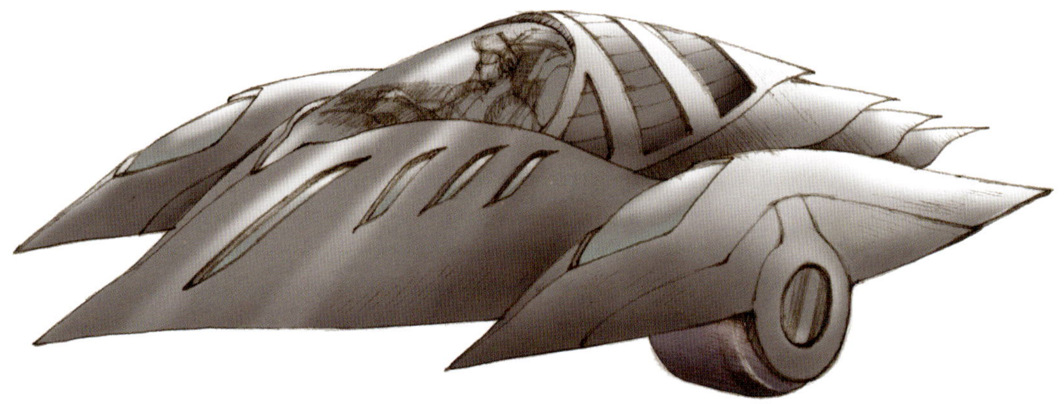

Layer works

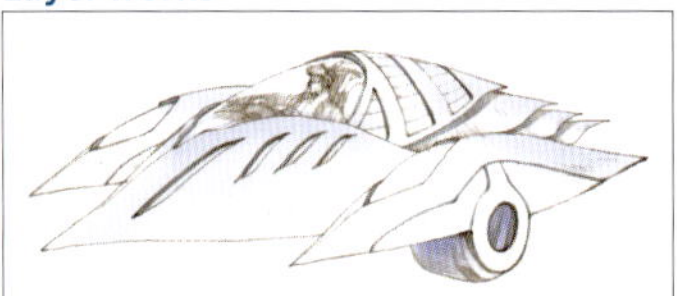

Body + Tire Shade (Multiply)

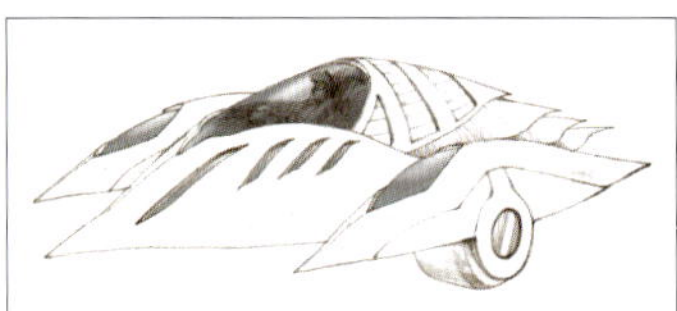

Glass section (Normal)

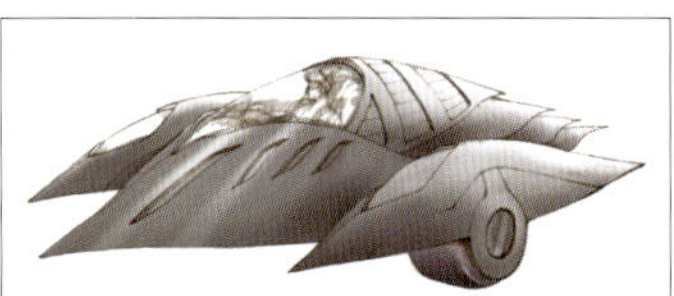

Body + Tire (Normal)

11 Coloring for Texture and Shadows

Color each layer. For a metallic texture on the body, use the gray tone layers as they are. Add detailed shadows with multiply layers for areas like the overlapping rear of the body and the tire sections.

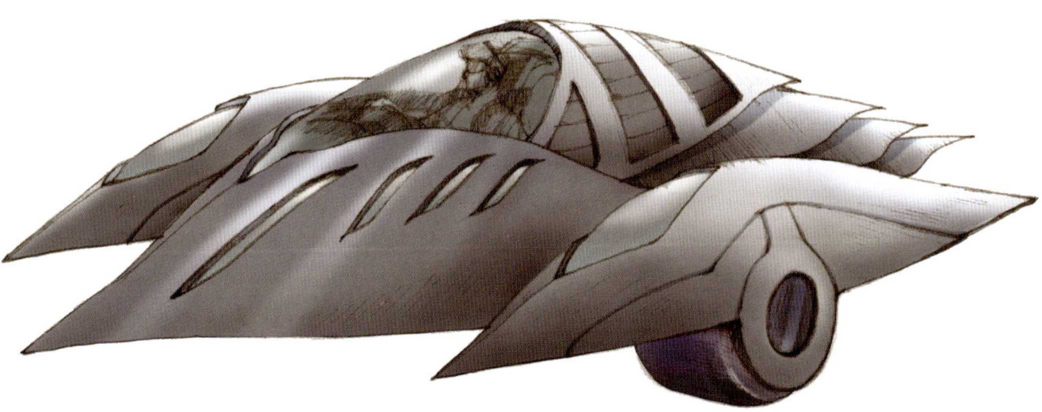

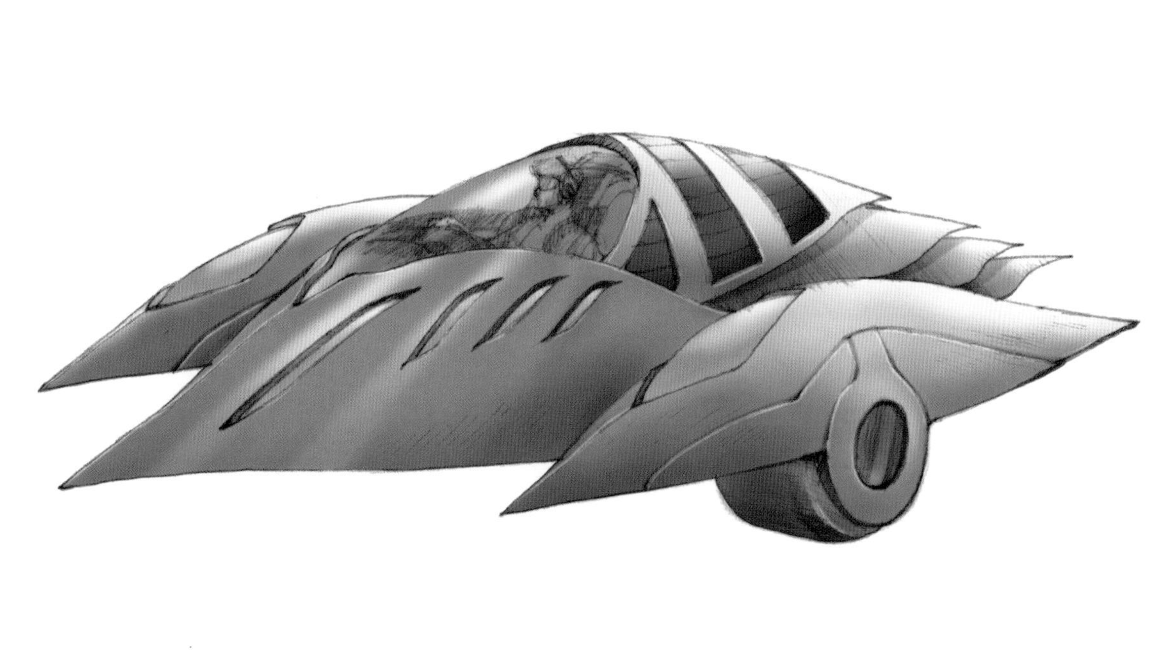

12 Finish

I added highlights by overlaying the layers and also adjusted the light and shadow on the solar panels.

Layer works

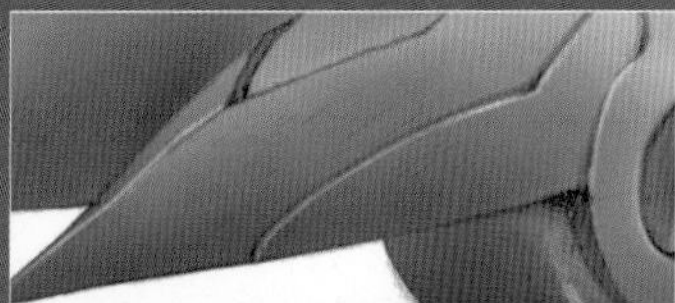

Highlights (Overlay)

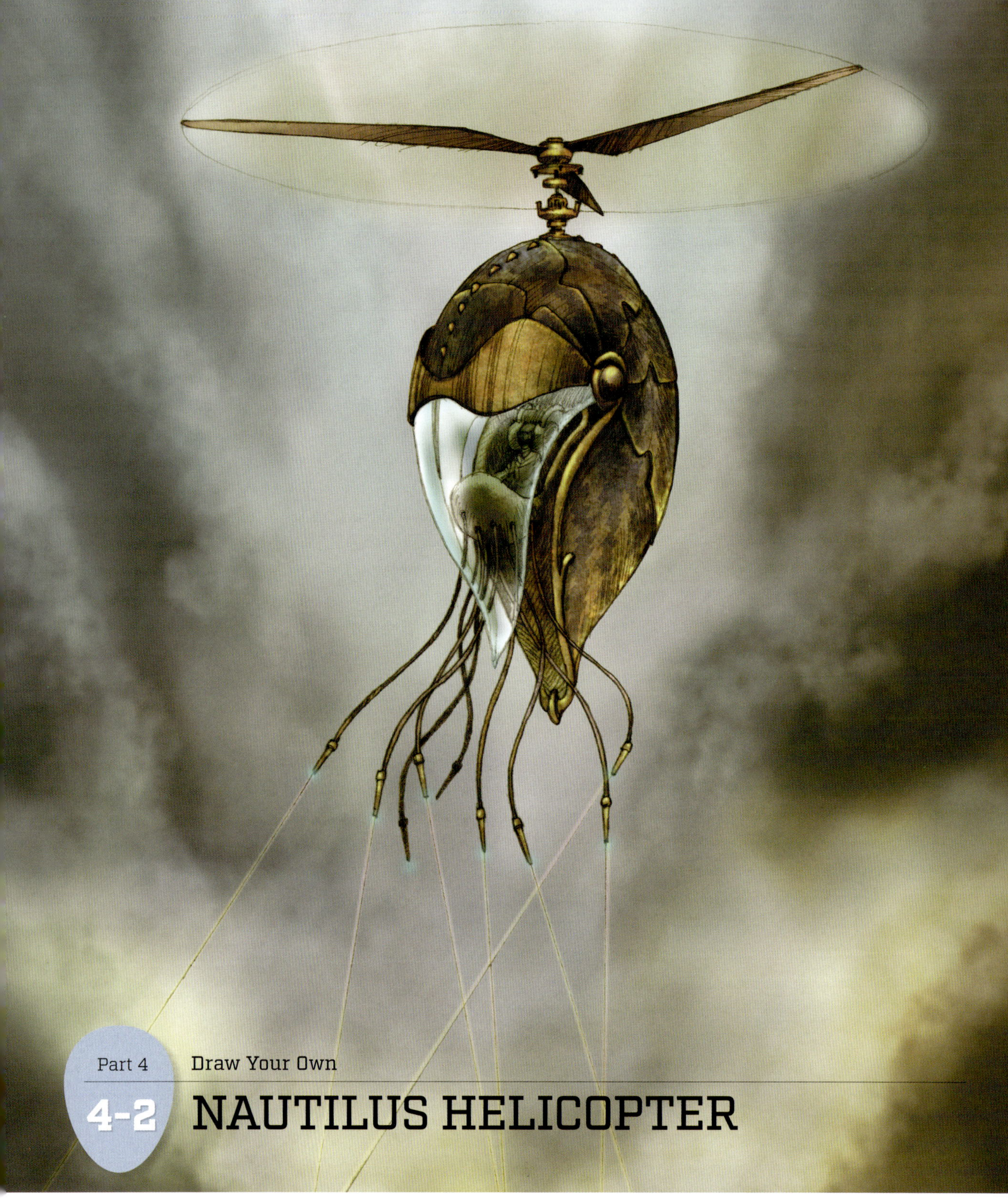

4-2 NAUTILUS HELICOPTER

This is a helicopter inspired by the nautilus. Although slow-moving typically in reality, it belongs to the cephalopod group, just like octopuses and squids, which can move freely and fluidly underwater. This association helped expand the design concept.

Developing Your Ideas

Think about the shape and style of the helicopter body. Here, animal forms are the inspiration.
Under the propeller, I considered adding the shapes of various animals to expand the concept.

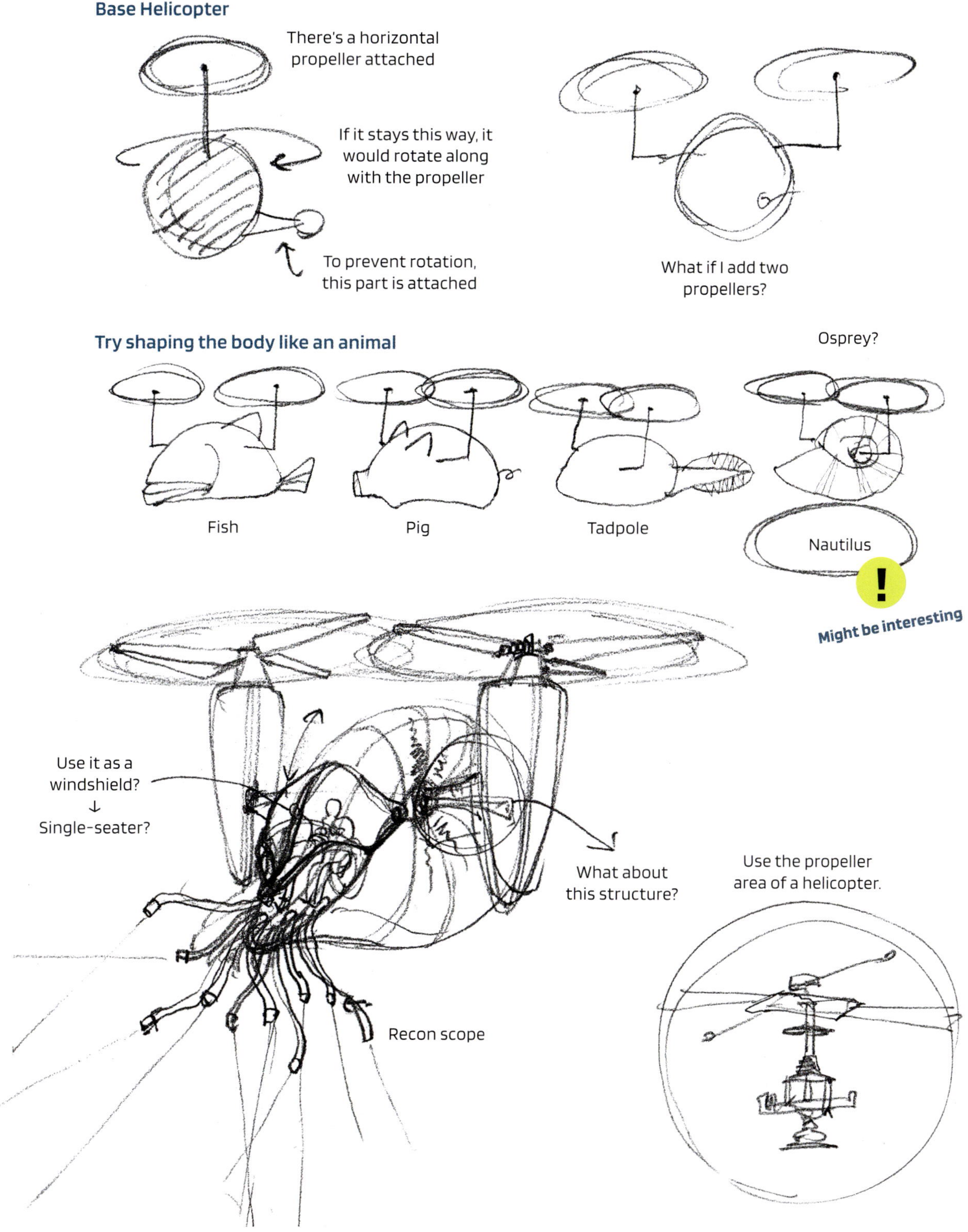

Nautilus

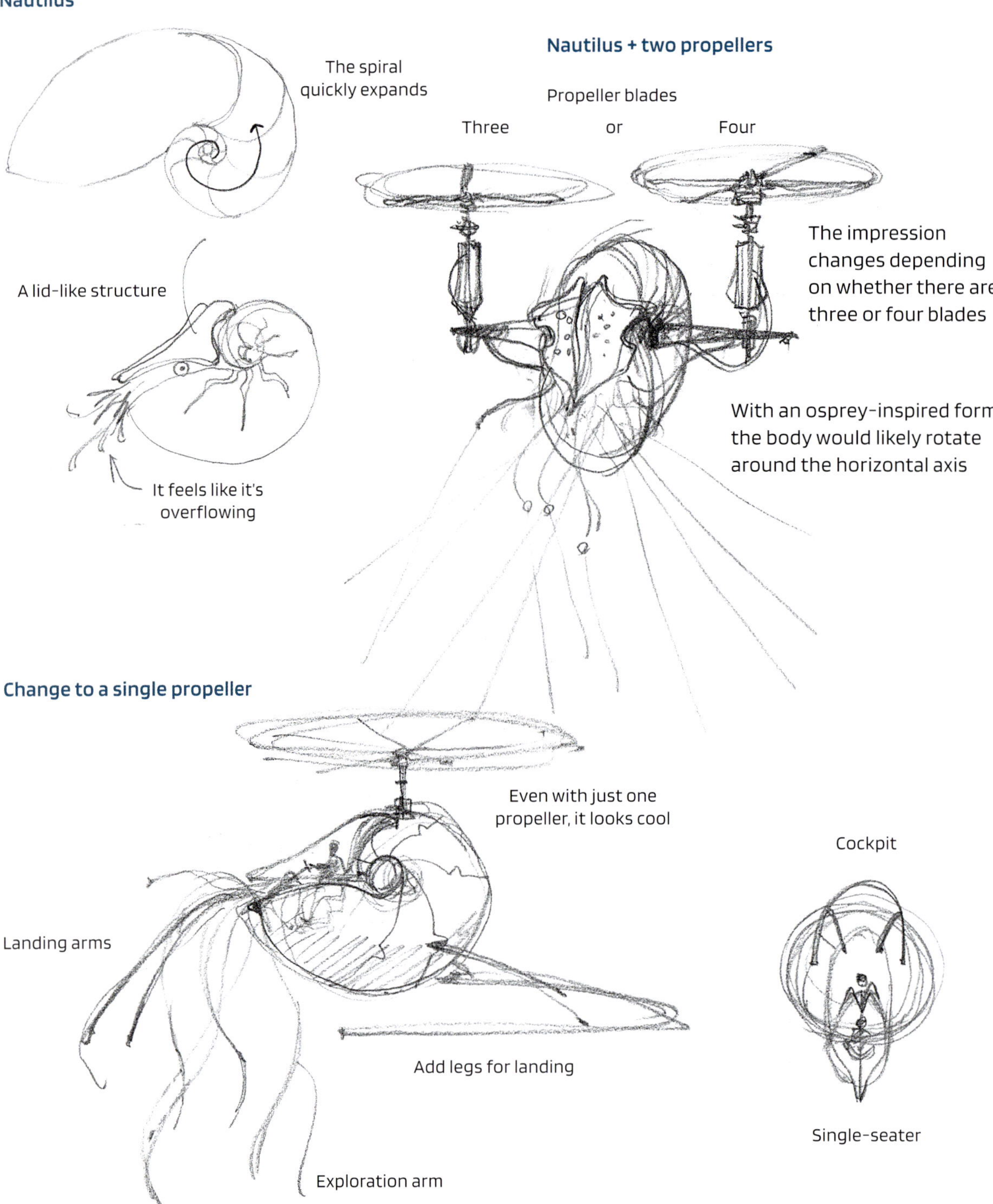

Forms and Rough Sketches

I decided to base the form on the nautilus and use rough sketches to study features that would allow it to function as a helicopter. I considered both flight and landing modes.

Structures and Basic Figures

Once the general design is captured in the rough sketch, create a front view and side view. Set up a grid in line with the nautilus form's proportions of height, width and depth.

Refine the structure

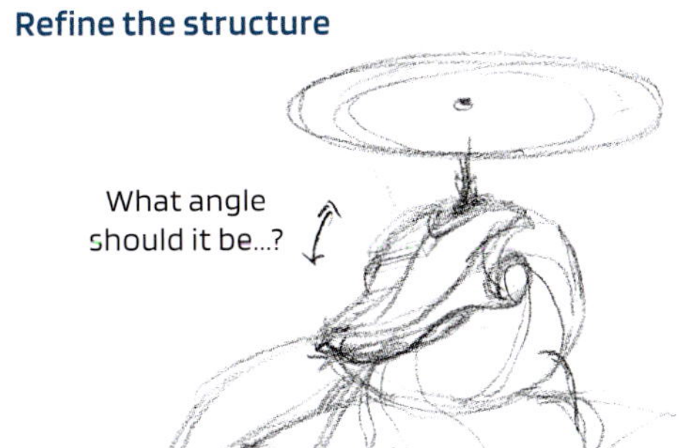

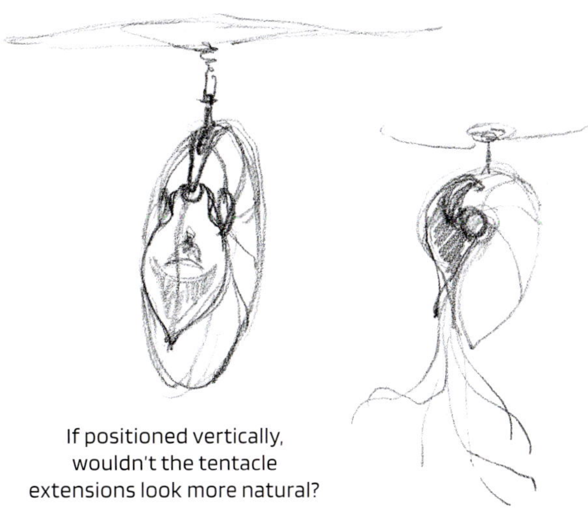

Landing leg structure

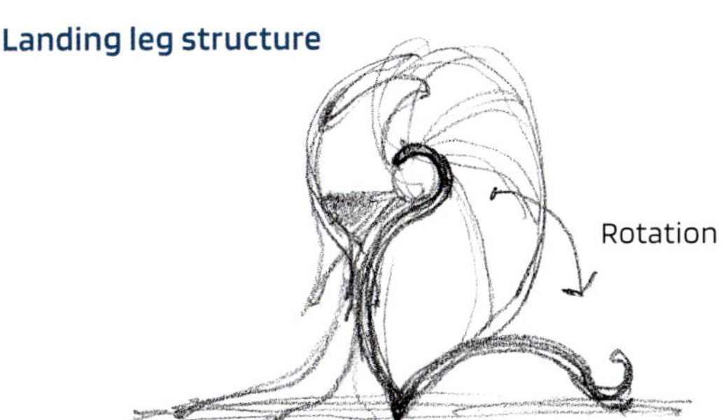

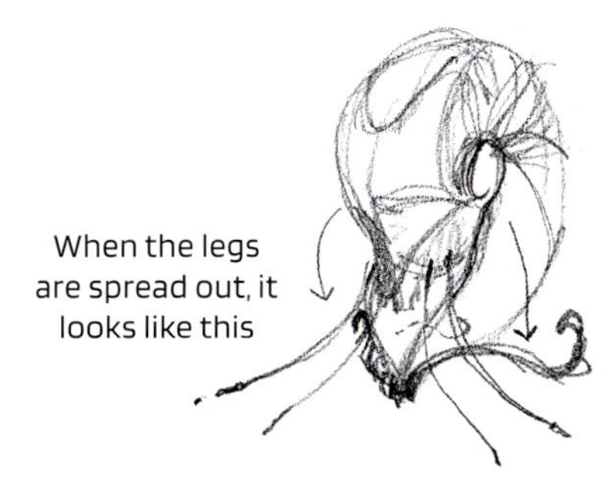

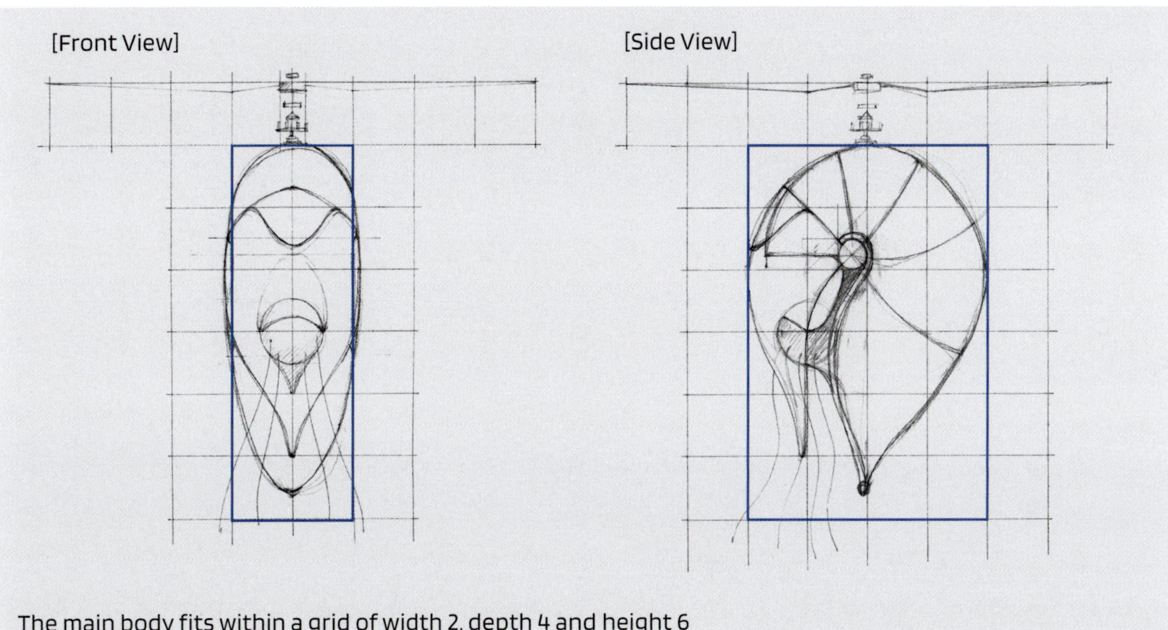

The main body fits within a grid of width 2, depth 4 and height 6

Drawing Steps

1 Creating the Grid

Draw the same square from the front view and side view onto the base perspective grid. The propeller area is at the very top horizontal plane, with the front and side view grids one level below.

The main body is within a grid of width 2, depth 4 and height 6, set one grid below the propeller grid.

Orange lines: grid from page 132

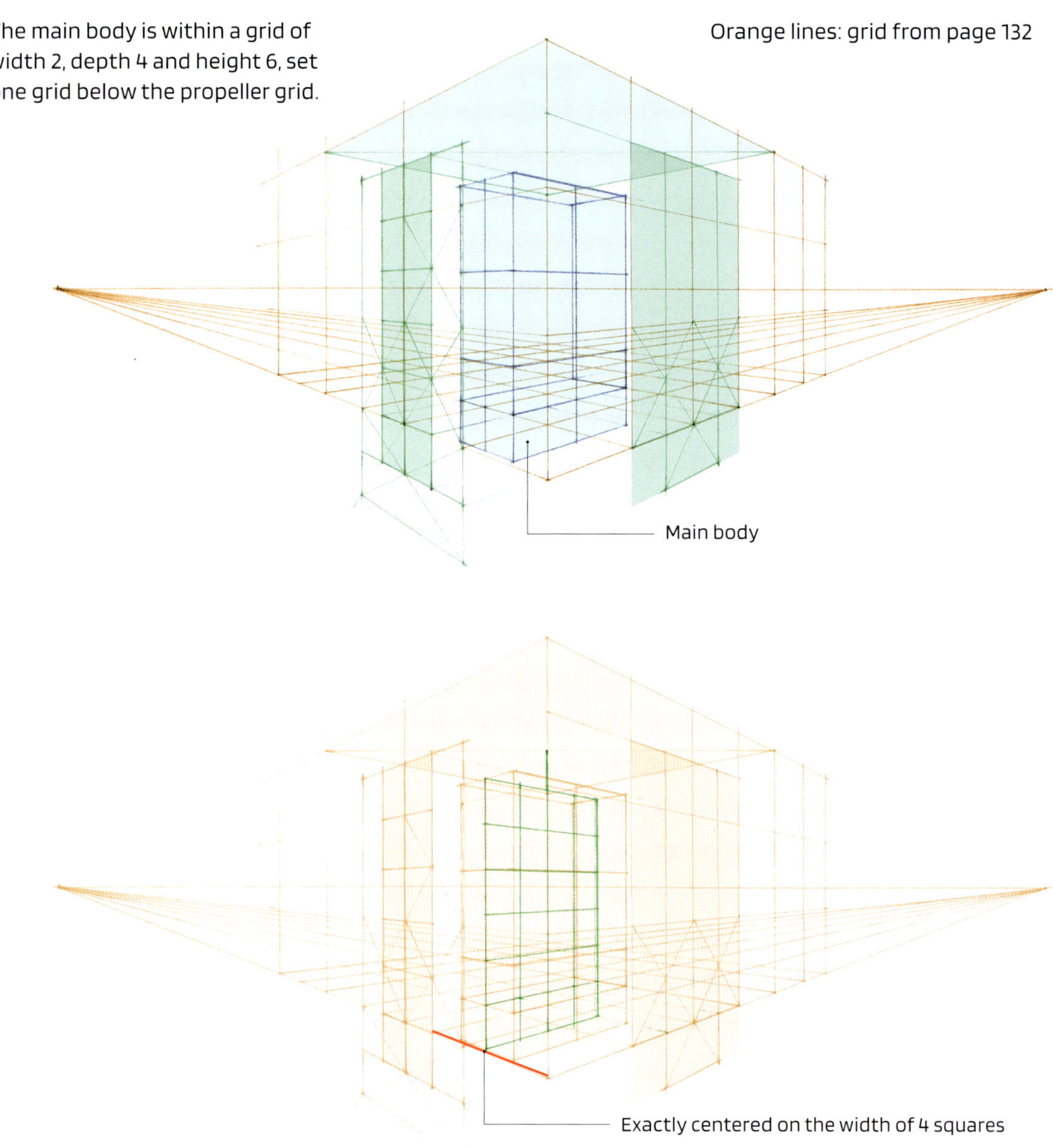

2 Creating the Side View Grid

Create a grid (6×4) for the side view in the center of the base perspective grid.

3 Drawing the Form to Fit the Grid
In the center grid, draw the side view. Focus on intersections to create the nautilus's characteristic curves.

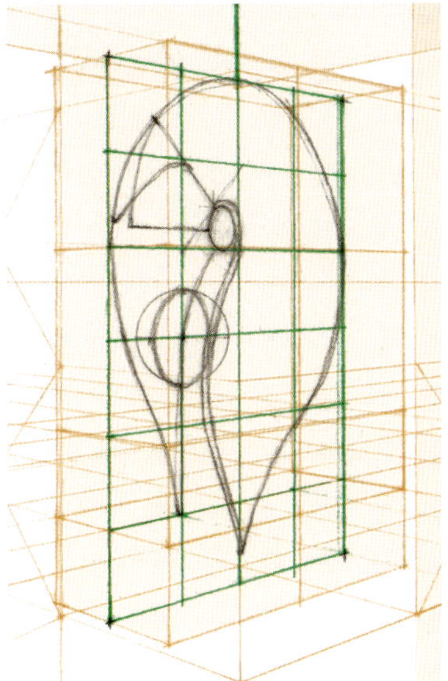

4 Drawing the Central Circles of the Form
Draw the central circles of the nautilus form on the front and back surfaces. Each circle fits within a square that's one-fourth the size of the base grid.

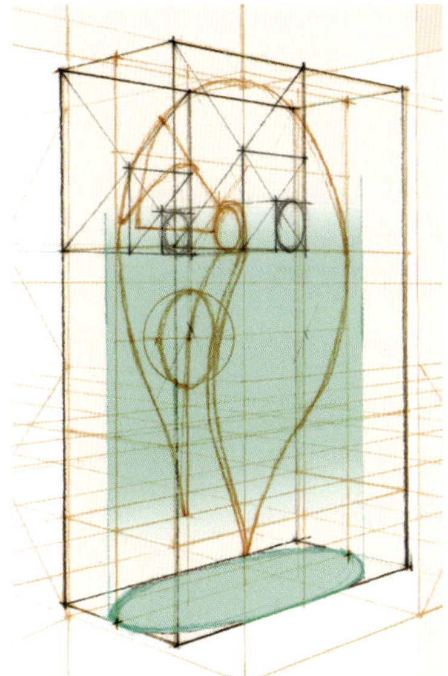

The propeller fits within an 8-by-8 square on the top. Though the square may be slightly distorted, ensure the ellipse remains perfectly symmetrical vertically and horizontally.

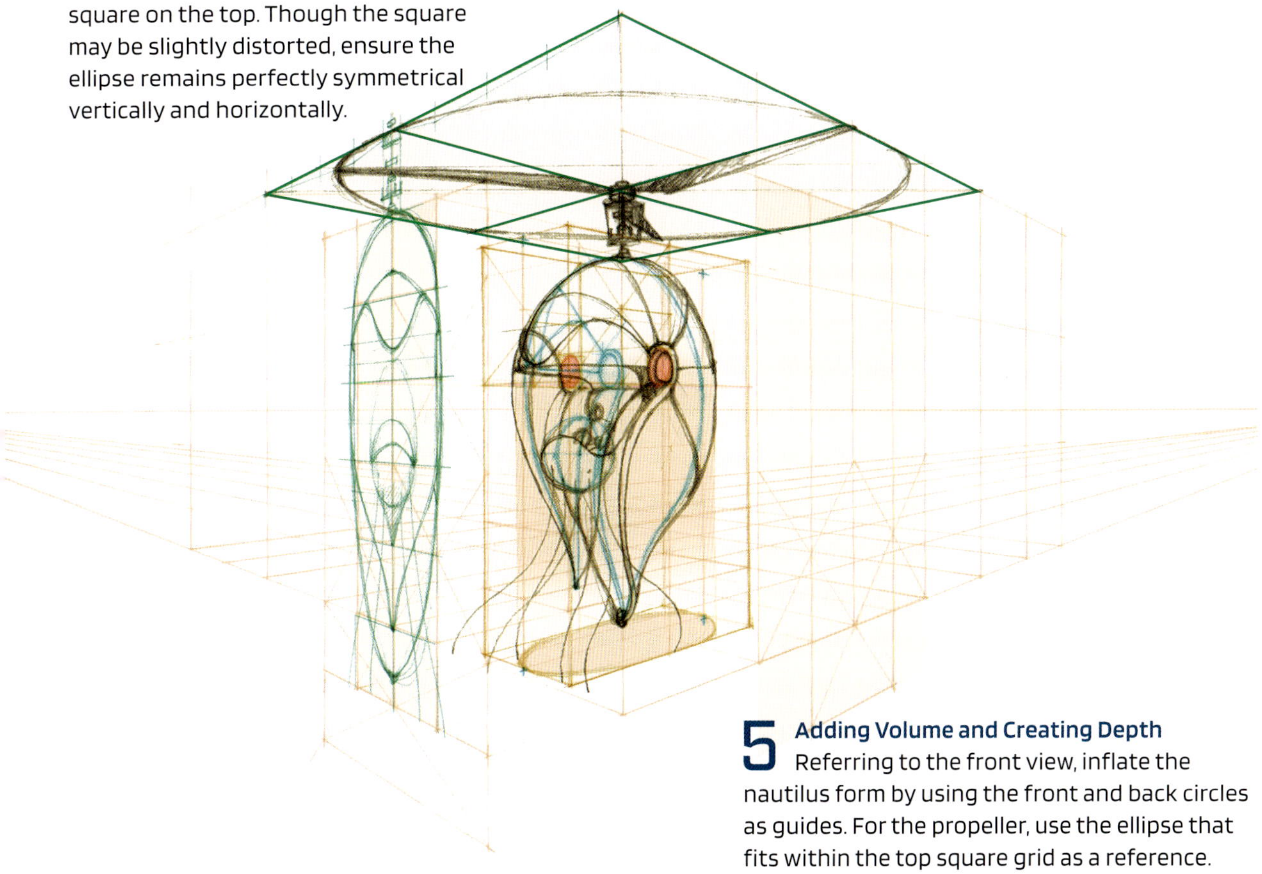

5 Adding Volume and Creating Depth
Referring to the front view, inflate the nautilus form by using the front and back circles as guides. For the propeller, use the ellipse that fits within the top square grid as a reference.

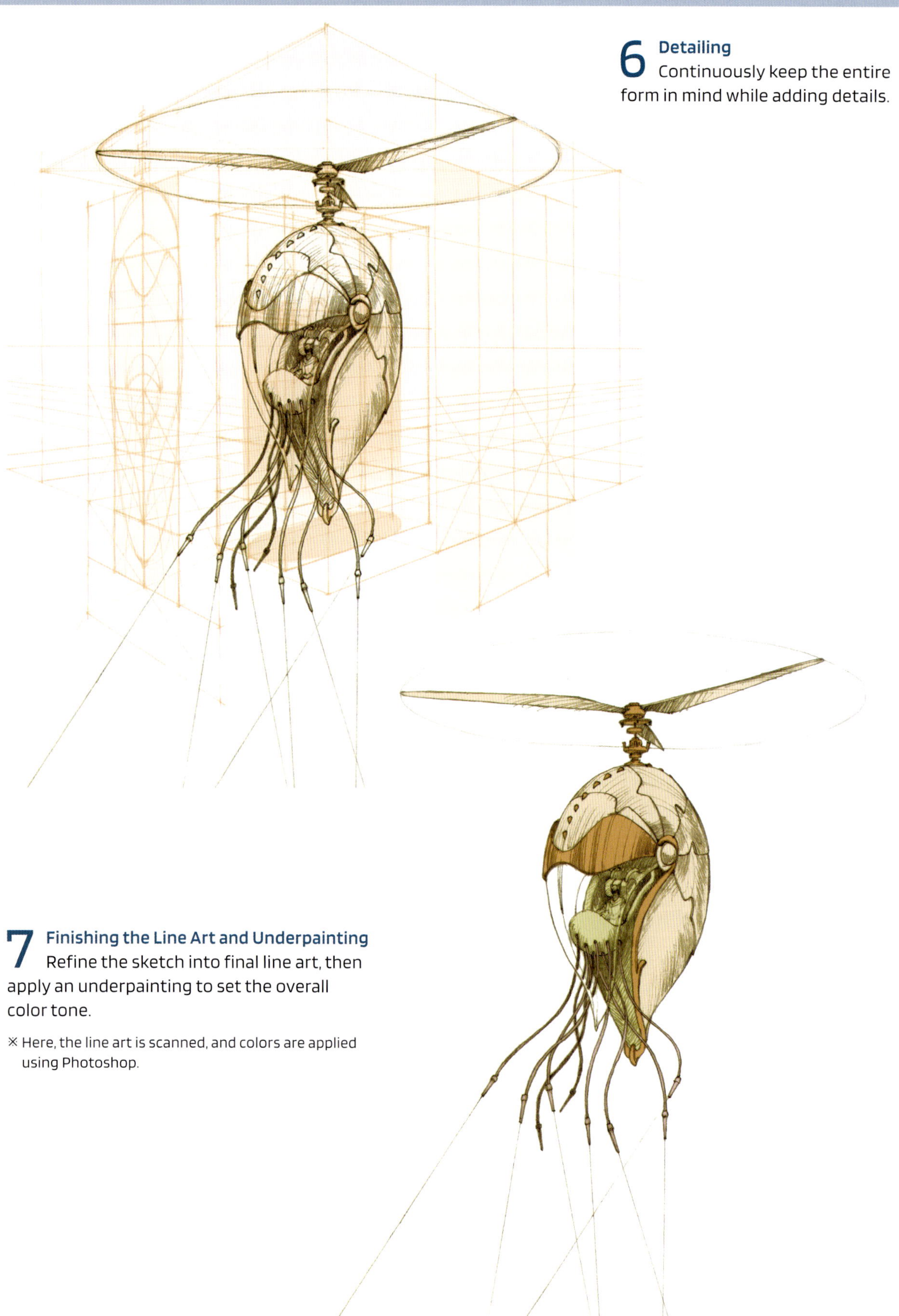

6 Detailing
Continuously keep the entire form in mind while adding details.

7 Finishing the Line Art and Underpainting
Refine the sketch into final line art, then apply an underpainting to set the overall color tone.

※ Here, the line art is scanned, and colors are applied using Photoshop.

8 Applying Tones – Main Body

Color each layer. Render a retro copper and brass texture, imagining the form's curves. For shading and atmosphere, use nautilus photos as reference. Since the windshield is on a separate layer, it won't be colored at this stage.

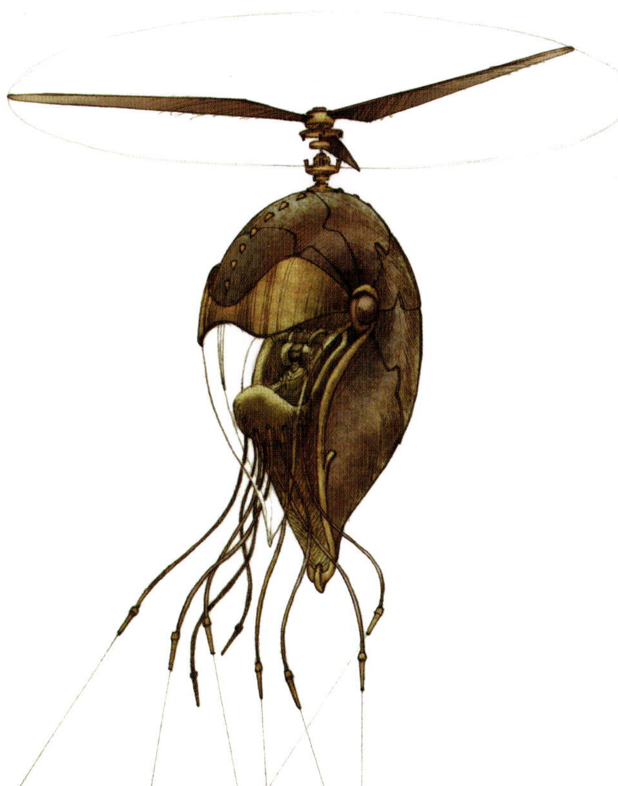

Layer works

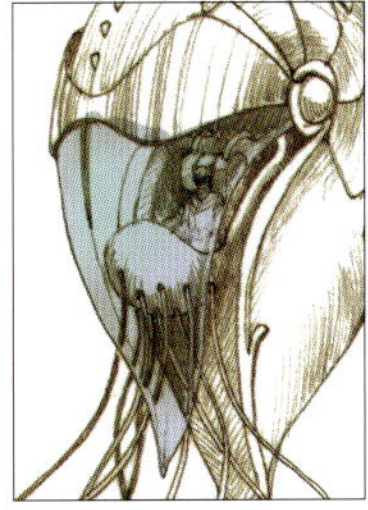

Front windshield
(multiply layer)

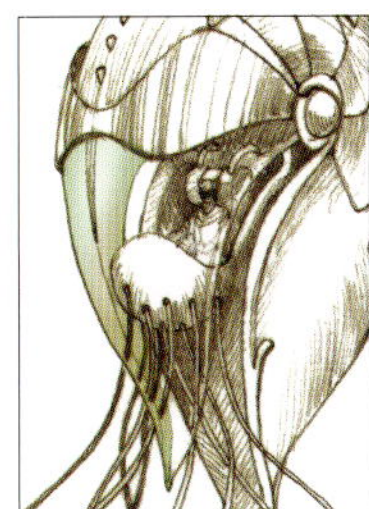

Far windshield
(multiply layer)

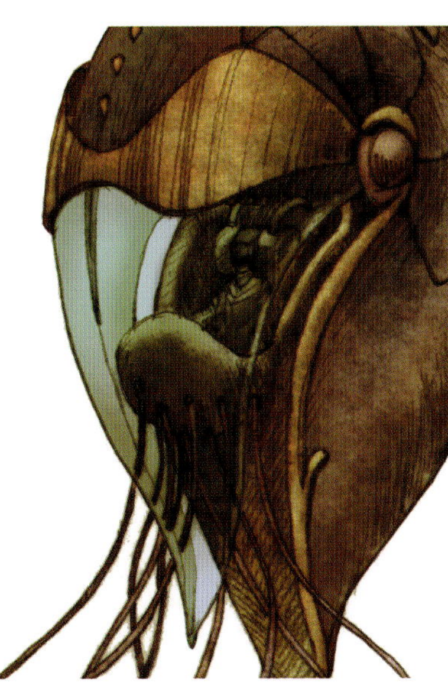

Layer works

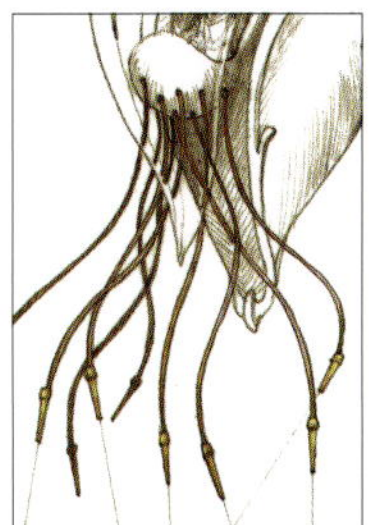

Legs (normal layer)

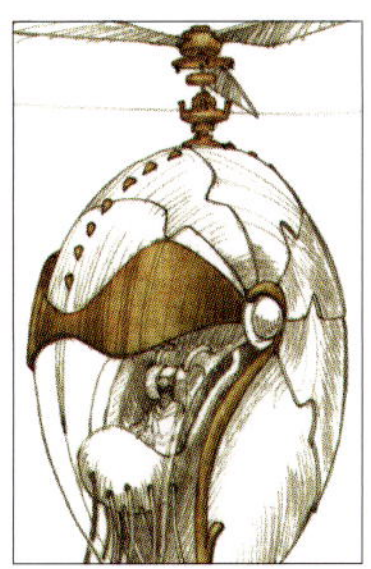

Details (normal layer)

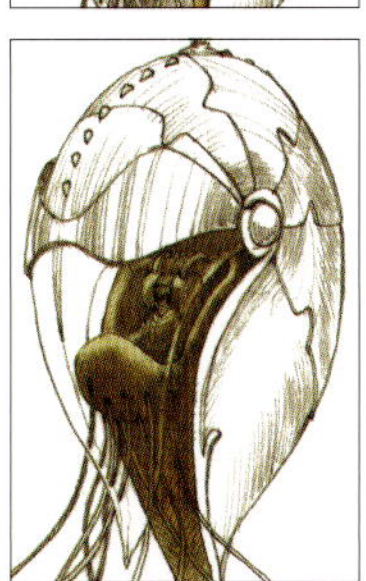

Cockpit (normal layer)

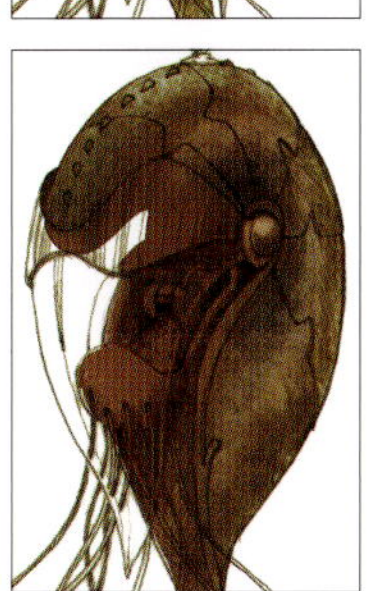

Body (normal layer)

9 Applying Tones – Windshield

Color the windshield using a multiply layer. Since it wraps around, overlap two multiply layers.

10   Adjusting the Tone of Glass and Other Parts
Use a screen layer to paint the windshield highlights.

Layer works

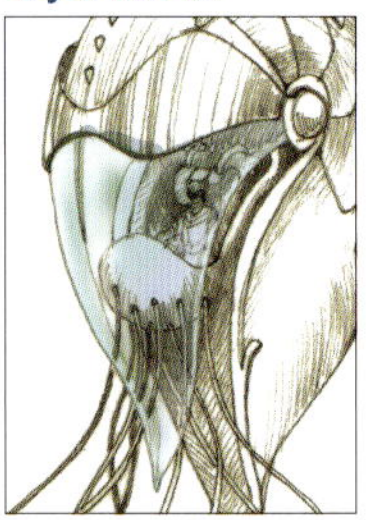

Highlight
(screen layer)

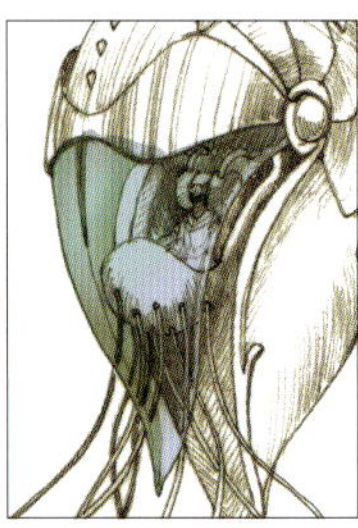

Front and far windshields
(two overlapping layers from step 9)

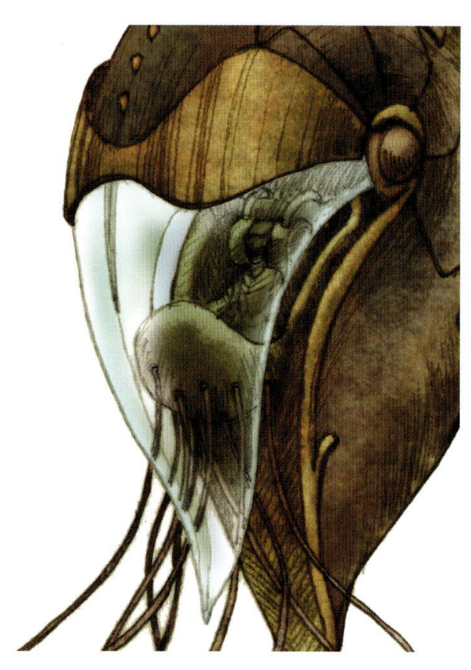

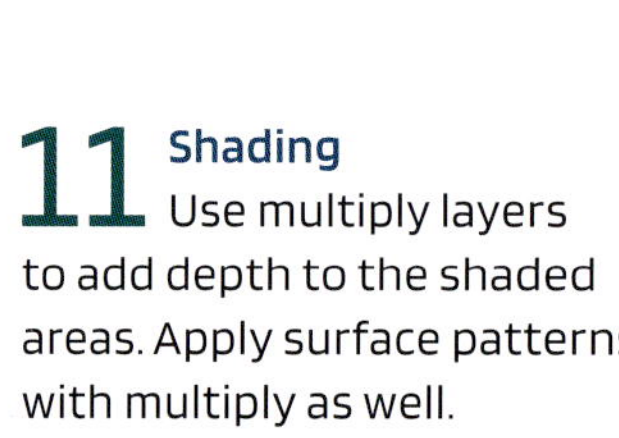

Layer works

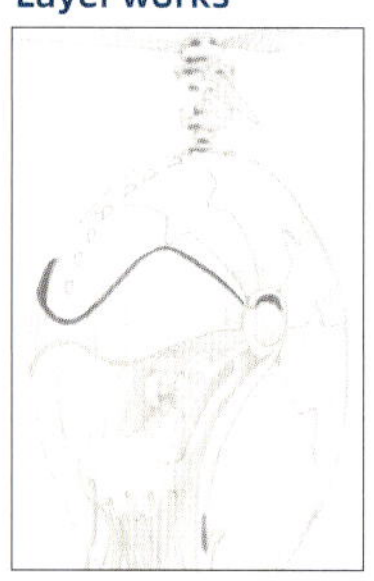

Shade for Accessories
(Multiply)

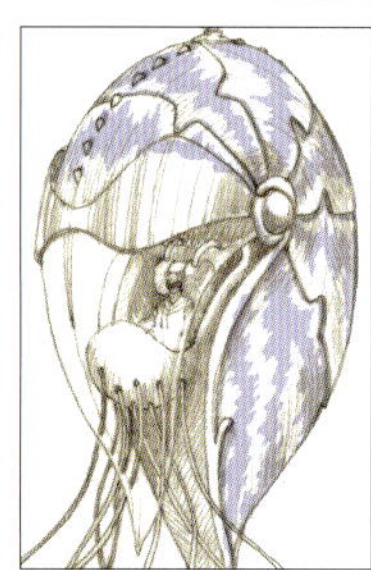

Shade and Pattern
(Multiply)

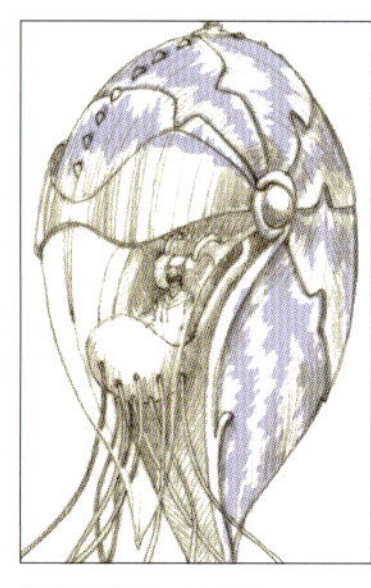

Shade
(Multiply)

11   Shading
Use multiply layers
to add depth to the shaded
areas. Apply surface patterns
with multiply as well.

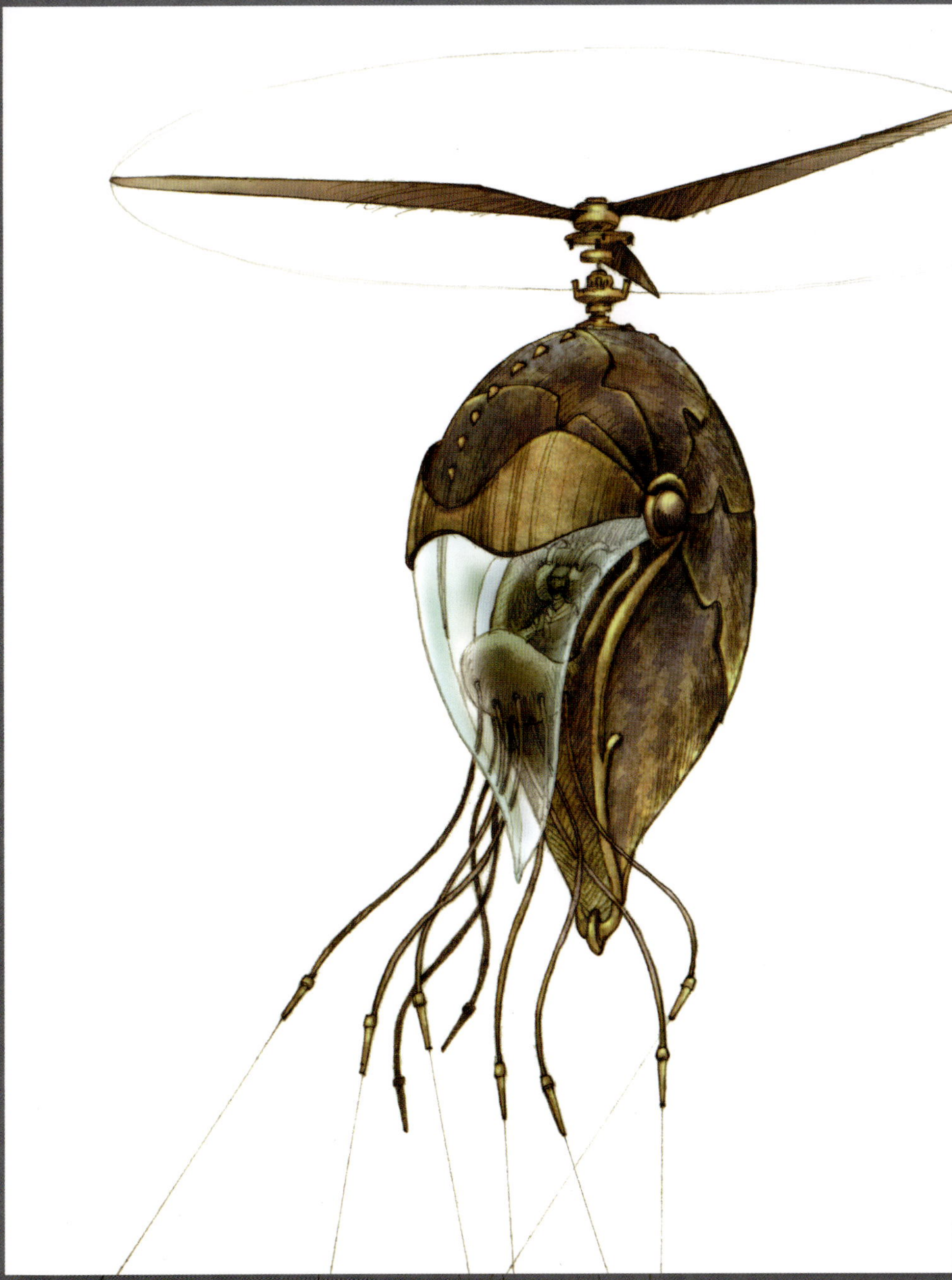

12 Adjustment of Highlight Areas
I'll draw in the highlight areas using an overlay.

Layer works

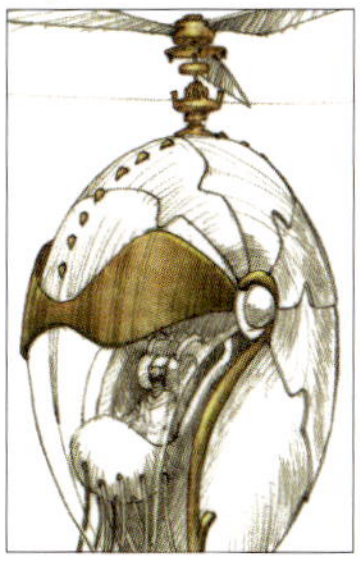

Accessory Highlights
(Overlay)

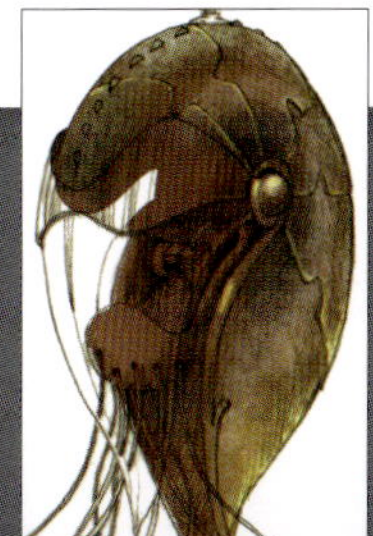

Highlights
(Overlay)

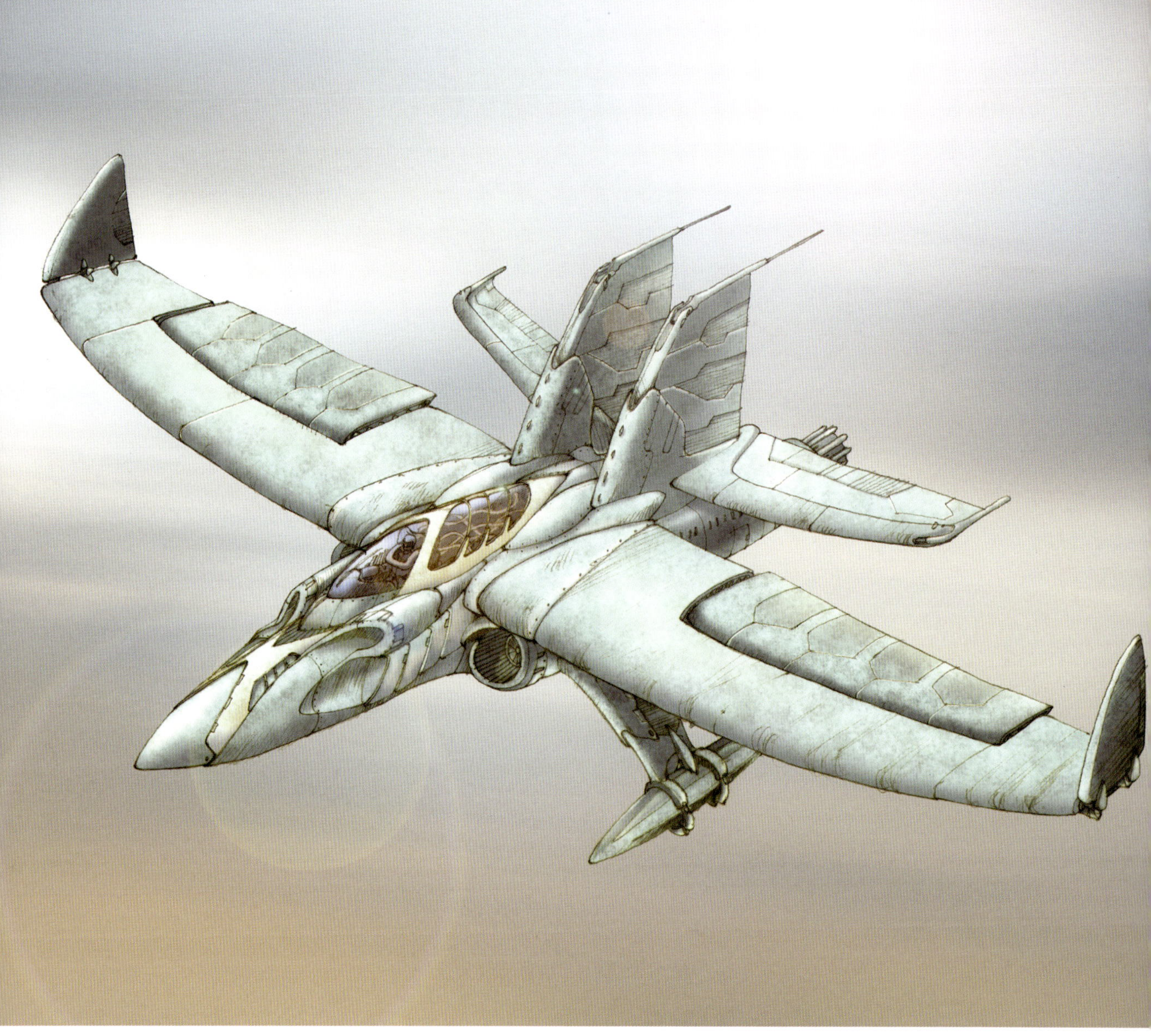

4-3 FLYING MANTIS

This is a high-speed fighter jet. Based on actual fighter jets, I superimposed and applied the silhouette and details of a mantis to create an original design.

Developing Your Ideas

I will use the MiG fighter jet developed in the former Soviet Union as the base form. Then, inspired by the thought that the shape of this fighter jet viewed from above resembles a mantis, I decided to add the silhouette and details of a mantis.

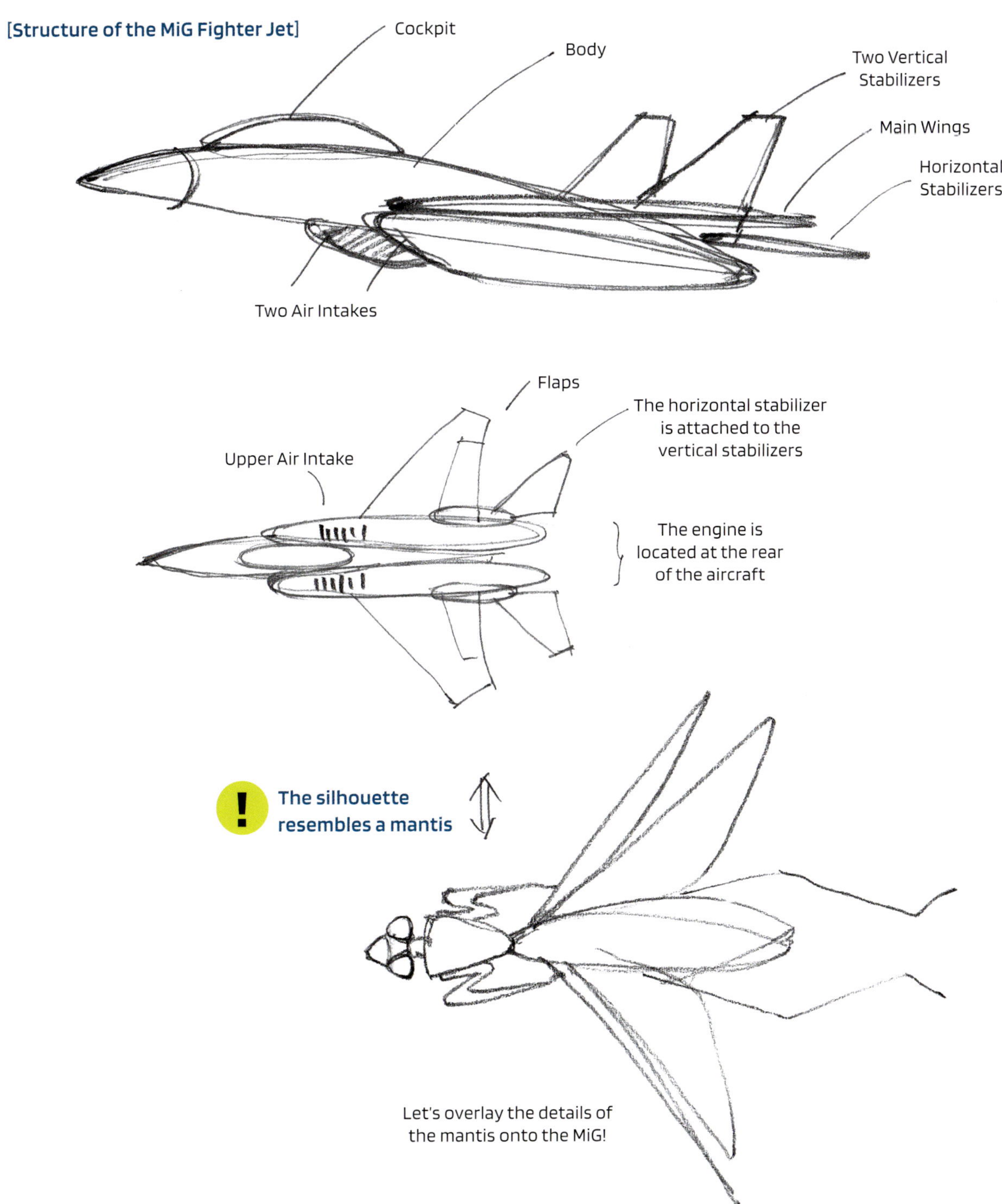

While sketching each part, consider where mechanical elements can be used.

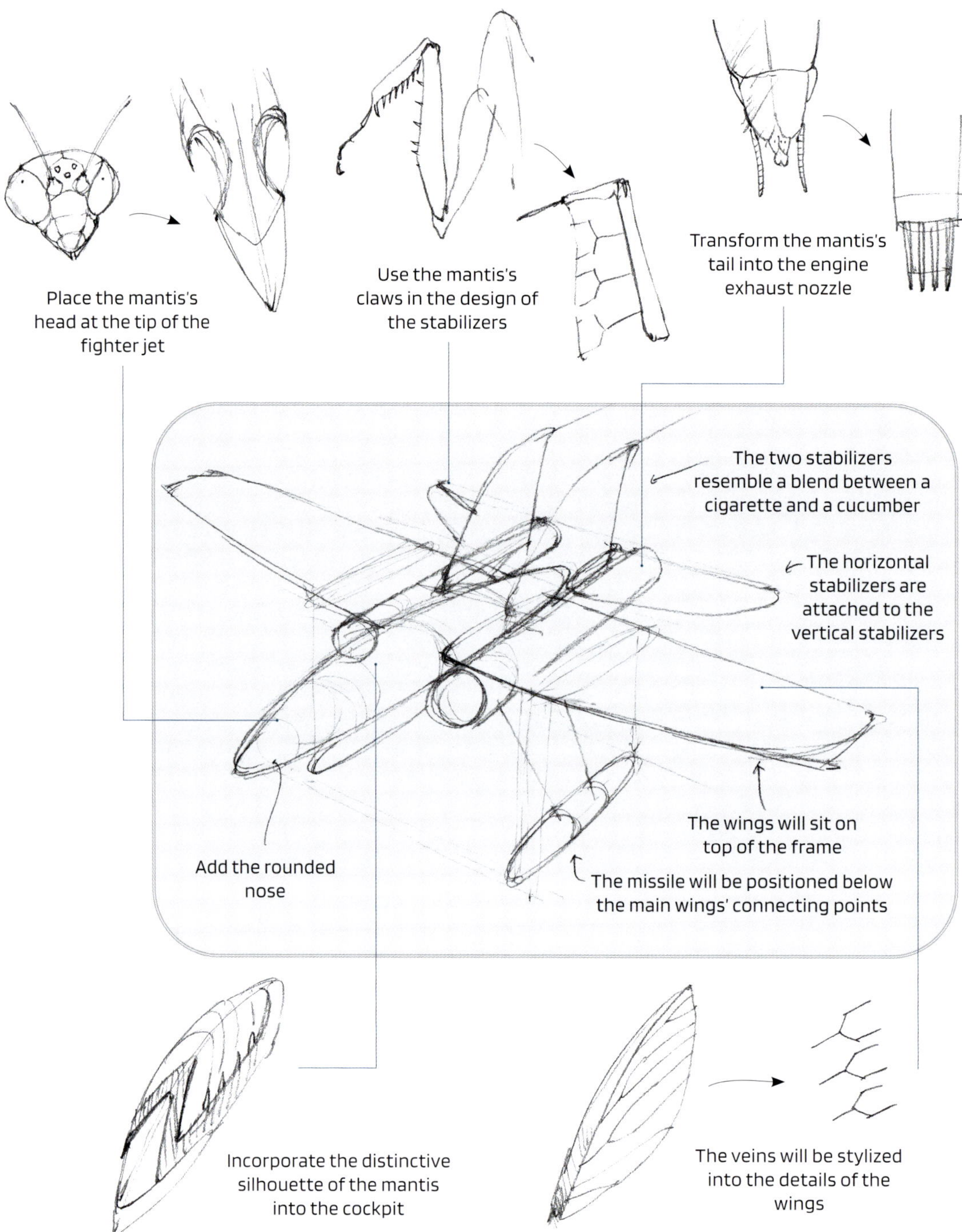

Forms and Rough Sketches

While rough sketching the silhouette and details of the mantis, I'll develop new ideas. Next, I'll use as simple, basic shapes as possible to consider the continuity and balance of the form.

Structures and Basic Figures

Develop the rough sketch and consolidate the image. Based on this sketch, create a rough front and side view. The body portion, excluding the wings, fits into a grid of approximately 7 aligned cubes.

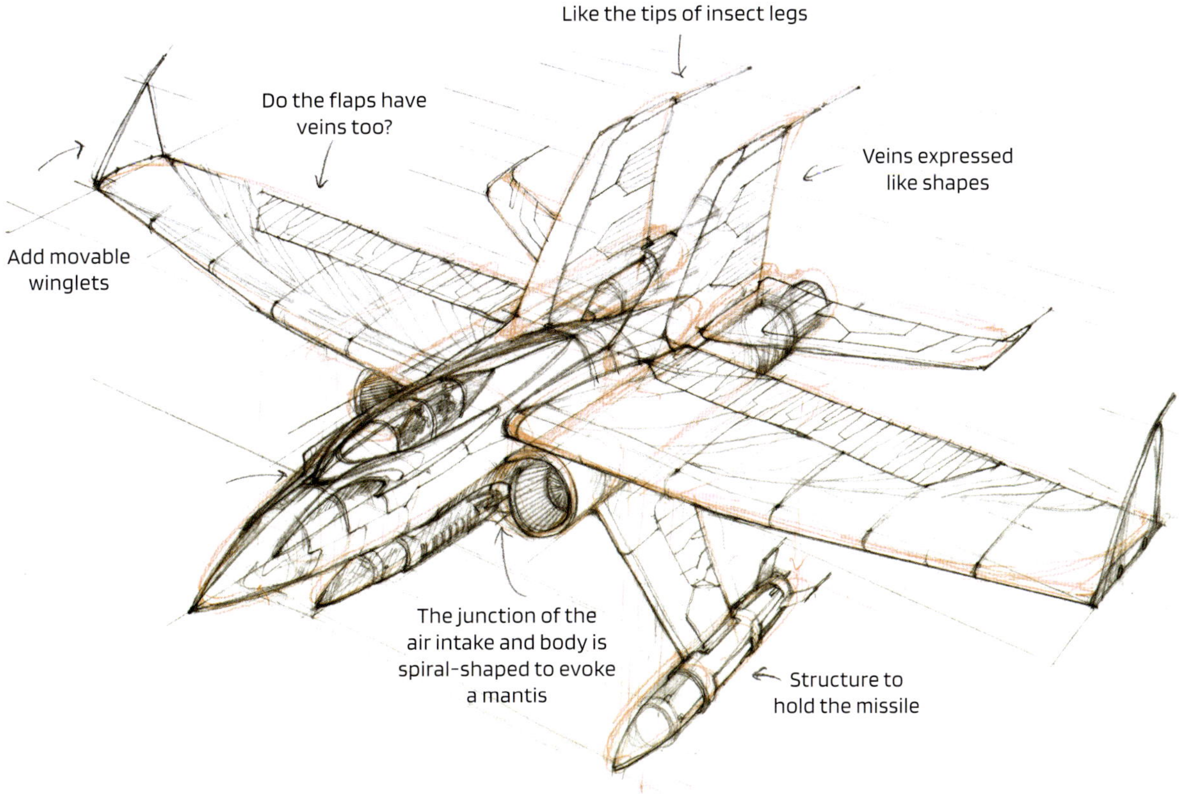

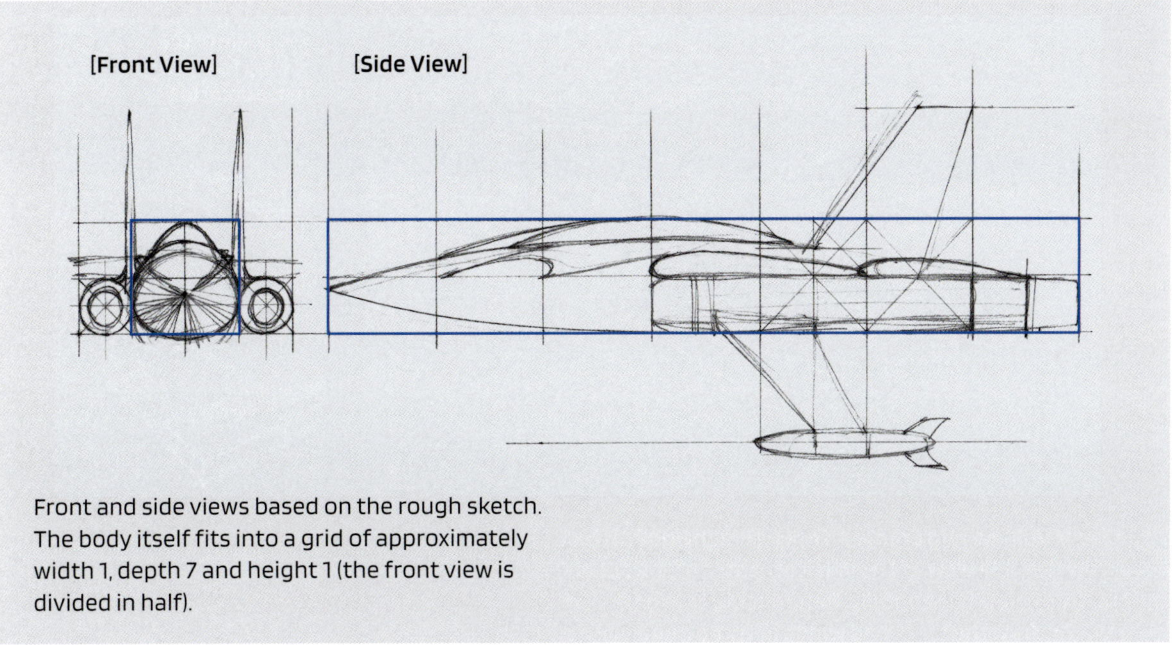

Front and side views based on the rough sketch. The body itself fits into a grid of approximately width 1, depth 7 and height 1 (the front view is divided in half).

Drawing Steps

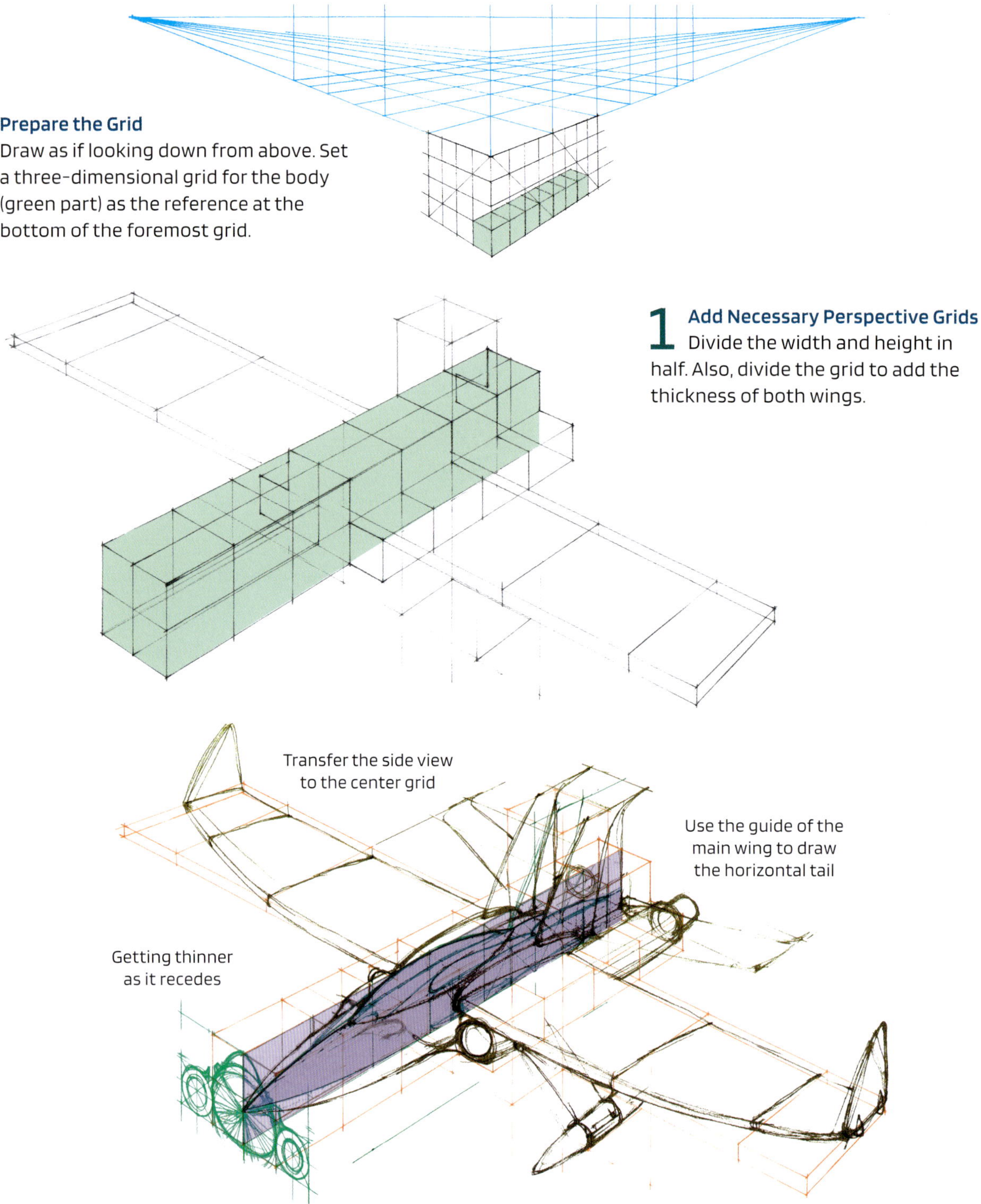

Prepare the Grid
Draw as if looking down from above. Set a three-dimensional grid for the body (green part) as the reference at the bottom of the foremost grid.

1 Add Necessary Perspective Grids
Divide the width and height in half. Also, divide the grid to add the thickness of both wings.

2 Give It Volume and Create a Three-Dimensional Effect
Draw the side view at the vertical center of the cube grid and the front view horizontally. Referencing these side and front views, draw the body and wings in three dimensions.

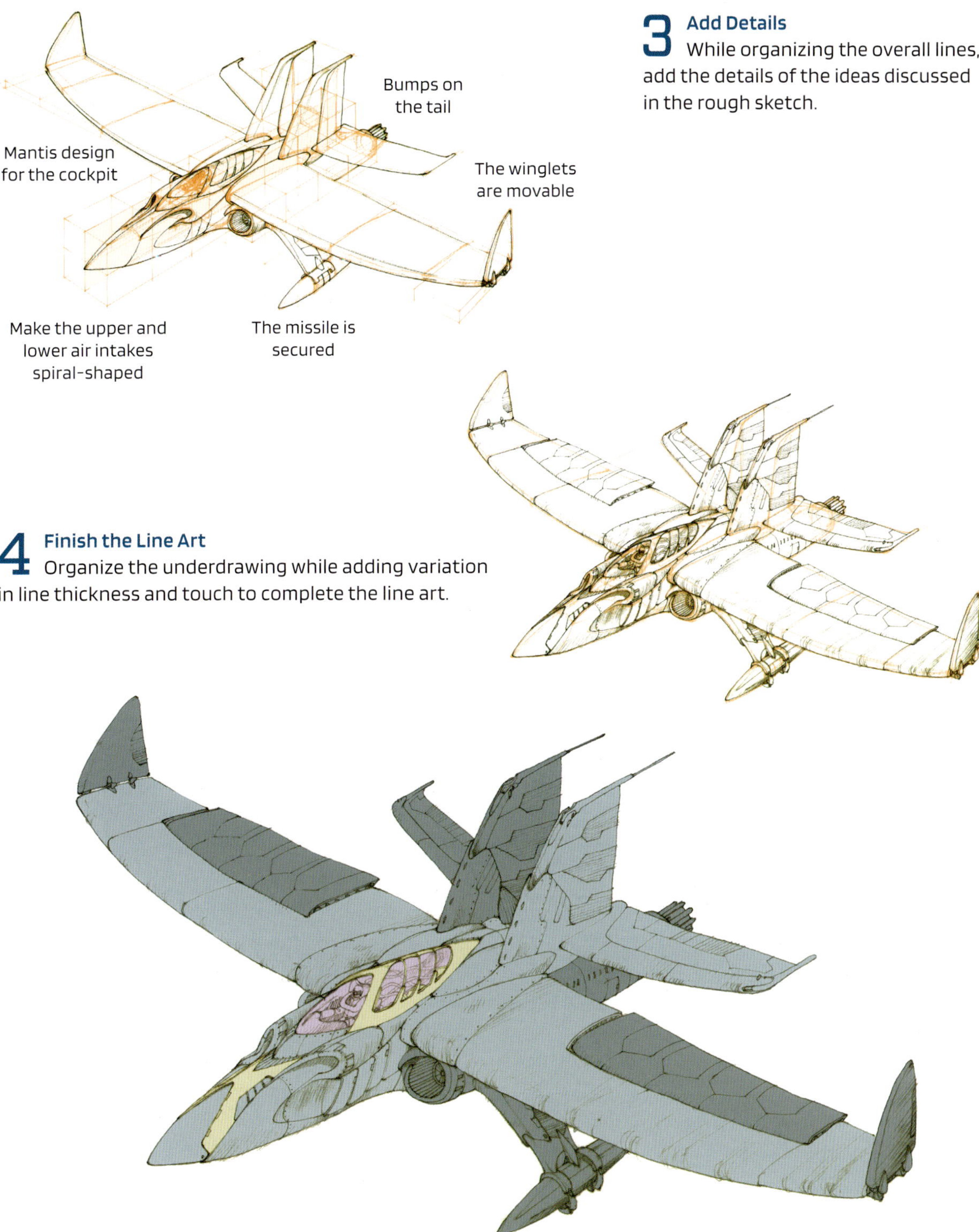

3 Add Details

While organizing the overall lines, add the details of the ideas discussed in the rough sketch.

4 Finish the Line Art

Organize the underdrawing while adding variation in line thickness and touch to complete the line art.

5 Create a Base Layer

Apply a base layer to set the overall color tone. While considering the image of light and shadow, separate areas where the contrast between light and dark may be strong. Also, separate areas where you want to change the material.

※ Here, the line art is scanned, and colors are applied using Photoshop.

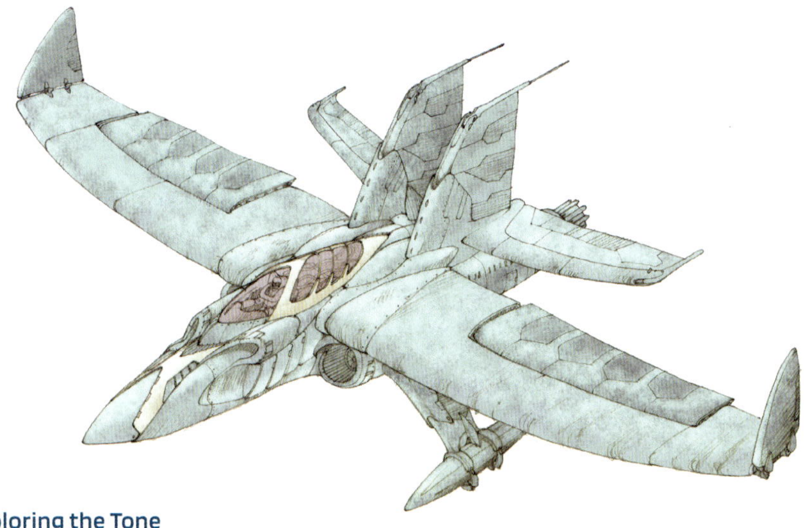

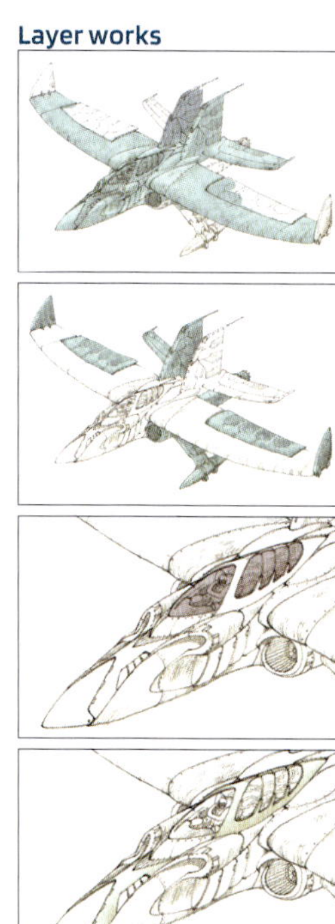

Layer works

6 Coloring the Tone

Roughly color the entire image. The expression of light and shadow will be done later, focusing on material texture.

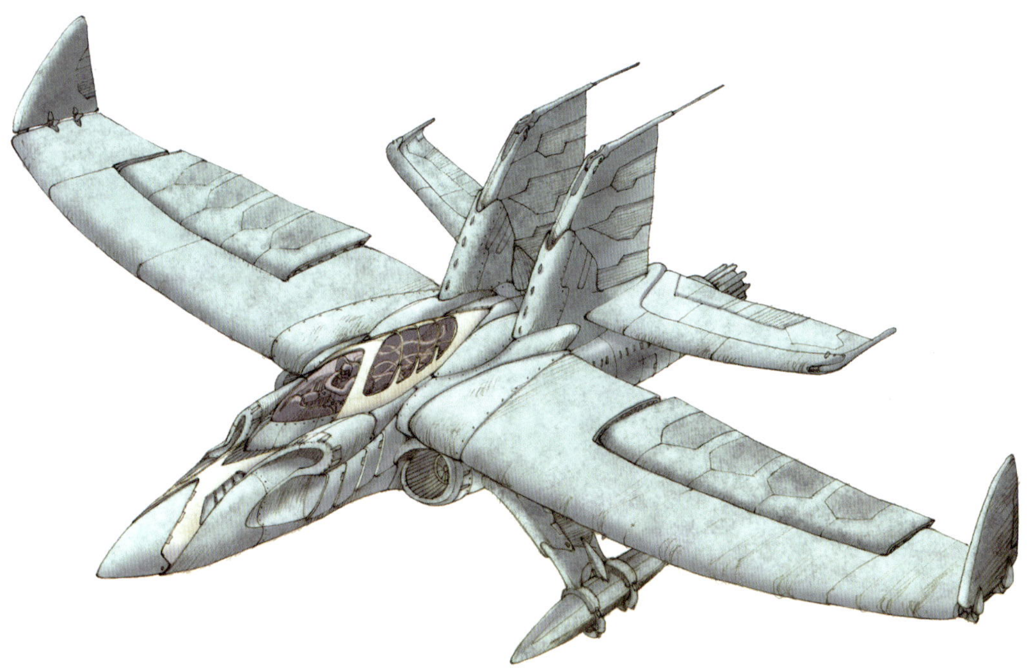

7 Adjusting Shadow Areas

Use a multiply layer to depict shadows. Assuming a cloudy sky while flying, keep the contrast low. The basic light comes from the upper-left front, but because the missile area will be in shadow, the light from the lower right is added to simulate reflected light.

Layer works

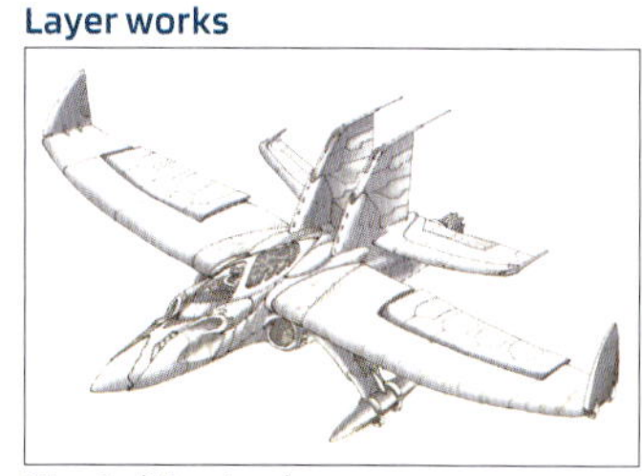

Shade (Shadow)

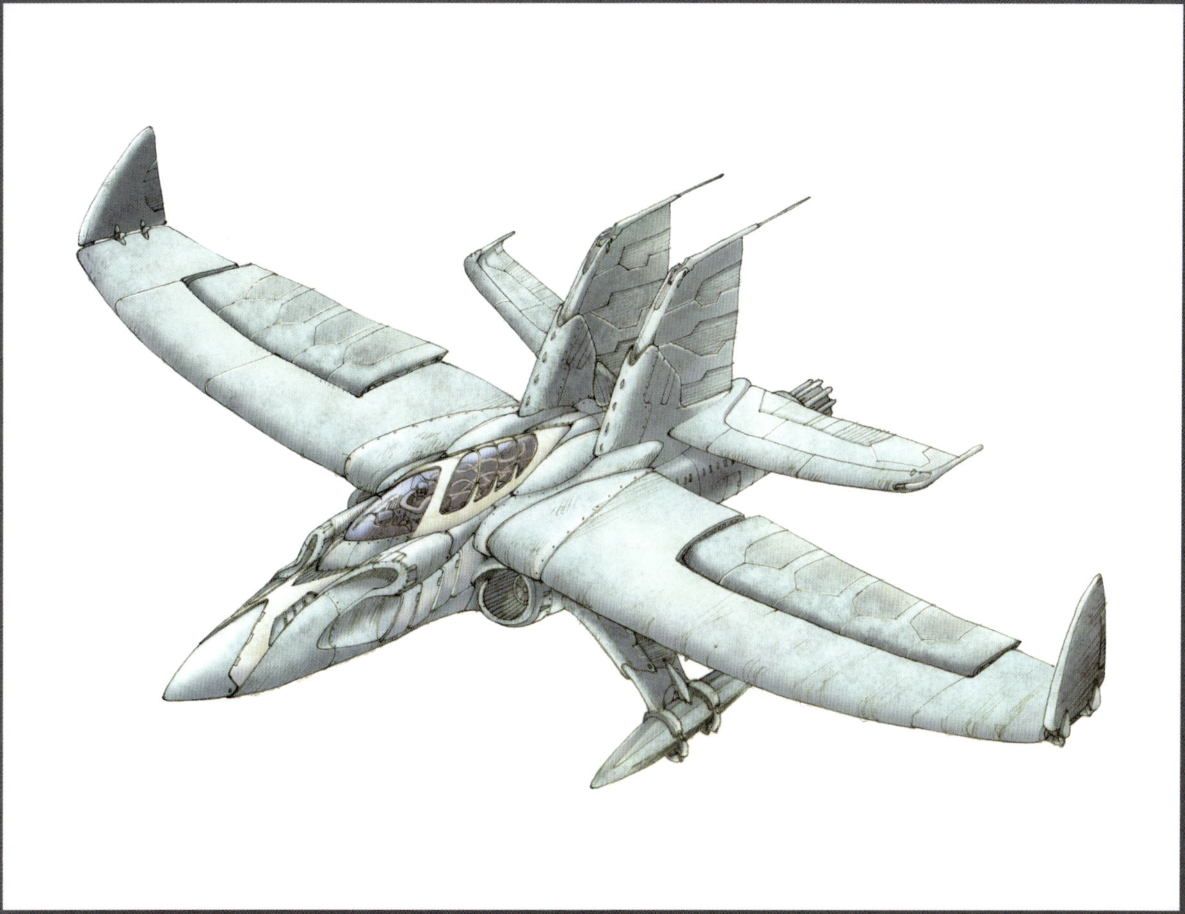

8 Adjusting Highlights

Overlay the layers to add highlights. Compared to screen layers, the drawing color appears more vivid, so be careful with color selection. This time, a light application is used on the main wing to express sky light.

Layer works

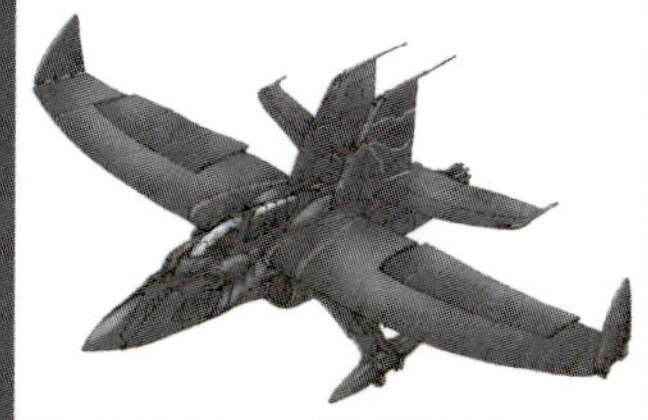

Highlights

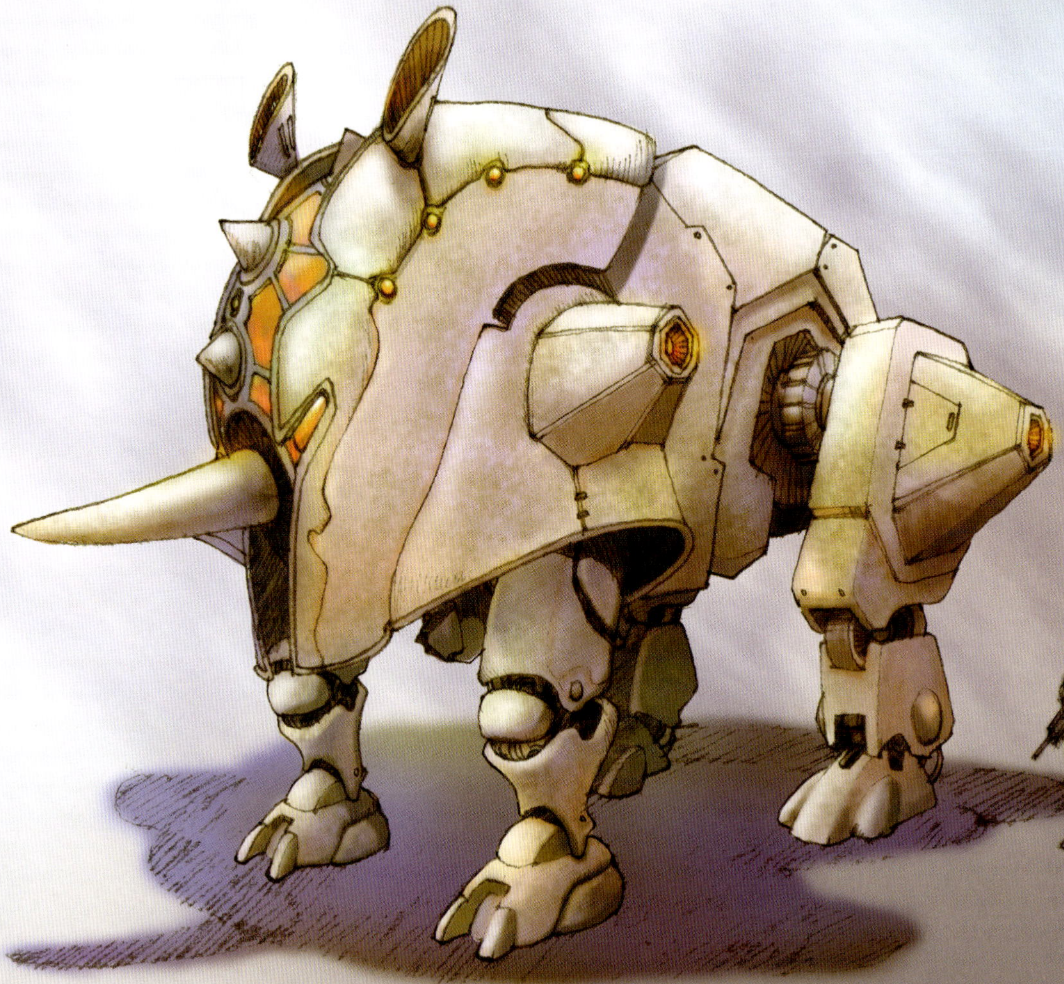

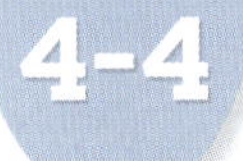

4-4 RHINO ROBOT

This is a four-legged robot. Inspired by the African white rhino, it's designed with a focus on a heavy, robust form while incorporating ideas for weaponry.

Developing Your Ideas

This mecha mashup is again inspired by animals, in this case the white rhino. Utilizing the creature's distinctive features, such as its sturdy body and the horn on the head, unique ideas will be emerge and be introduced.

Carefully observe the features of the rhino

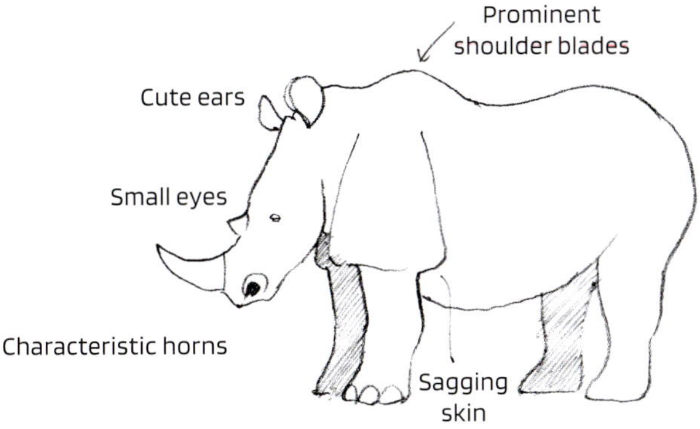

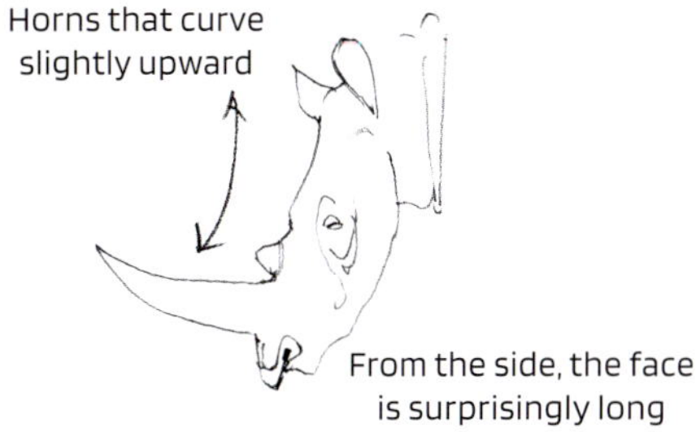

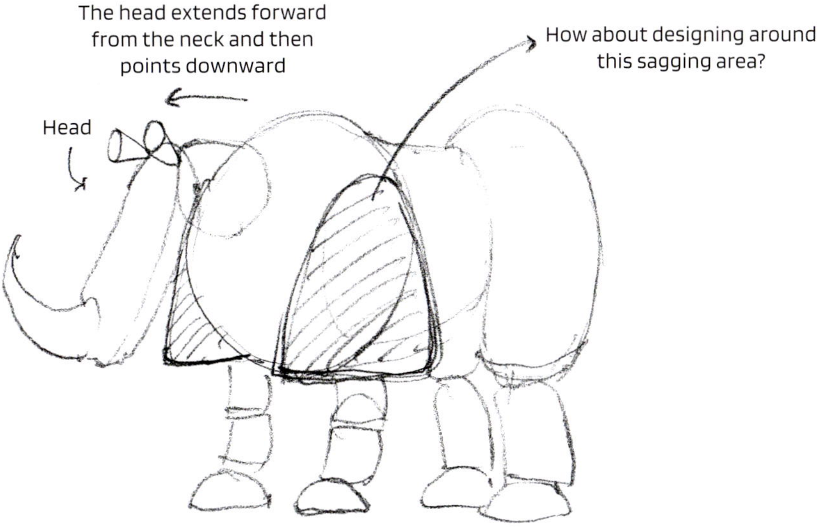

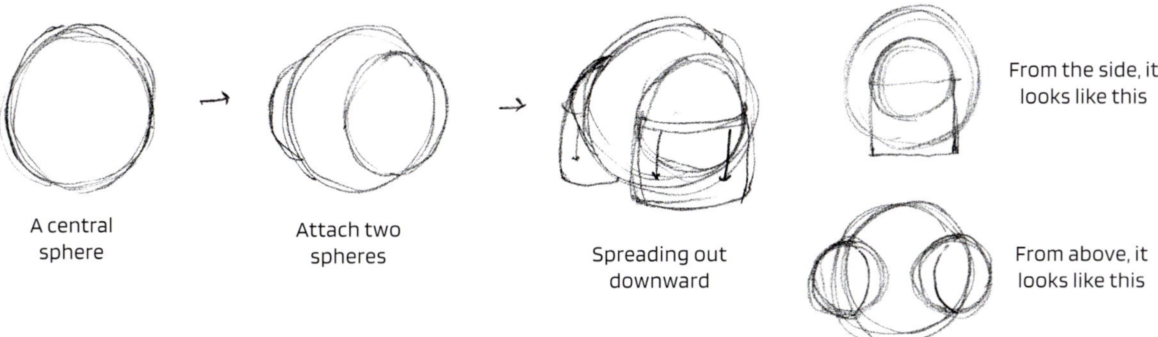

Let's start designing from the mechanical head

Attach the neck

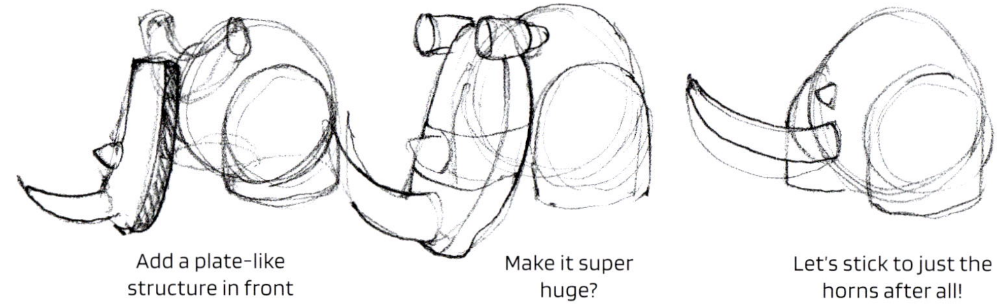

Add a plate-like
structure in front

Make it super
huge?

Let's stick to just the
horns after all!

A twist with the horns

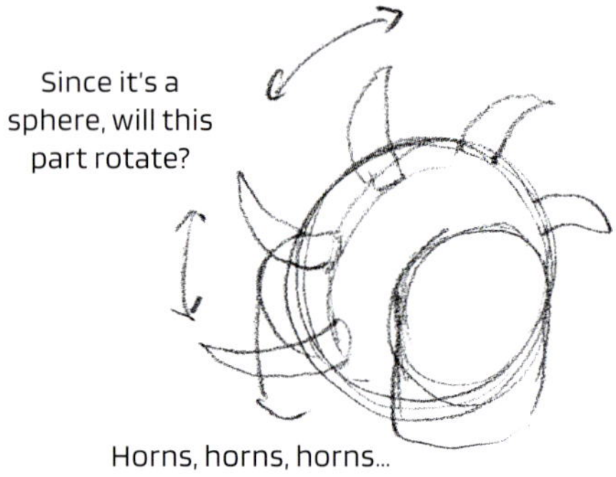

Since it's a
sphere, will this
part rotate?

Horns, horns, horns...

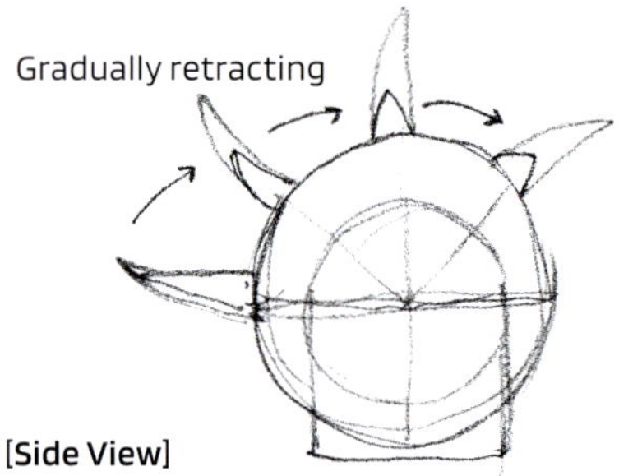

Gradually retracting

[Side View]

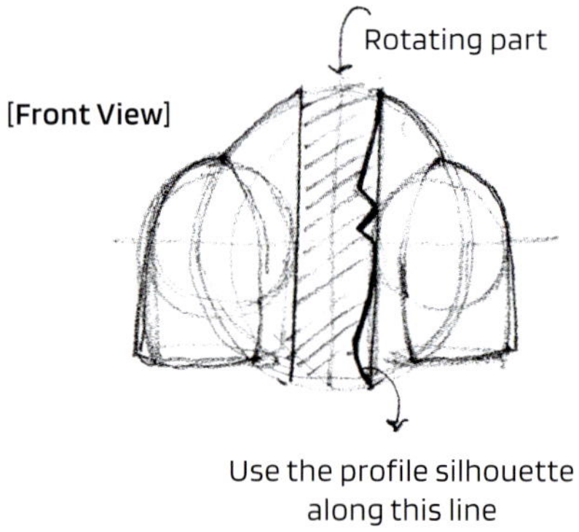

[Front View]

Rotating part

Use the profile silhouette
along this line

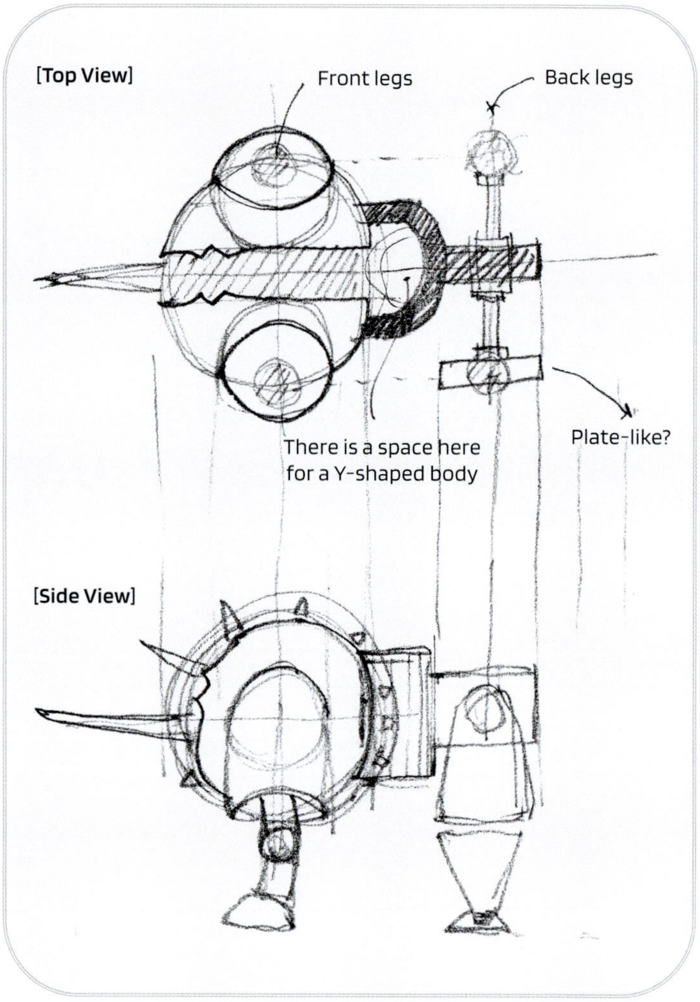

[Top View]

Front legs

Back legs

There is a space here
for a Y-shaped body

Plate-like?

[Side View]

Forms and Rough Sketches

Sketch the overall rough composition. Use the simplest basic shapes possible to establish a sense
of the connection and balance of the form.

Structures and Basic Figures

Develop the rough sketch and confirm the shape of the sci-fi vehicle you're designing.

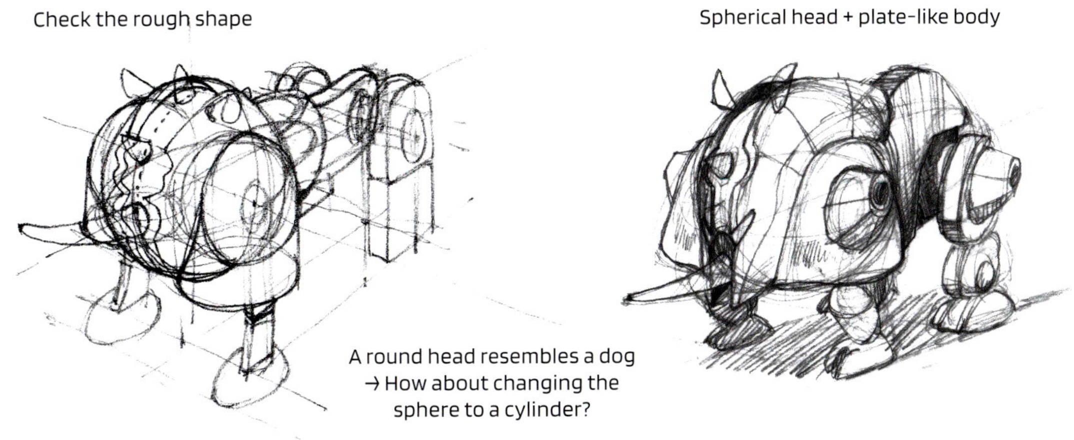

[Plan View]

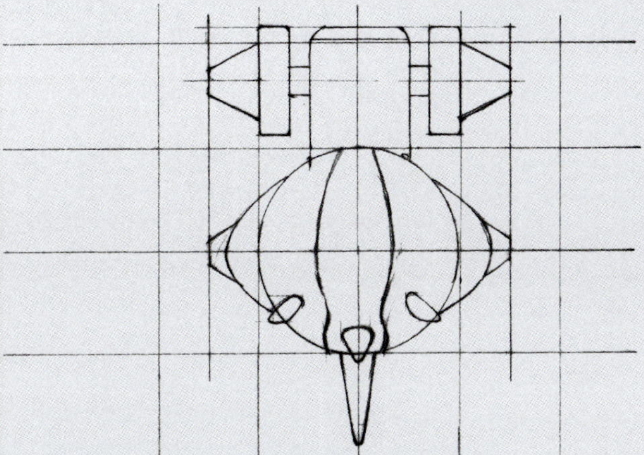

Create three views. The overall volume fits within a cubic grid of width 3, depth 3 and height 3.

[Front View]

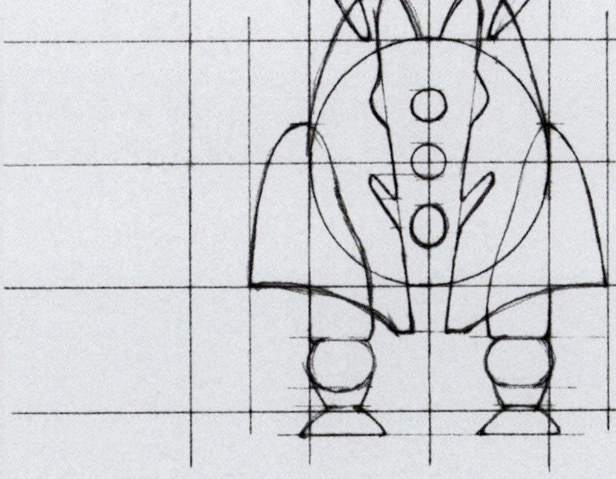

[Side View]

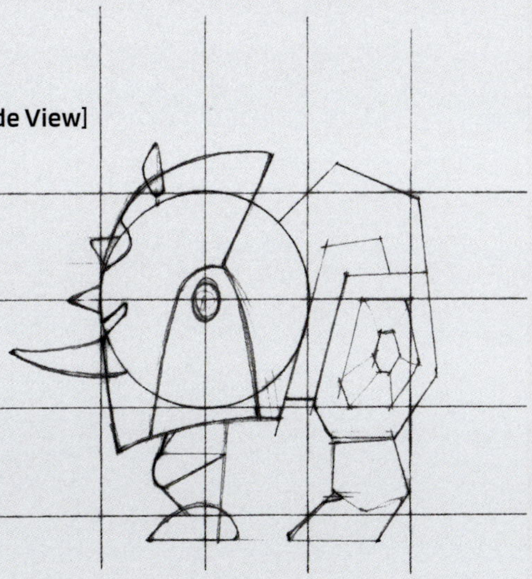

Drawing Steps

Preparation of the Grid
Create it based on the
grid on page 132

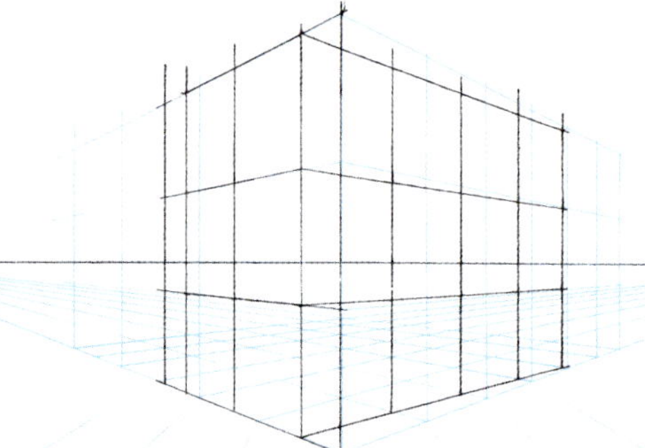

Blue lines: grid from page 132
Black lines: grid used this time

1 Grid Drawing – Draw the Form According to the Grid

Transform the grid from the three views
into a three-dimensional grid. Next, place
an oval for the head in the central grid and
outline the shape of the legs on the right
side. Draw the oval representing the sphere
and the shape of the side view according to
the three-dimensional grid.

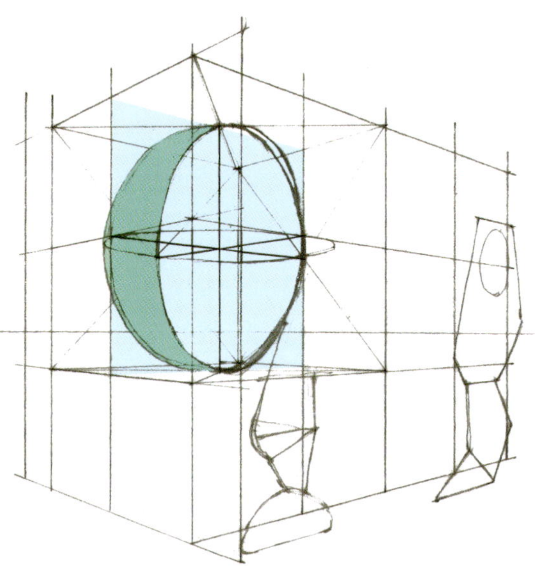

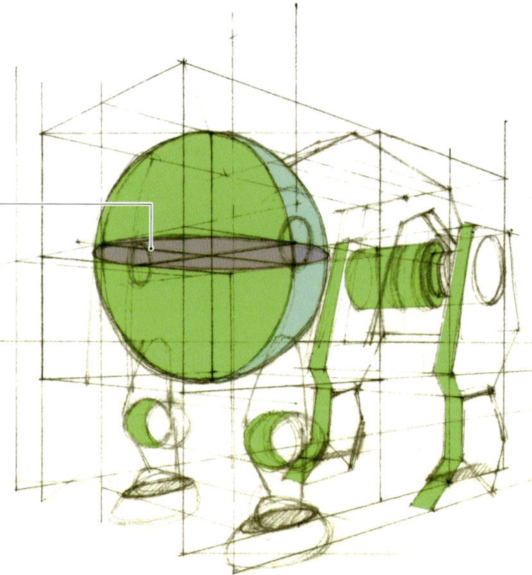

Use a 2-by-2 grid for
the center of the head
to check the volume.

2 Add Volume and Create a Three-Dimensional Form

Give volume and thickness to the
flat shape (the oval) and side shape
(the legs) transferred to the three-
dimensional grid. At the same time, add
the back legs, referring to the grid.

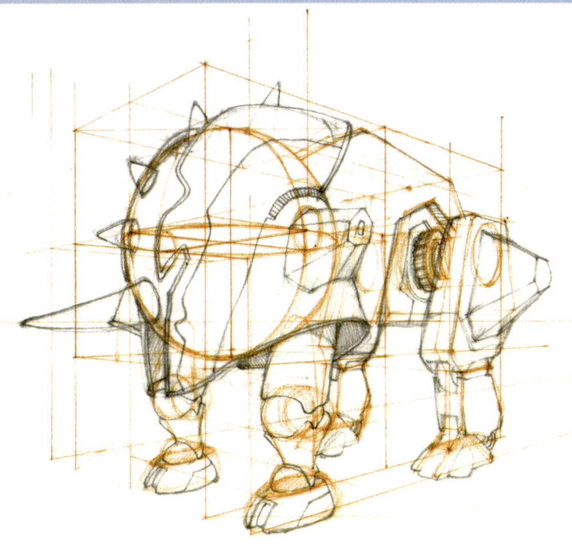

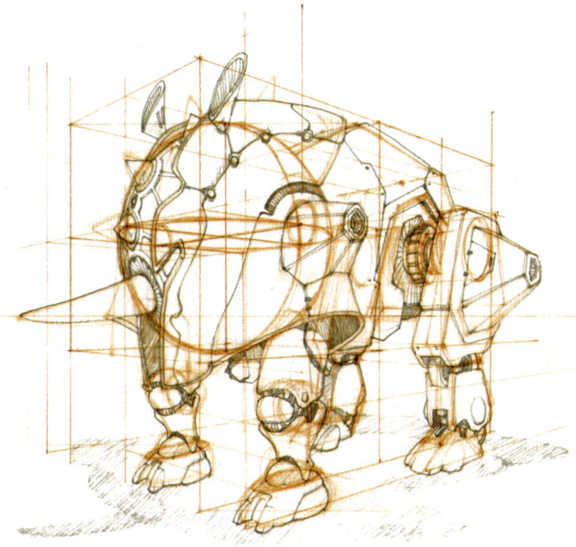

3 Add Parts

While being aware of each three-dimensional shape, such as the spherical part of the head, add the smaller parts.

4 Add Details

Add additional smaller parts and the details of the seams between the components on the three-dimensional surface.

5 Finish the Line Art

Organize the sketches and guide lines while adding strength and variation to the lines to complete the design.

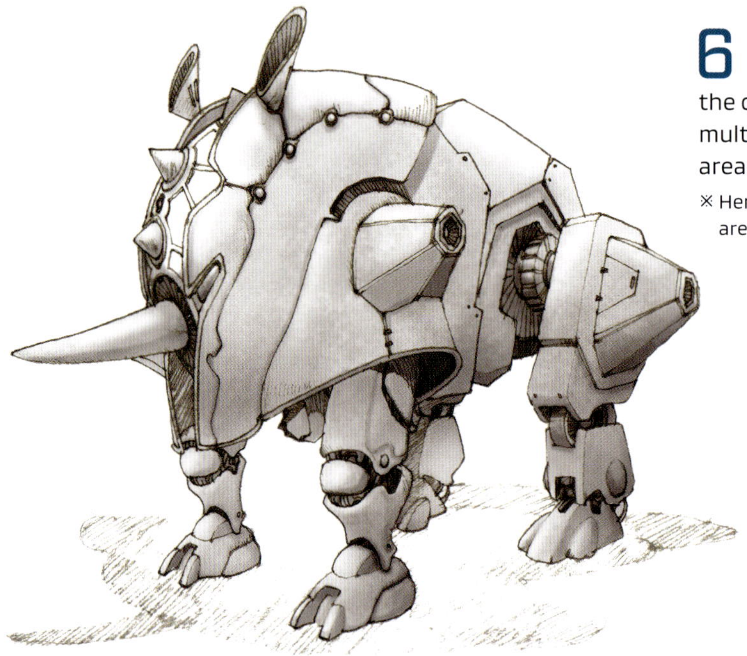

6 Base Color – Tone Coloring

Apply a base color to determine the overall tone. Then, use color multiplication to color the shaded areas, giving the entire piece depth.

※ Here, the line art is scanned, and colors are applied using Photoshop.

Layer works

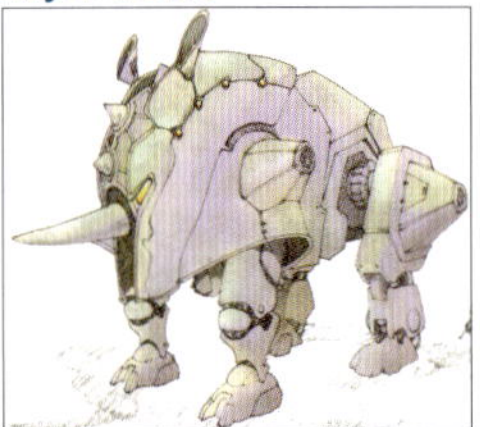

Body Coloring (Multiply)

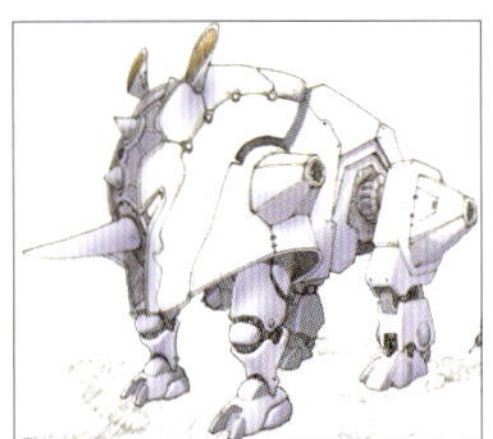

Shadow (Multiply)

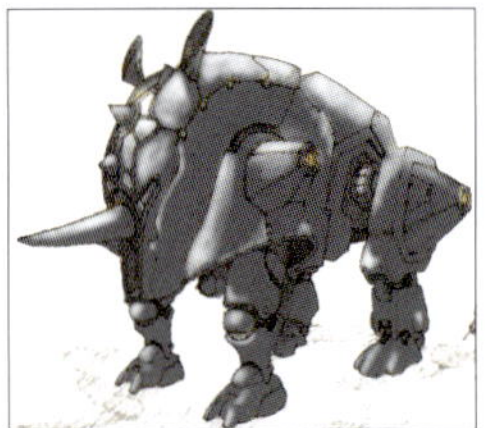

Highlight (Overlay)

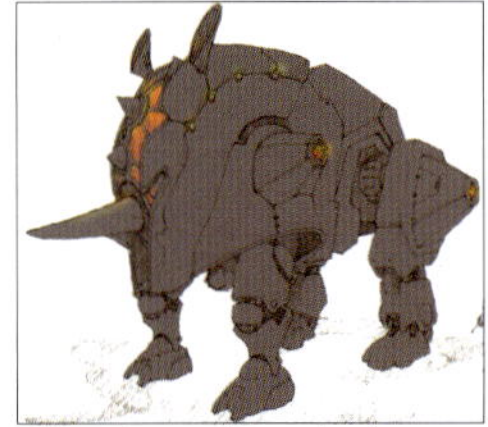

Glow Areas (Overlay)

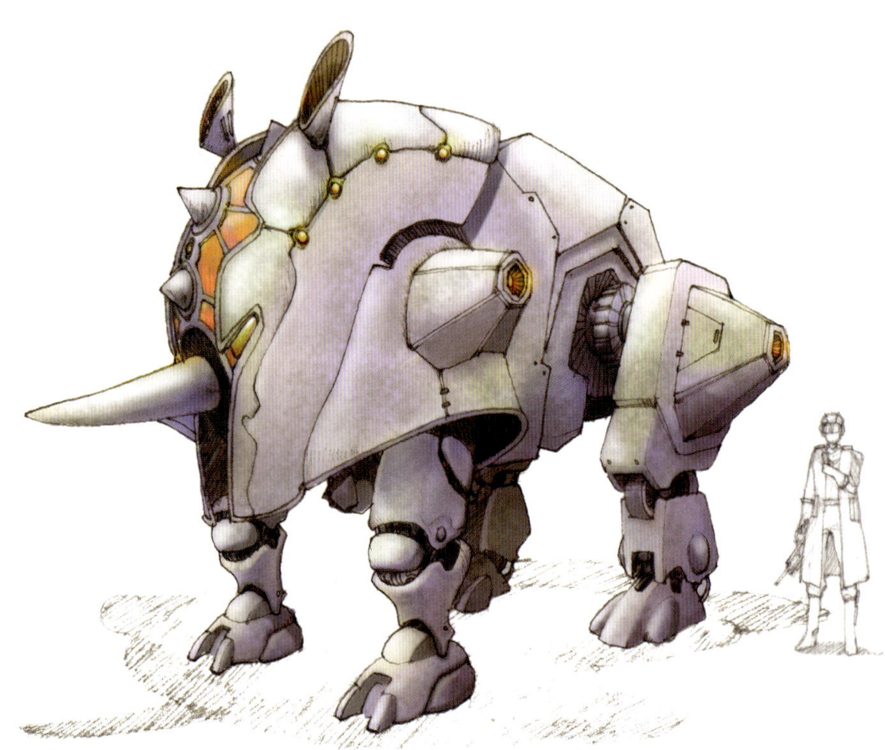

7 Body Coloring and Tone Adjustment

Color the body using multiply and adjust the tones for highlights and reflective parts. Also, add accents to the glowing areas using overlays.

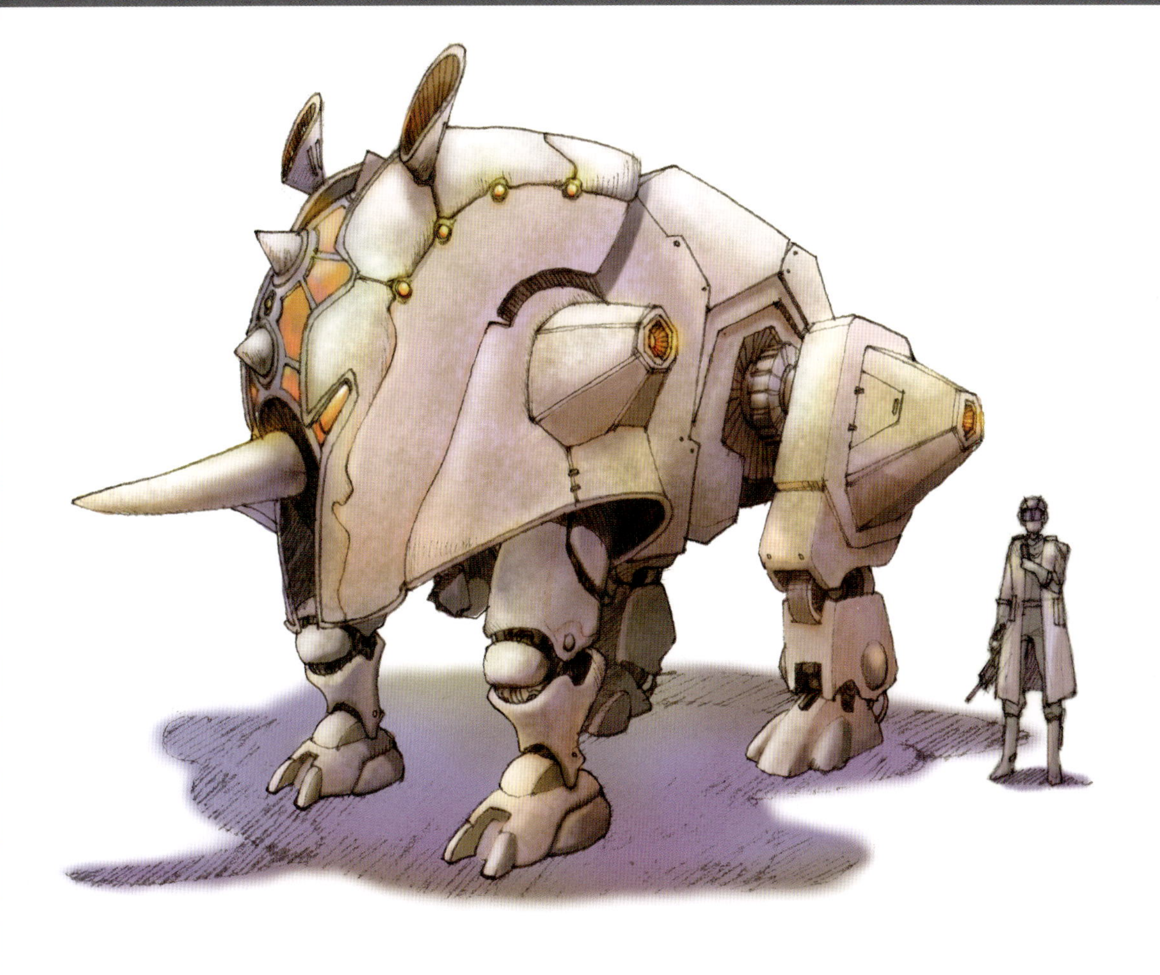

8 **Coloring Shadows – Final Touches**
Color the shadowed areas,
including the surrounding scenery, to
complete the entire illustration.

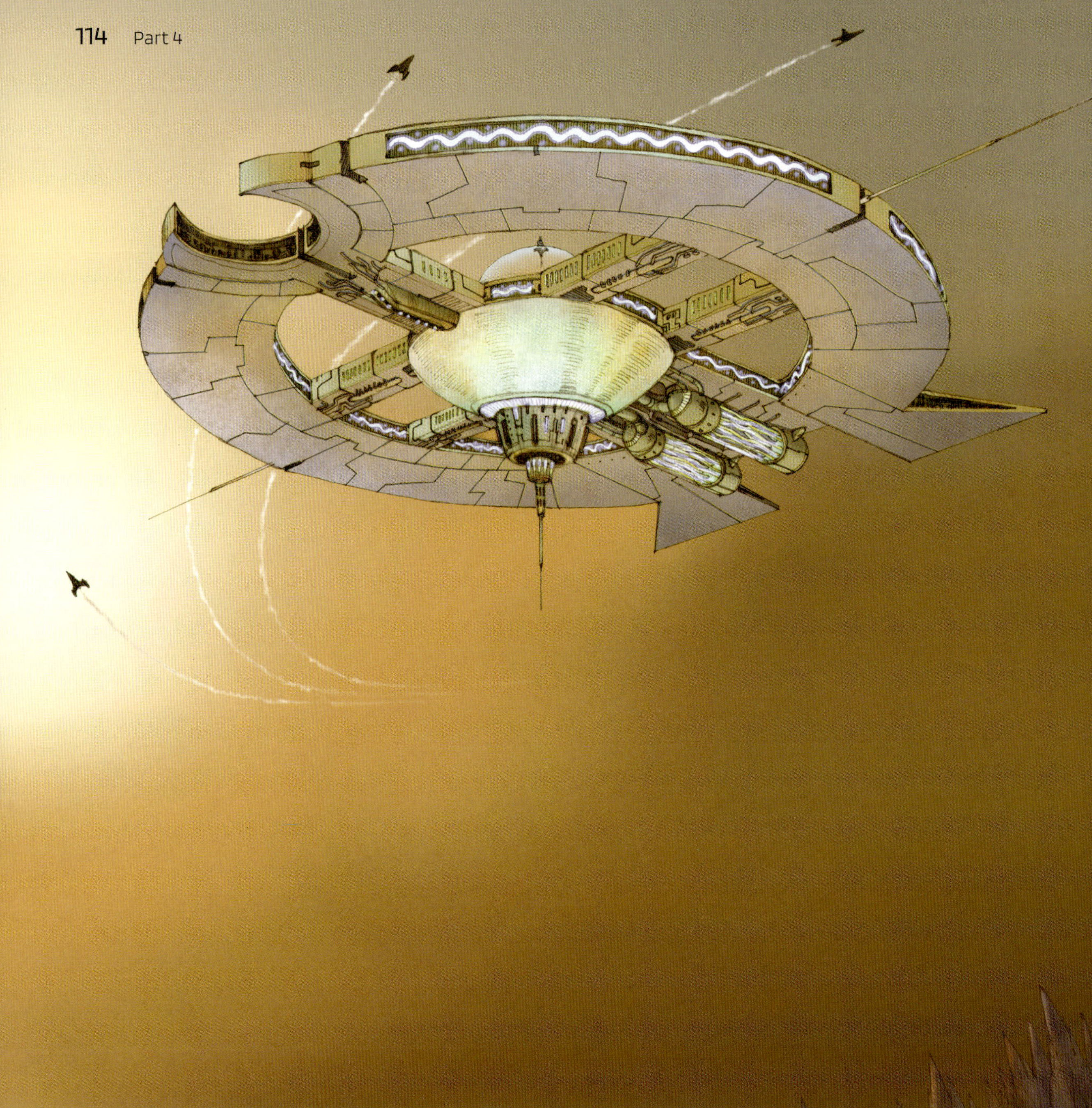

Part 4   Draw Your Own

4-5 LARGE INTERSTELLAR SPACECRAFT

This is a large spaceship that travels between galaxies. It's modeled on a giant scallop, using circles and ovals extensively and drawn using a one-point perspective grid.

Developing Your Ideas

The design is a giant disc inspired by a scallop shell. First, the shape is roughly defined, and then the smaller parts are embellished with details and visual information.

Decide on the Base Shape

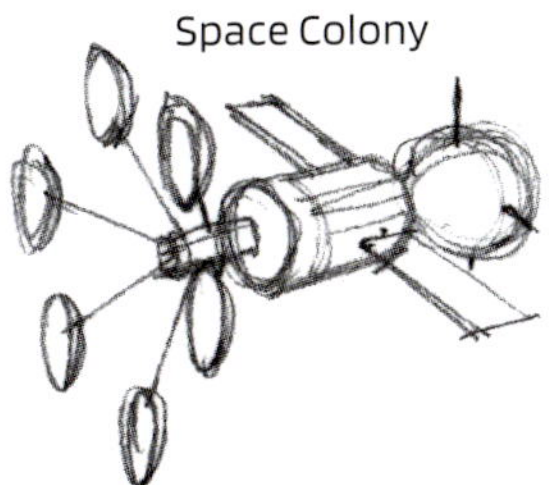

Space Colony

This type has powerful propulsion.

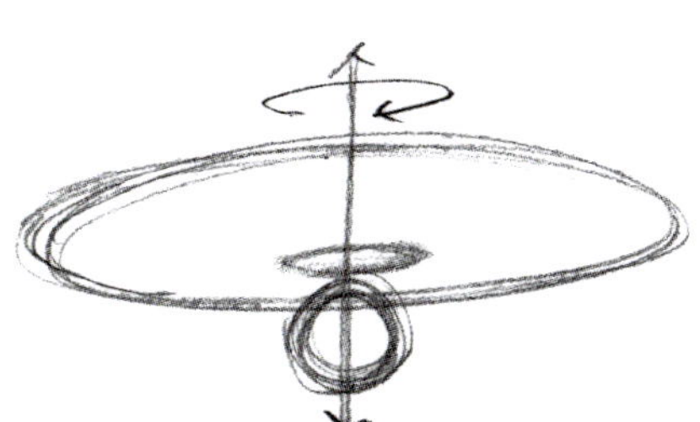

Suspend the power unit away from the living quarters.

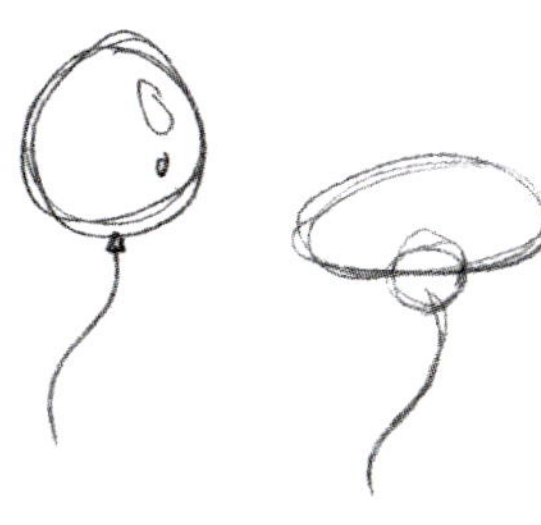

The image is of it just floating without much movement.

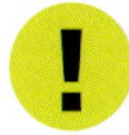

It resembles something...

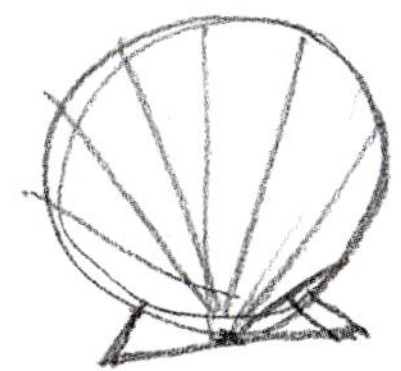

A scallop!

Draw inspiration from the scallop.

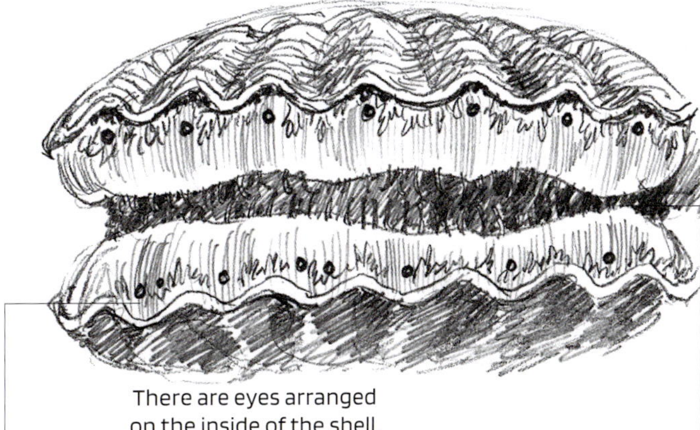

There are eyes arranged on the inside of the shell.

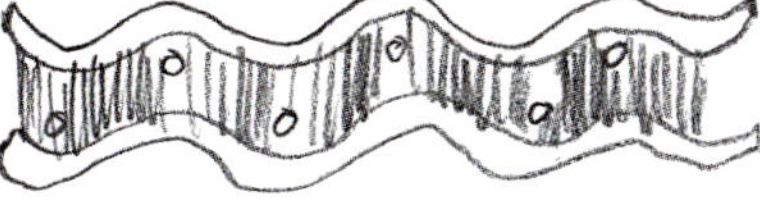

Slits and eyes.

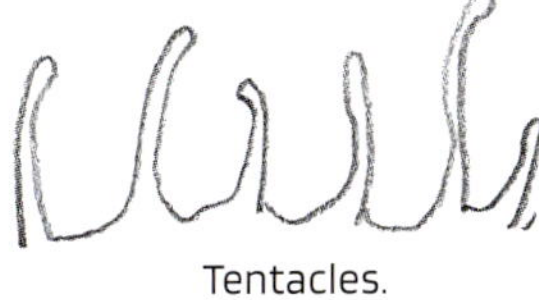

Tentacles.

Prepare parts to be combined.

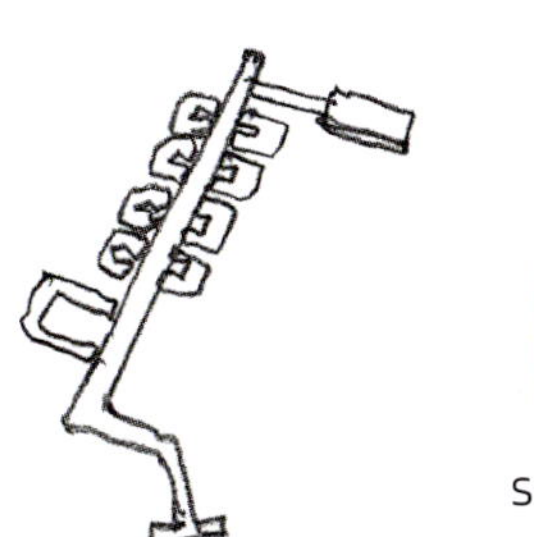

Something is attached to the piping.

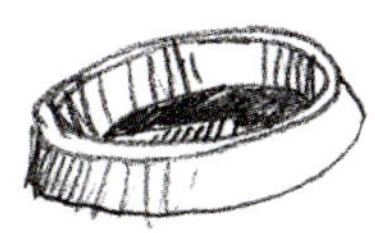

S-curve.

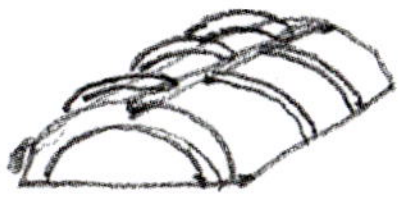

Something can be seen inside the hole.

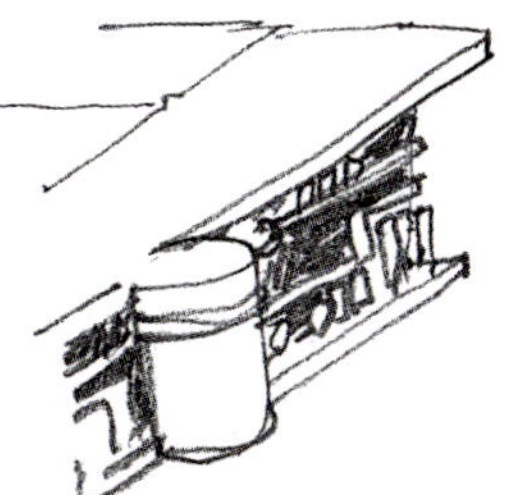

Kamaboko (steamed fish cake).

Piping in cross-section.

Create from Basic Shapes

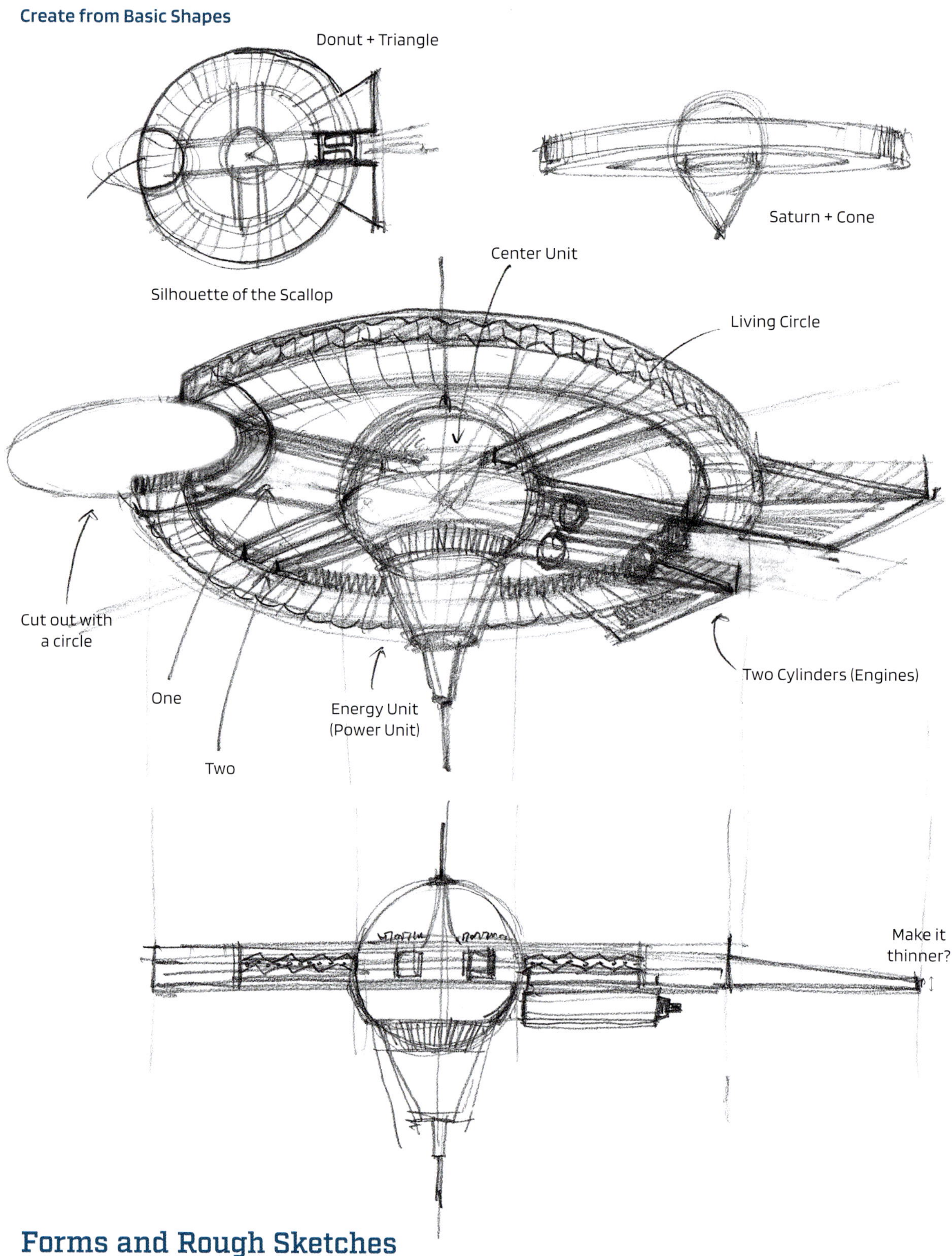

Forms and Rough Sketches

The basic shape is a cylinder without thickness, with the central part and tip hollowed out in a circular shape. A sphere is also placed in the center to create a more voluminous, defined form.

Structures and Basic Figures

Once you've captured the overall basic design in the rough sketch, a floor plan is created. Since the basic form is a cylinder, we'll proceed using only a one-point perspective floor plan.

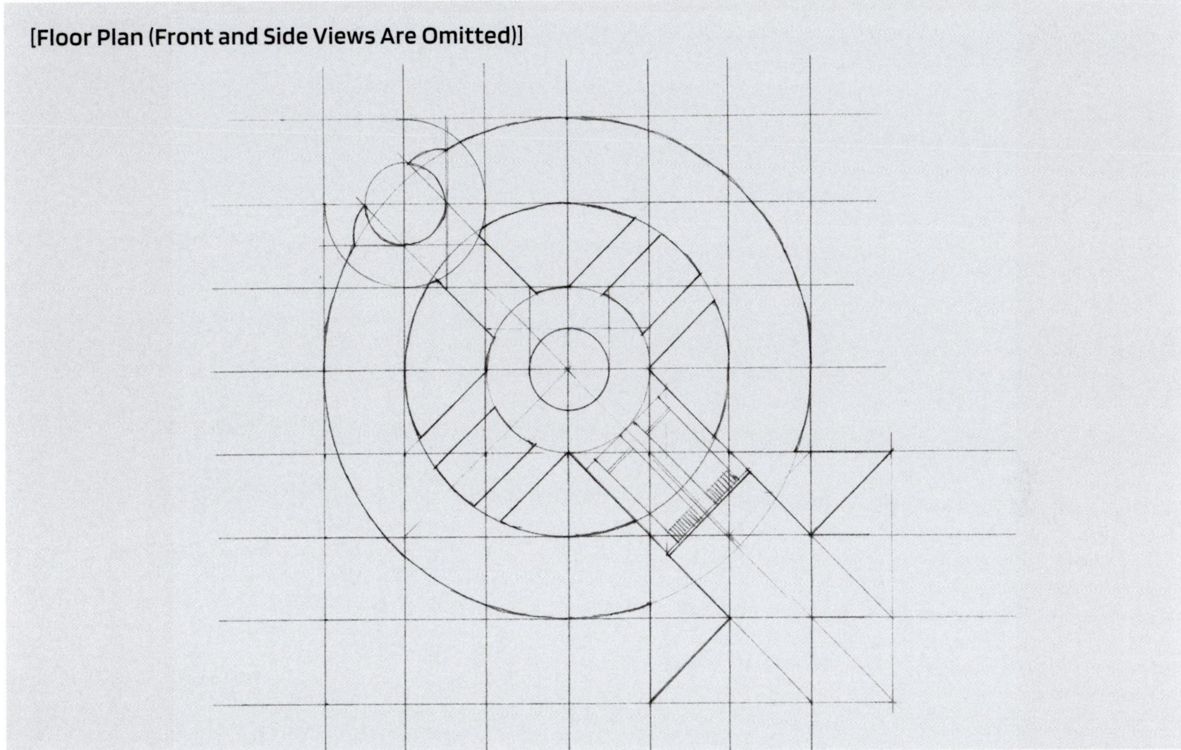

For this design, the view from below gives a better sense of scale, so we first create an arbitrary square with a one-point perspective below. Divide the lines of the vanishing direction into six equal parts with a ruler, and draw diagonals (in green) to utilize each intersection point to add horizontal lines (divided into six parts), preparing a 6-by-6 perspective grid.

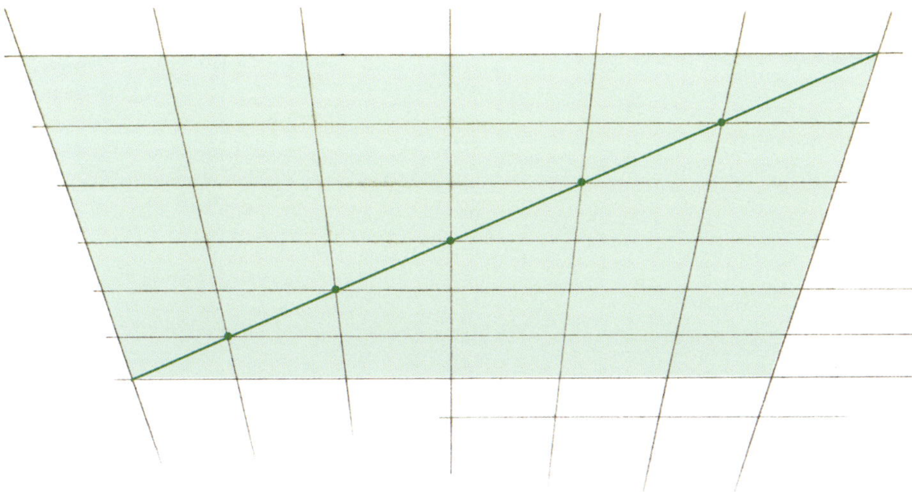

Drawing Steps

1 **Transfer the Floor Plan to the Grid**
First, the floor plan is transferred onto the grid, carefully picking up the intersection points. It's helpful to add guide lines for ½ and ¼ divisions to the floor plan in advance. Here, the central axis of the circles is all vertical lines, and the ellipses will also be horizontal. Detailed proportional adjustments can be made after the overall rough shape has been established.

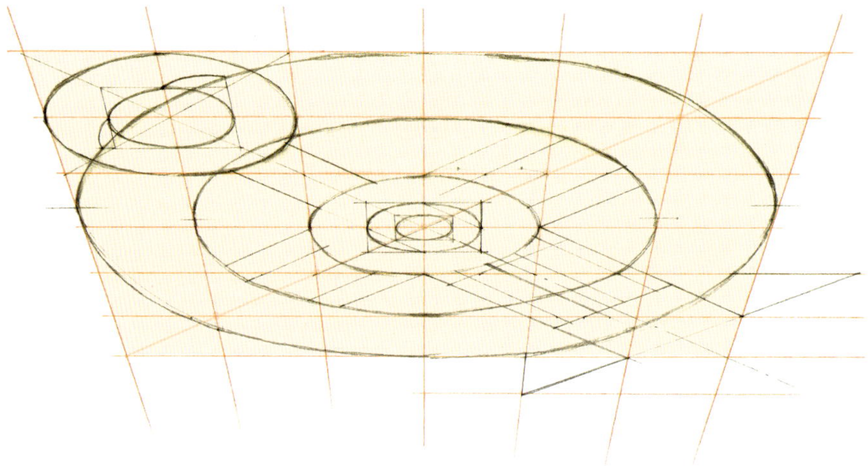

2 **Create the Three-Dimensional Shape (Add Thickness)**
Draw a guide line for the thickness of the hull above the left vanishing point. It will narrow in the direction of the vanishing point. Next, move horizontally from the point where the thickness is to be measured (the green dots) toward the direction of the guide line, then move vertically from the point where it hits the left edge of the grid line. Returning to the original point at the intersection of the guide line will indicate the thickness (the green line).

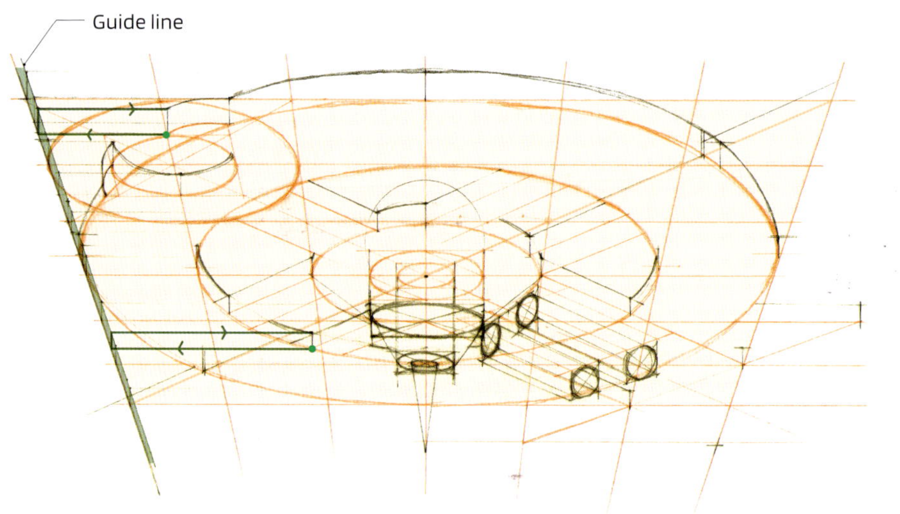

3 Finish the Line Drawing

Add details to the drawing. At this stage, freely incorporate parts that spring to mind, and don't worry too much about minor distortions.

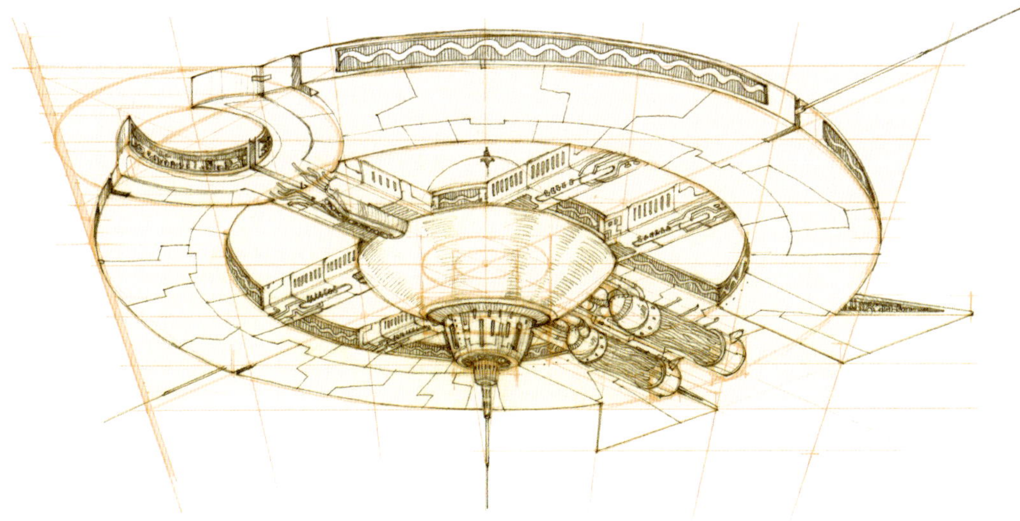

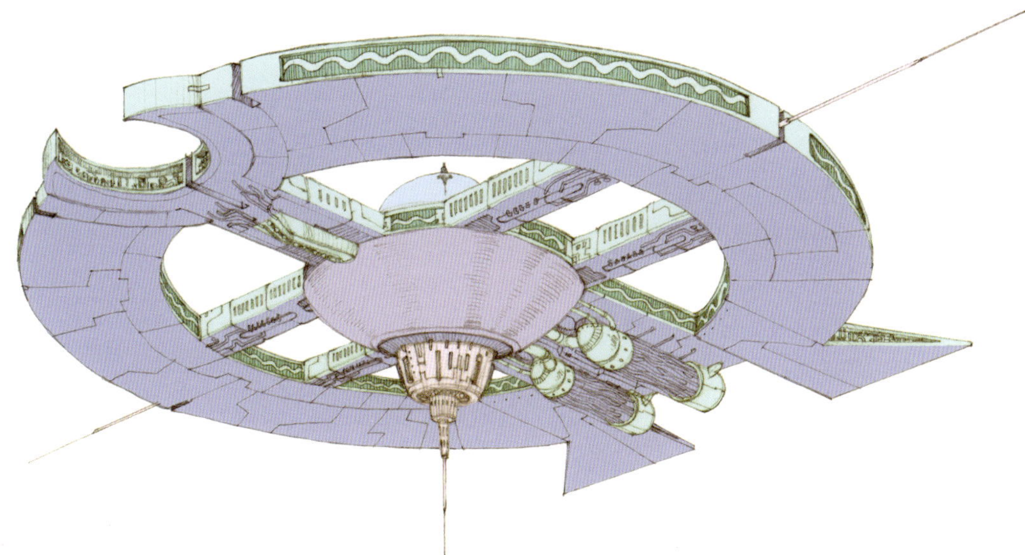

4 Base Layer

Paint by separating layers for each surface. I divided them broadly into the bottom surface, side surface and central energy unit. Since the area around the windows is supposed to glow, I separate it into a different layer. If the layers are divided too finely, the coloration can become monotonous, so I avoid separating the details of external units like the pipes.

※ Here, the line drawing is scanned, and colors are applied using Photoshop.

5 Coloring by Layer

Each layer is colored. This time, I set the scene to be flying through the planet's atmosphere and preparing to land. I colored the base blue with an orange sunset. The central part is grouped with complementary colors like blue and orange to avoid monotony.

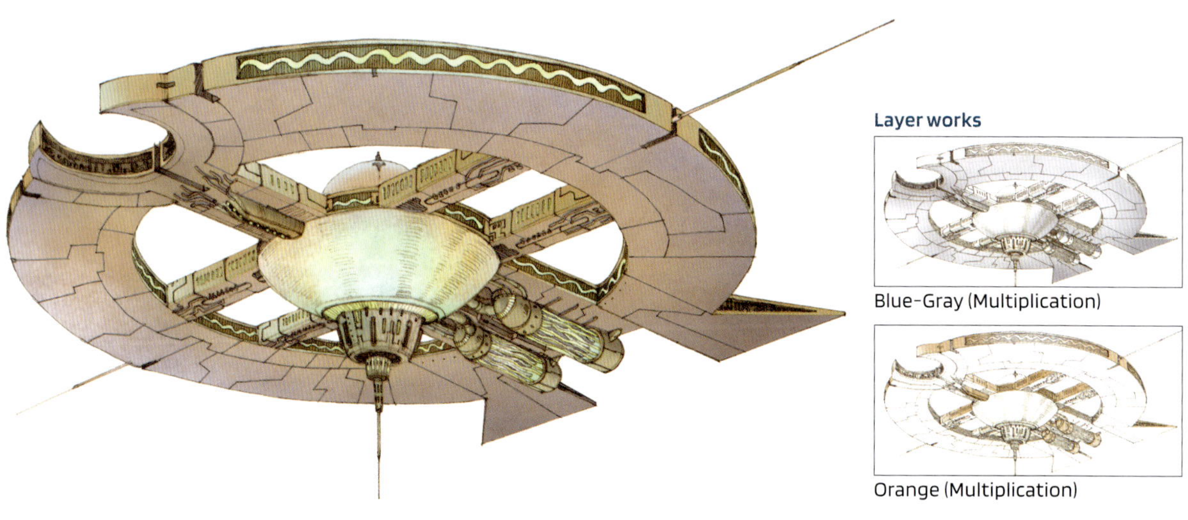

Layer works

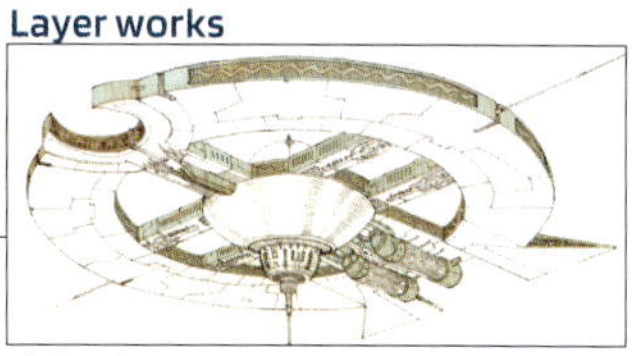

Side View

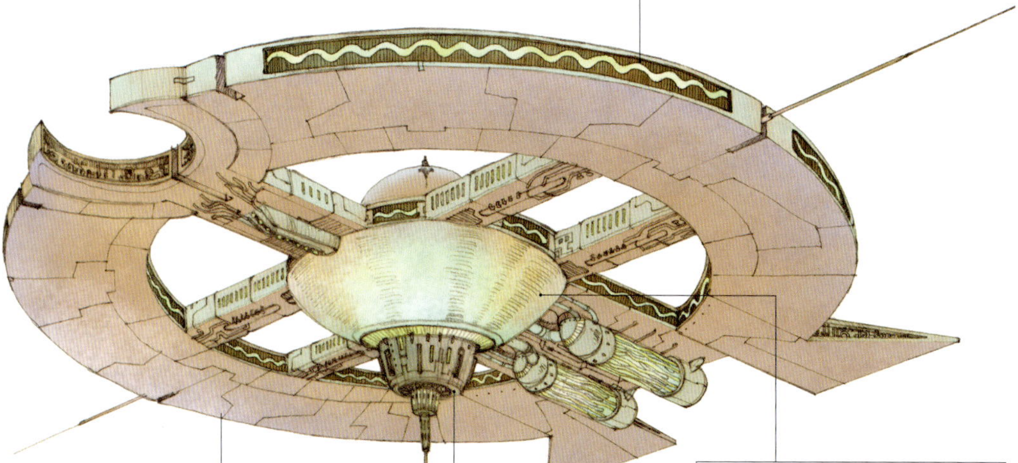

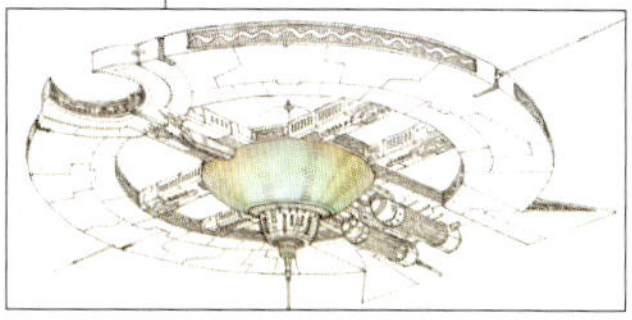

Bottom View

Details

Energy Unit (Power Section)

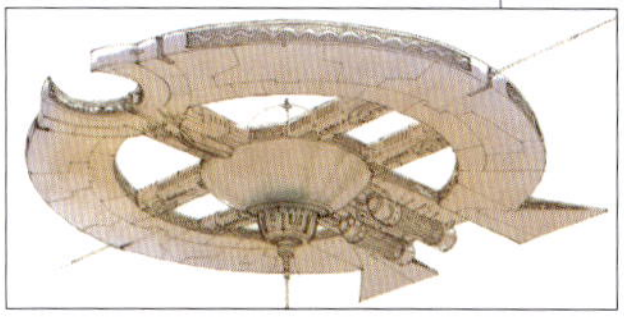

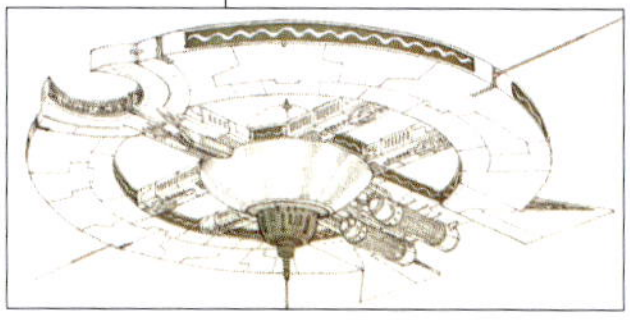

6 Shading Coloring

Here, I create a multiplication layer and fill out the shape with blue-gray.

Layer works

Blue-Gray (Multiplication)

Orange (Multiplication)

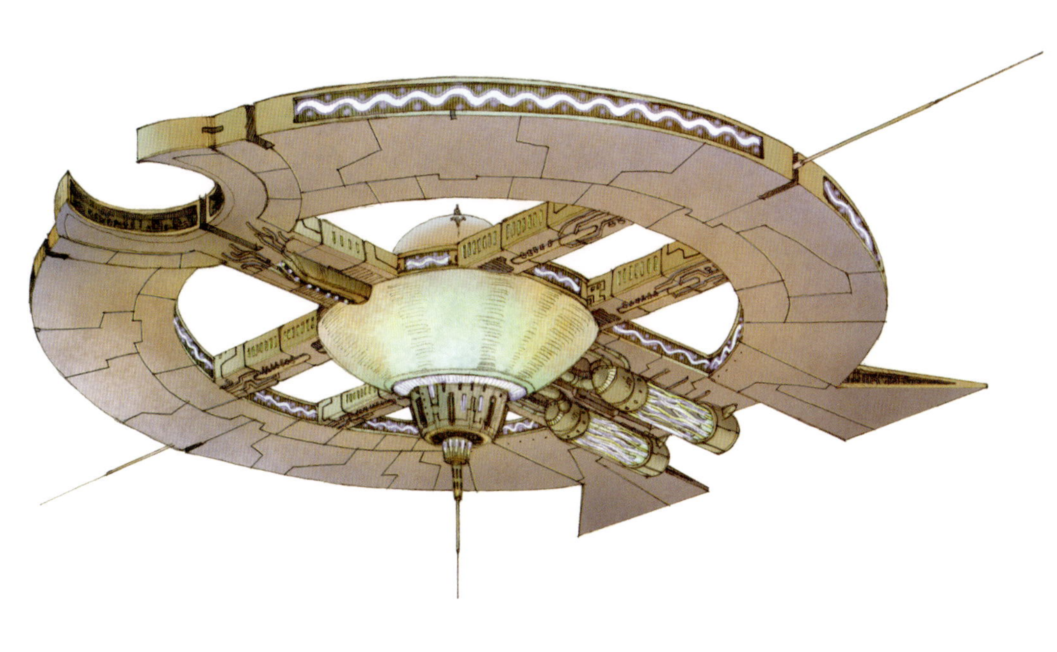

7 Highlight Adjustment
Finally, highlights are introduced in the overlay layer.

Layer works

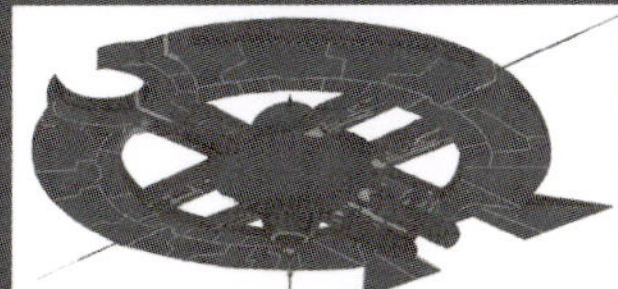

Highlight (Overlay)

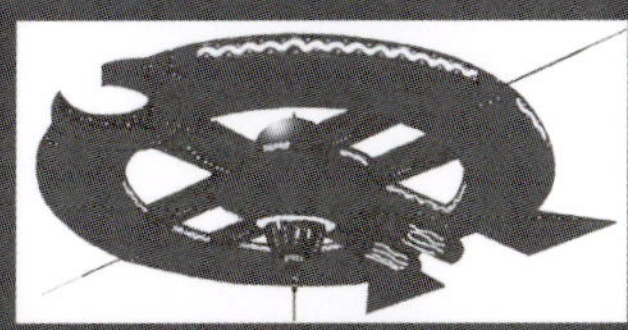

Glow (Overlay)

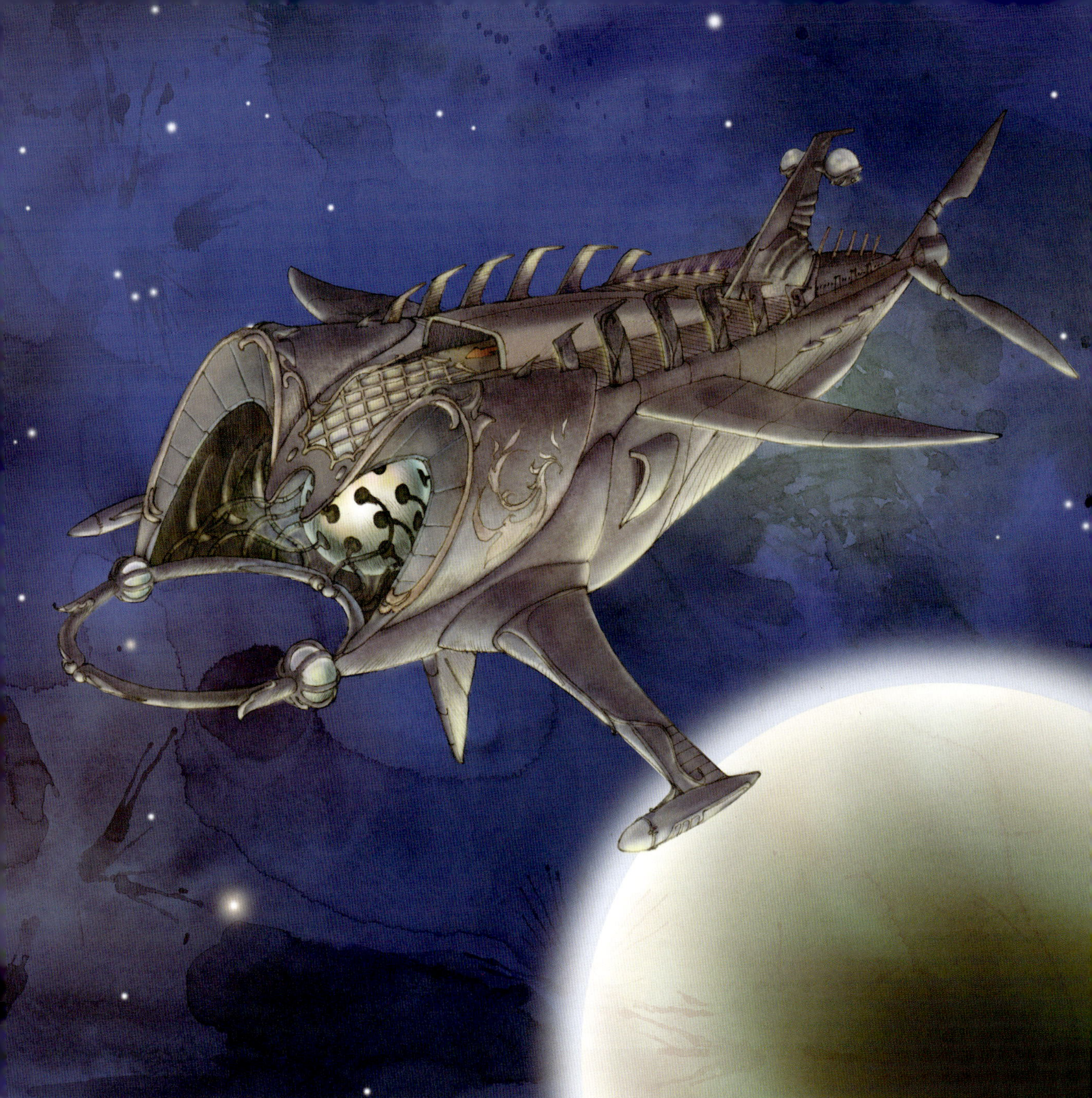

4-6 TUNA BATTLESHIP

This is a space cruiser and battleship suggested by the movement of a tuna swimming in the ocean. This mecha mashup seems at home in steampunk stories or space operas.

Developing Your Ideas

The design of the spaceship is inspired by fish with streamlined bodies. Since it's a battleship, I chose a hefty and weighty tuna. I capture the roundness of the cross-section, the shape of the tail fin and the characteristics of the gills. In a bold, I'll then turn the shape upside down.

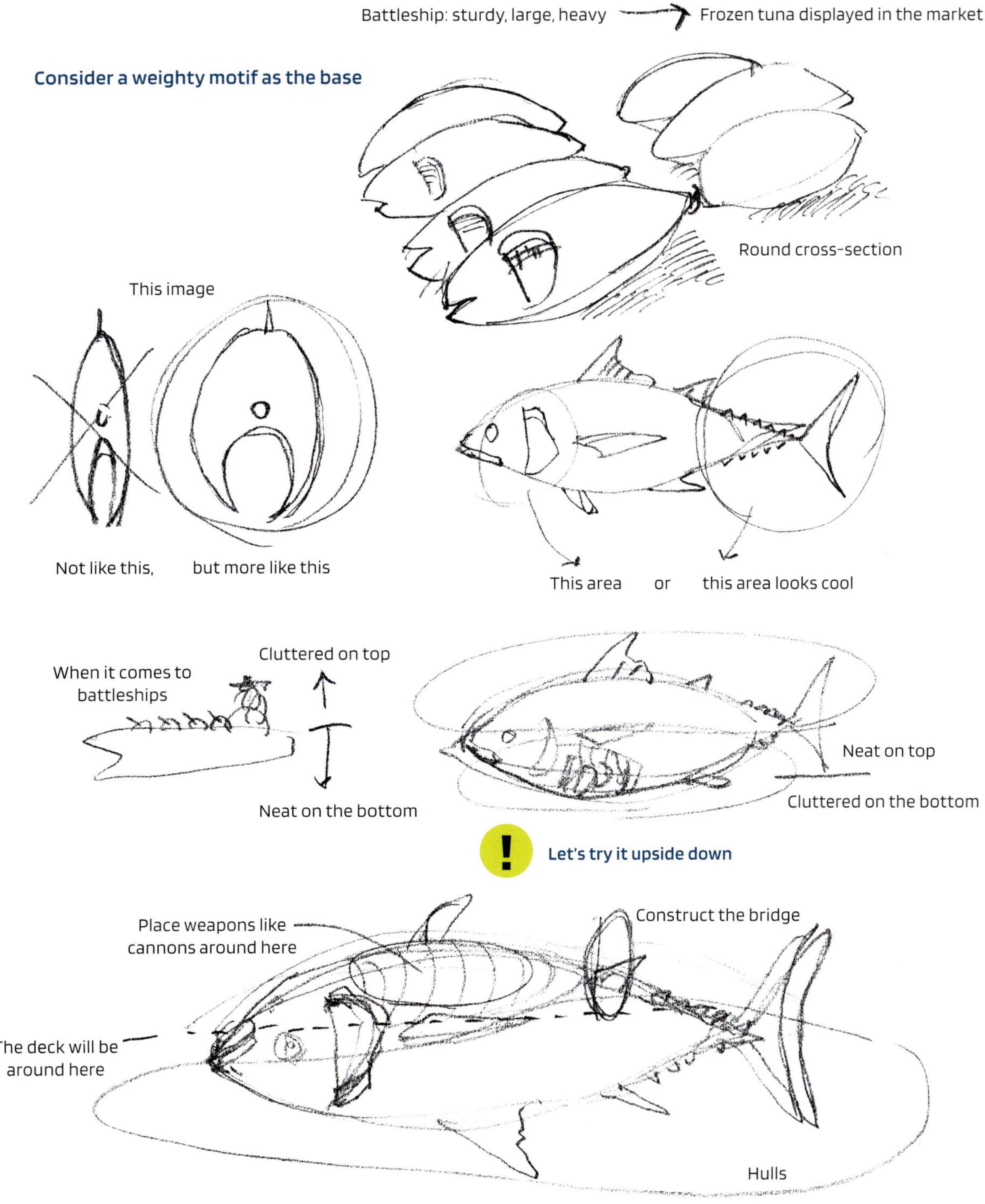

Roughly sketch the tuna upside down

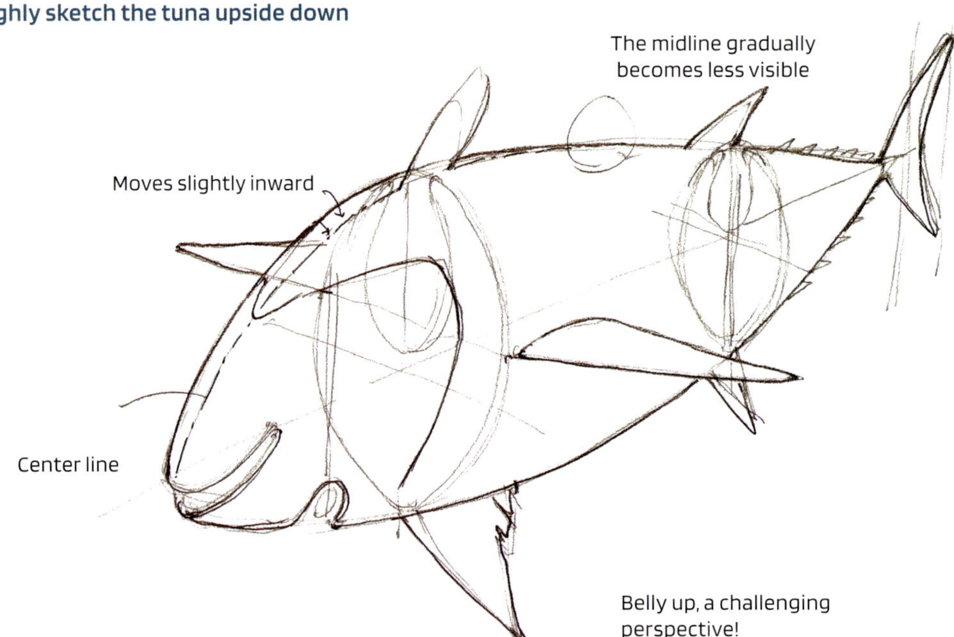

Create the deck

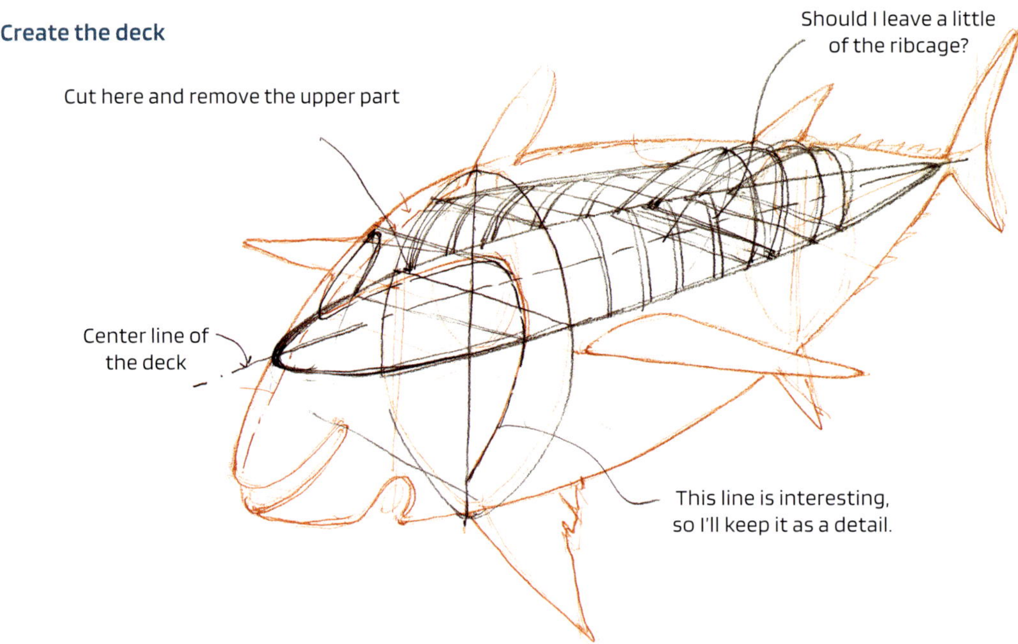

Forms and Rough Sketches

Create in the sketch a sense of the overall large volume. While imagining the cross-section, draw the form upside down. From there, create the shape of the hull. The head is removed from the nape, and then the upper part is finalized.

Structures and Basic Figures

While developing the basic form of the rough sketch, study the details. Once the overall image starts to emerge, organize it once and create a top view and a side view from a straight-on angle. Since the angle of this drawing doesn't require a front view, it's omitted.

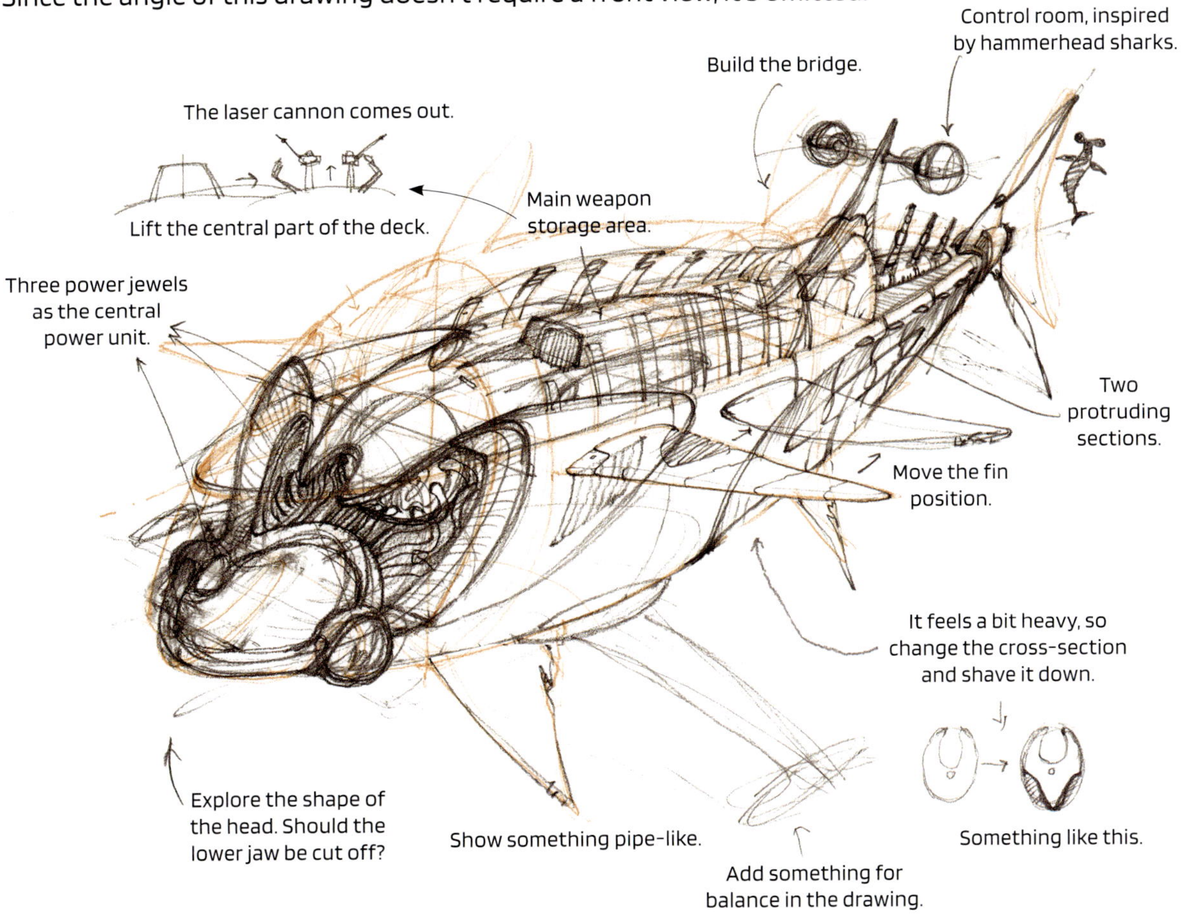

The laser cannon comes out.

Lift the central part of the deck.

Build the bridge.

Control room, inspired by hammerhead sharks.

Main weapon storage area.

Three power jewels as the central power unit.

Two protruding sections.

Move the fin position.

It feels a bit heavy, so change the cross-section and shave it down.

Explore the shape of the head. Should the lower jaw be cut off?

Show something pipe-like.

Add something for balance in the drawing.

Something like this.

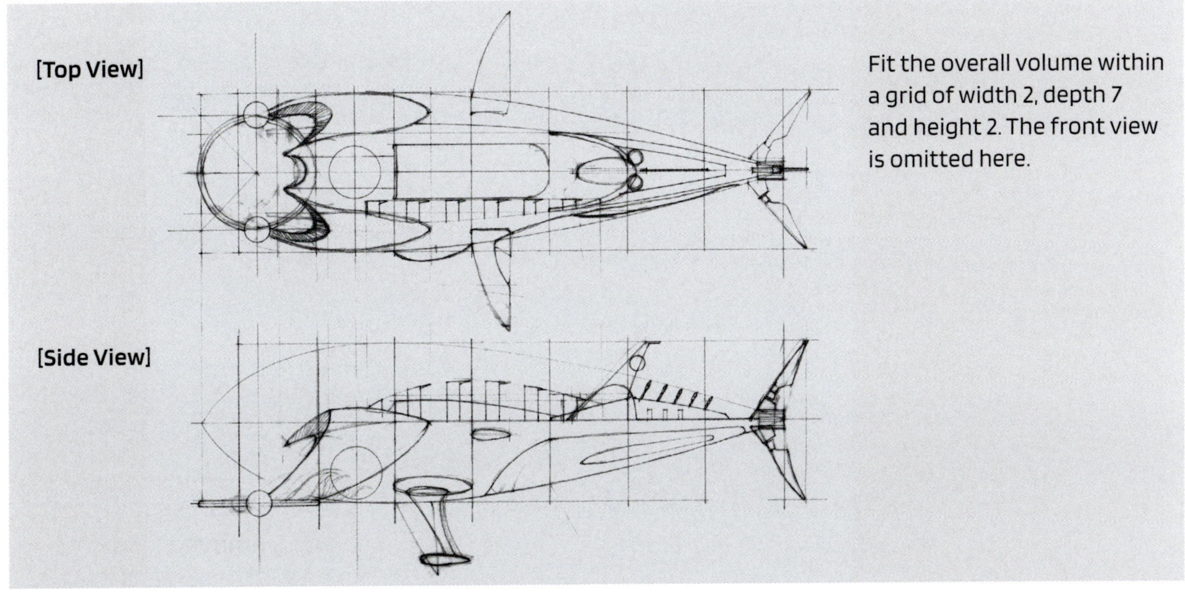

[Top View]

[Side View]

Fit the overall volume within a grid of width 2, depth 7 and height 2. The front view is omitted here.

Drawing Steps

1 Determine the Two-Point Perspective Vanishing Points

When viewing a massive object like a battleship up close, the perspective can become significantly distorted toward the foreground. In such cases, place the sketch in the center of the paper, then determine the vanishing points so that the top and side views approximately align. For large motifs, it's important to keep the distance between the vanishing points appropriately spaced.

Start by sketching roughly on a large sheet of paper and then reduce the scale it to make it easier to work with.

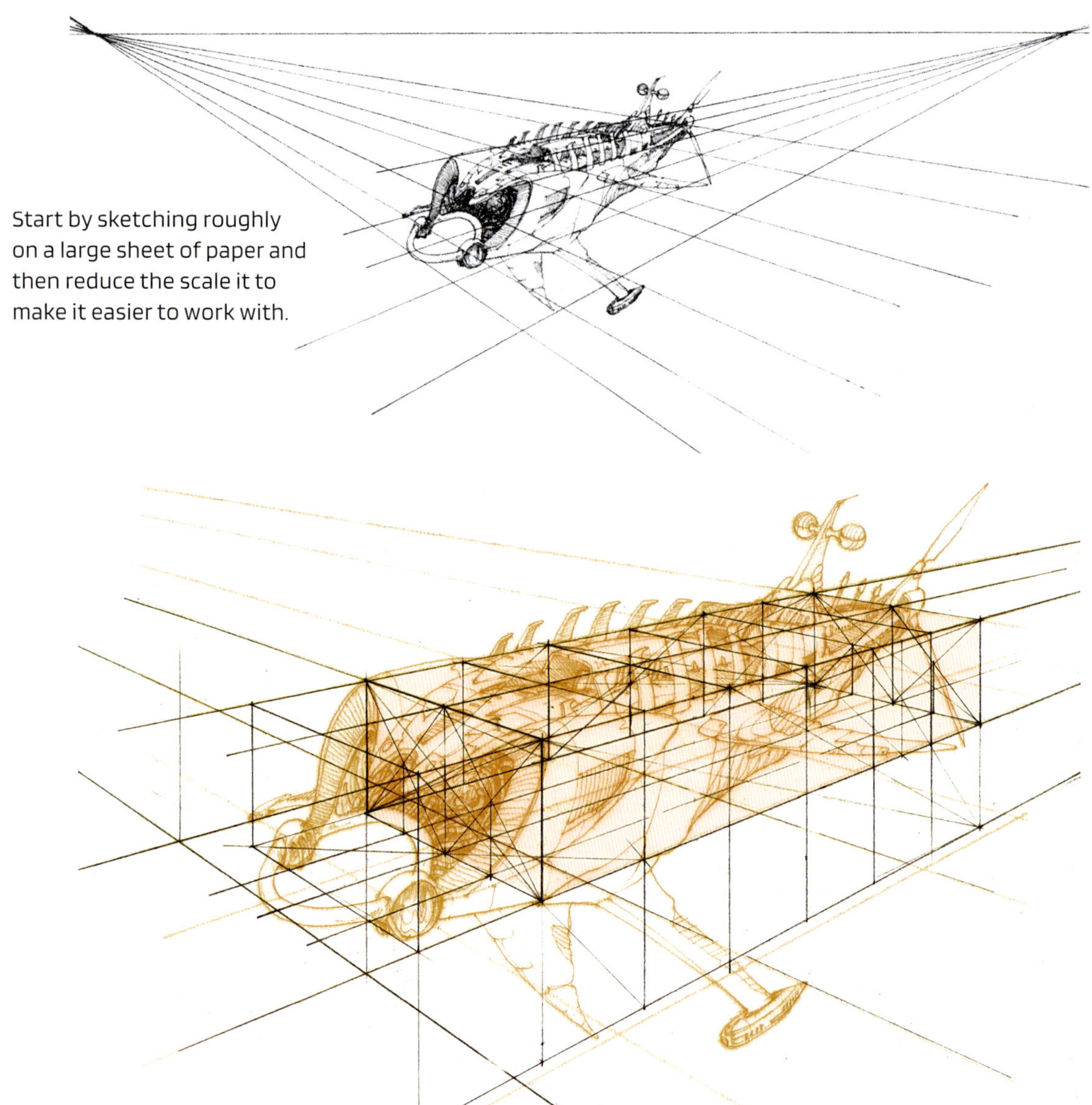

2 Create the Grid

Using the perspective grid of the top view as a base, first create a grid of width 2 and depth 6. Use the methods of grid division and proliferation. Since the front part has a slightly unique shape, create it as a different grid at the end.

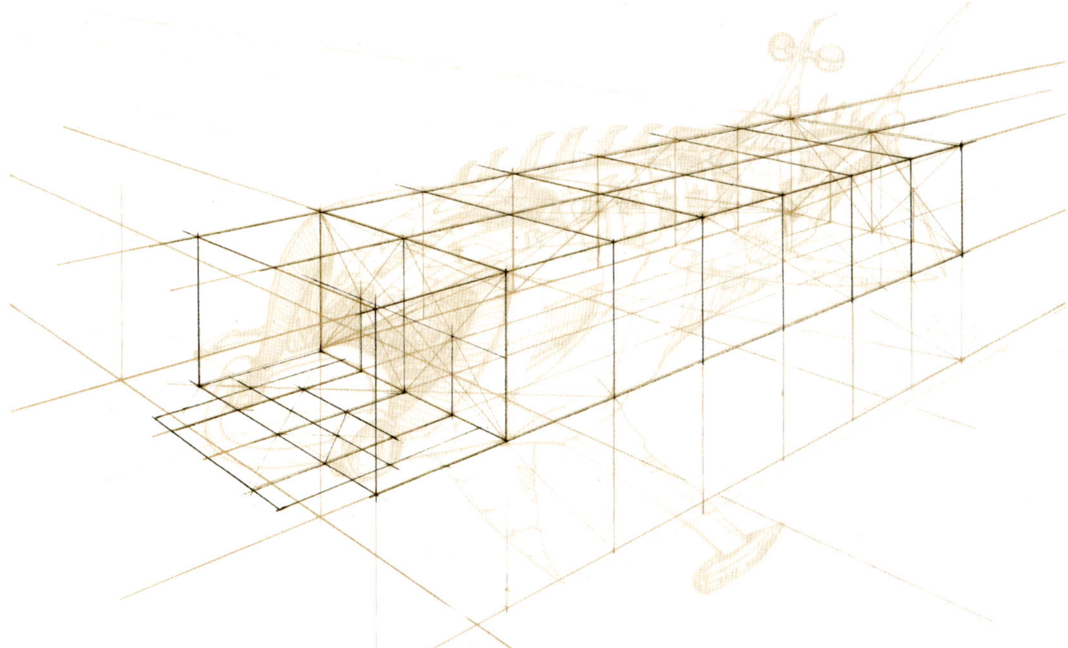

3 **Clean up the Drawing for the Perspective Grid**
At this stage, don't worry about the misalignment between the 3D perspective grid and the sketch, and proceed to the next step.

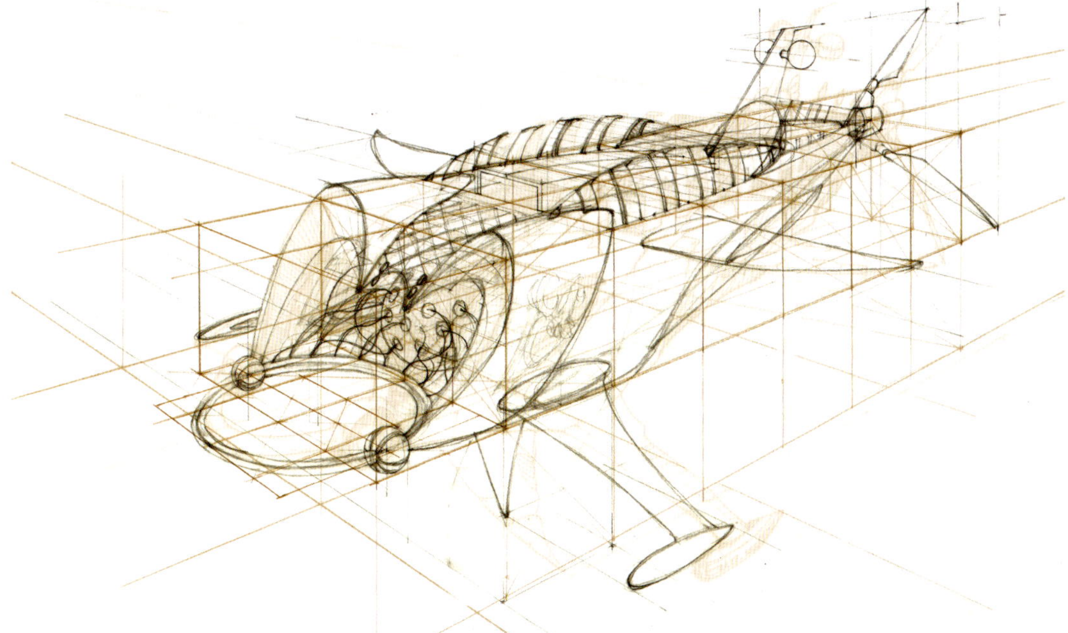

4 **Draw the Form According to the Grid**
Draw the elements of the previously created top view and side view according to the perspective grid. By relying on the grid, the overall shape will remain intact and solid. For curved and rounded parts, don't be overly restricted by the grid and draw with a sense of momentum.

5 Finish the Line Drawing

After adding details like the hull parts and patterns, organize the rough sketch and add varying line weights to complete the line art.

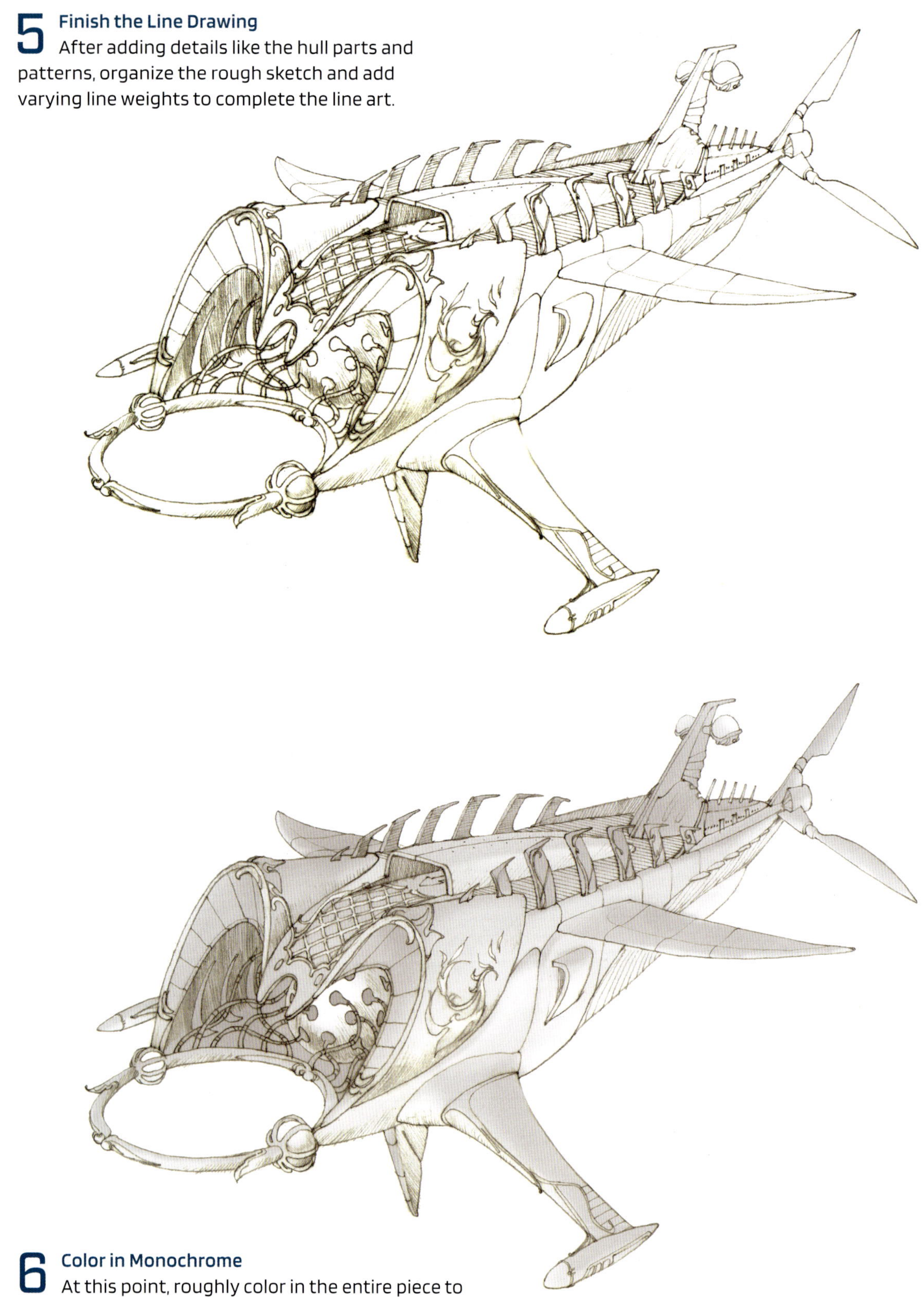

6 Color in Monochrome

At this point, roughly color in the entire piece to determine the monochromatic tone.

※ Here, the line art is scanned and colored using Photoshop.

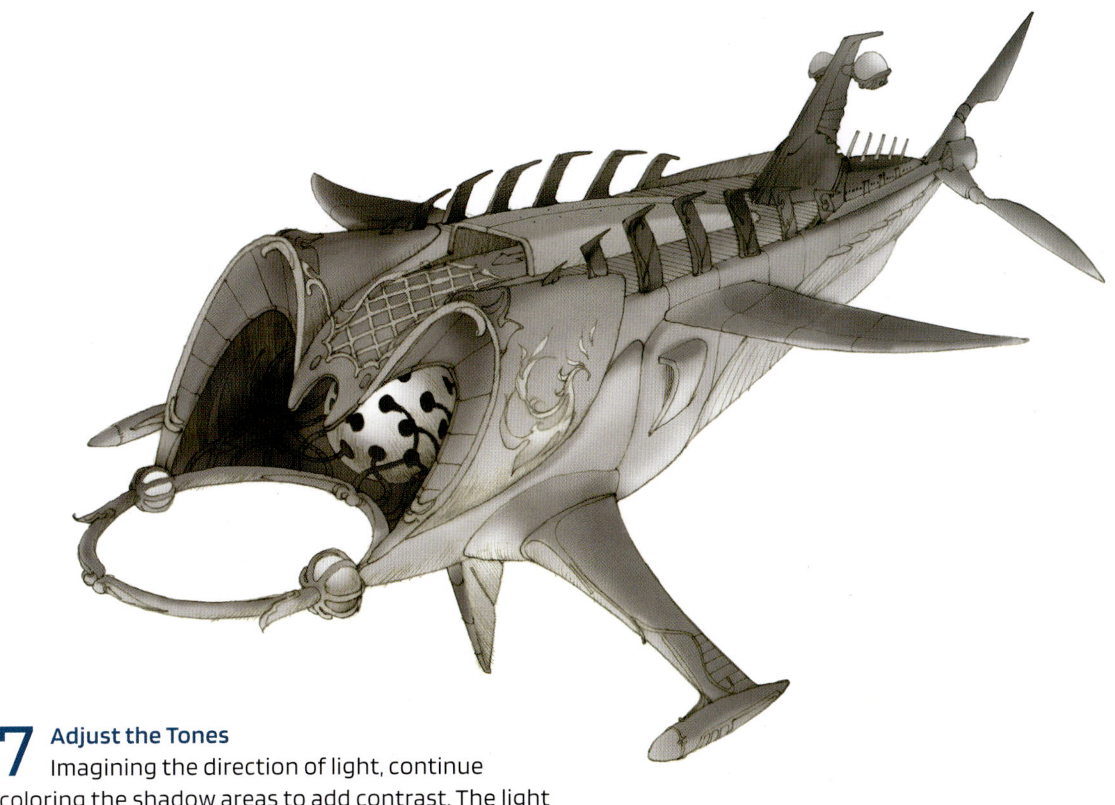

7 Adjust the Tones
Imagining the direction of light, continue coloring the shadow areas to add contrast. The light source is assumed to be coming from underneath.

8 Color the Overall Image
The hull has a rough metallic feel. A mix of gray transitioning from purple to blue is used, with some beige incorporated.

9 Add Tones and Color the Highlights

While emphasizing the hull's shading, add tones. The energy ball at the bow is painted in a more saturated color to represent a glowing object in the dark space.

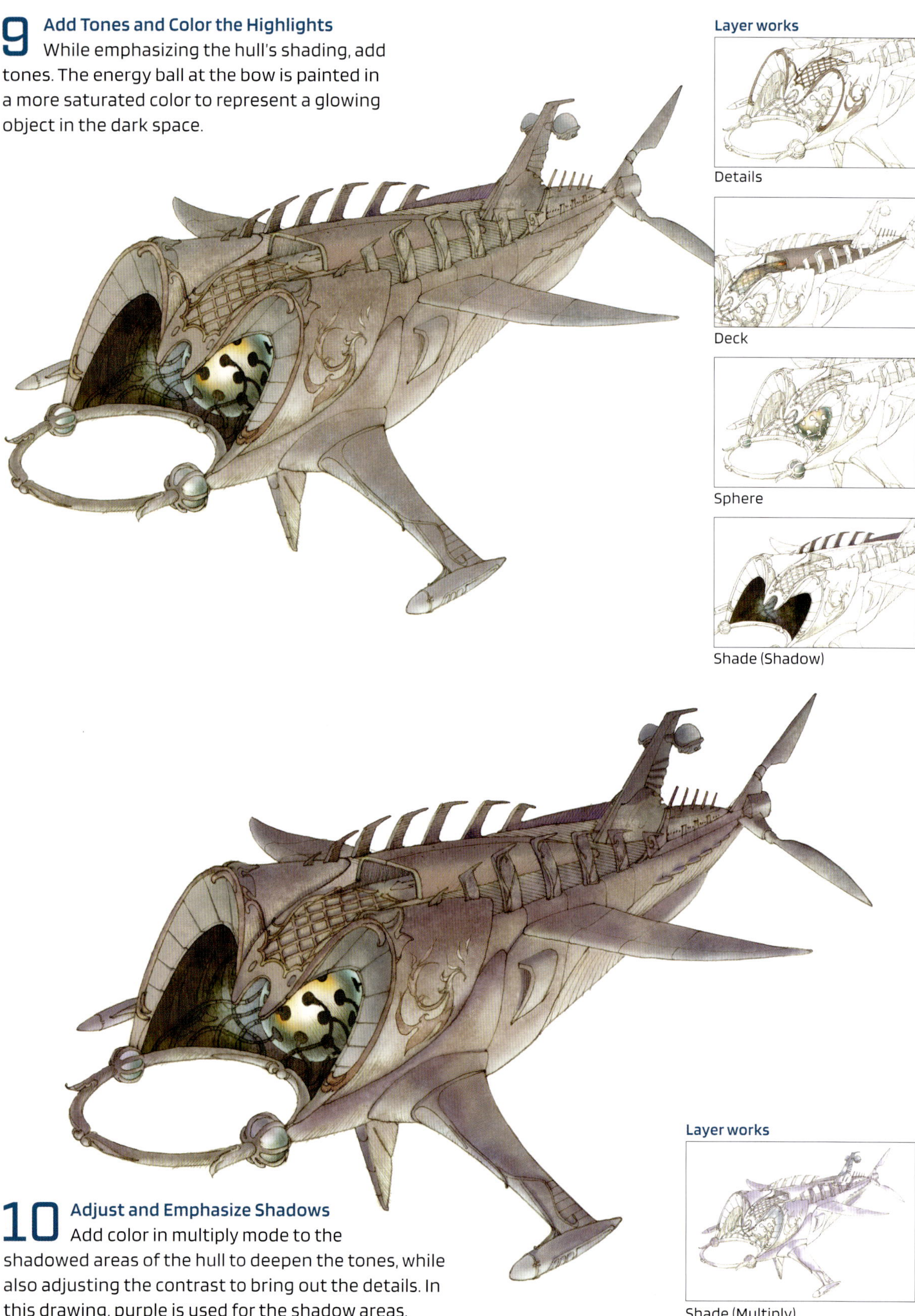

10 Adjust and Emphasize Shadows

Add color in multiply mode to the shadowed areas of the hull to deepen the tones, while also adjusting the contrast to bring out the details. In this drawing, purple is used for the shadow areas.

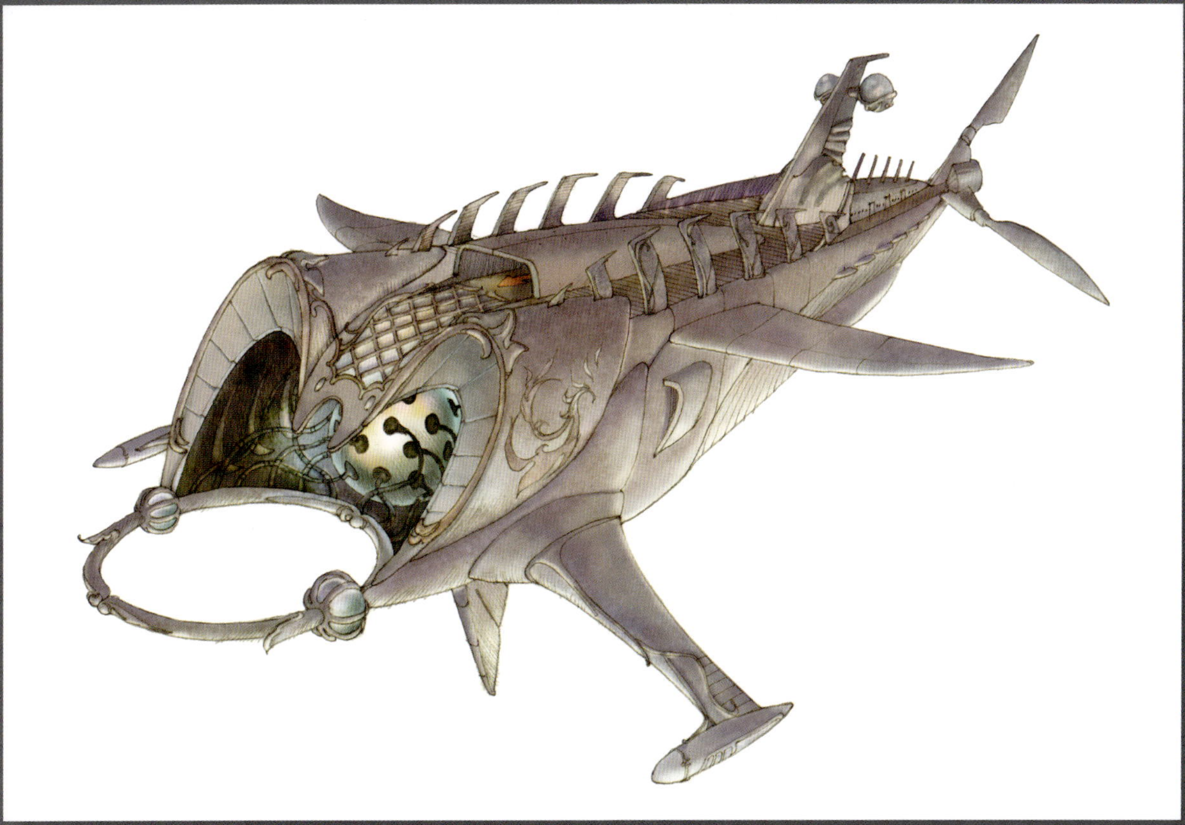

11 Highlight the Adjustments and Finish
Finally, add highlights to complete the piece. In the finished artwork on page 122, light is shining from below the hull, and a star is drawn in the lower-right corner of the background.

Layer works

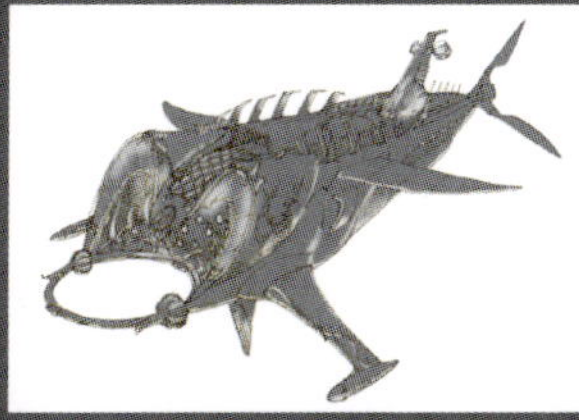

Highlight (Overlay)

Basic Three-Dimensional Perspective Grid

Please enlarge and copy this page to 120%.
For details on increasing or decreasing
the grid, refer to page 23.

SPECIAL THANKS

- **Editing Assistance and Image Contributions**
  Uraba Research Institute (Railstation.net) Kaneyoshi Uraba
    Tōkaidō and Sanyō Shinkansen (pages 26–27) / DD51 Diesel Locomotive (page 40)

  Kōji Morikawa
    Lloyd Reconnaissance Aircraft (pages 30–31)

  Mittan Tank Factory
    Tiger II (page 9)

  Ta. gucci – My Home Hobby World
    Zero Fighter (page 11)

  Uniphoto Press
    René Lalique Perfume Bottle (page 46) /
        Honoré Daumier "French Republic. Their Support is Deceptive" Lithograph (page 58)

- **Image Contributions (In Order of Appearance)**
  Medieval Cannon (page 6) © stocksolutions/Fotolia.com
  Colt M1911 (page 8) © Gary Blakeley/Fotolia.com
  Steam Locomotive (page 16) © reb/Fotolia.com
  Large Motorcycle (page 34) © Kana/PIXTA
  Paris Metro (page 37) © aloha2014/Fotolia.com
  Victorian Design (page 38) © Petkov/PIXTA
  Steampunk (page 38) © Andrey Kiselev/Fotolia.com
  Cyberpunk (page 38) © La cage aux poupées/Fotolia.com
  Gothic Fashion (page 39) © Choreograph/PIXTA, © Nejron Photo/PIXTA
  Gothic and Lolita (page 39) © Choa/PIXTA
  Scorpion Fish (page 50) © ftlaudgirl/Fotolia.com
  Dragonfly (page 51) © Magdziak Marcin/Fotolia.com

- **Reference Books**
  "Product Design: For Everyone Involved in Product Development"
  JIDA "Product Design" Editorial Committee (Works Corporation) 2009
  "Diagram of Sculpture" Kiyoo Koyama & Kazuko Mende (Japan Publishing Service) 1982
  "Perspective Techniques" Kenichi Somemori (Ohmsha) 2009
  "Easy to Trace! Three-Dimensional Sketch Practice Notebook" Kenichi Somemori (Ohmsha) 2011

AUTHOR & ILLUSTRATOR BIOS

Author

Kenichi Somemori
Graduated from the oil painting department of Tama
Art University and completed the Graduate School of
Art Research, master of arts, at the same university. He
participated in numerous projects as a landscape architect.
Registered Civil Consultant Manager (RCCM).
Major Works: "Perspective Techniques," "Perspective
Expressions," "Easy to Trace! Three-Dimensional Sketch
Practice Notebook," "Easy to Trace! Plant and Animal Sketch
Practice Notebook."

Illustration

Shin Yoshimura
Graduated from the department of agricultural biological
sciences, faculty of agriculture, University of Tokyo.
Engaged in urban planning and landscape design at EPI
Co., Ltd. Later established MEGA DRAWING, focusing on
illustration and perspective creation. Awarded the Jury
Prize at the 30th JARA Grand Prize in 2010.

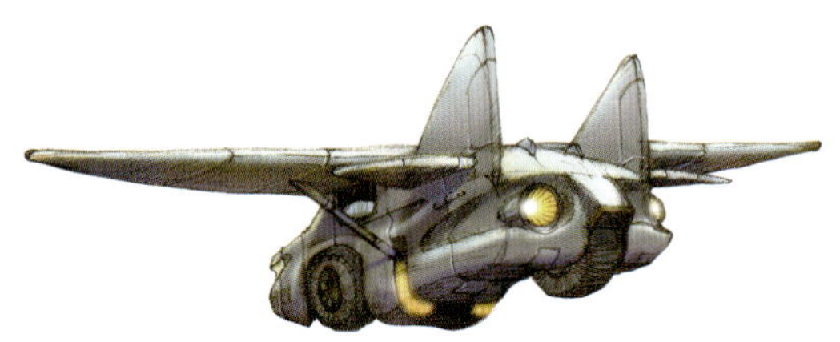

"BOOKS TO SPAN THE EAST AND WEST"

Tuttle Publishing was founded in 1832 in the small New England town of Rutland, Vermont [USA]. Our core values remain as strong today as they were then—to publish best-in-class books which bring people together one page at a time. In 1948, we established a publishing outpost in Japan—and Tuttle is now a leader in publishing English-language books about the arts, languages and cultures of Asia. The world has become a much smaller place today and Asia's economic and cultural influence has grown. Yet the need for meaningful dialogue and information about this diverse region has never been greater. Over the past seven decades, Tuttle has published thousands of books on subjects ranging from martial arts and paper crafts to language learning and literature—and our talented authors, illustrators, designers and photographers have won many prestigious awards. We welcome you to explore the wealth of information available on Asia at **www.tuttlepublishing.com**.

Published by Tuttle Publishing, an imprint of Periplus Editions (HK) Ltd.

www.tuttlepublishing.com

SF Fantasy Mecha to Norimono wo Kaku
© 2015 Kenichi Somemori, Shin Yoshimura, Becom plus
English translation rights arranged with MAAR-sha Publishing Co., Ltd
through Japan UNI Agency, Inc., Tokyo

English Translation @2025 Periplus Editions (HK) LTD

ISBN: 978-4-8053-1946-8
Library of Congress Control Number: 2025932244

All rights reserved. No part of this publication may be reproduced or utilized in any form or by any means, electronic or mechanical, including photocopying, recording, or by any information storage and retrieval system, without prior written permission from the publisher.

Distributed by

North America, Latin America & Europe
Tuttle Publishing
364 Innovation Drive
North Clarendon
VT 05759-9436, USA
Tel: 1 (802) 773 8930
Fax: 1 (802) 773 6993
info@tuttlepublishing.com
www.tuttlepublishing.com

Japan
Tuttle Publishing
Yaekari Building 3rd Floor
5-4-12 Osaki, Shinagawa-ku
Tokyo 141-0032
Tel: (81) 3 5437-0171
Fax: (81) 3 5437-0755
sales@tuttle.co.jp
www.tuttle.co.jp

Asia Pacific
Berkeley Books Pte. Ltd.
3 Kallang Sector #04-01
Singapore 349278
Tel: (65) 67412178
Fax: (65) 67412179
inquiries@periplus.com.sg
www.tuttlepublishing.com

28 27 26 25   10 9 8 7 6 5 4 3 2 1
Printed in China   2505EP

TUTTLE PUBLISHING® is a registered trademark of Tuttle Publishing, a division of Periplus Editions (HK) Ltd.